DOLPHINS

AND THEIR POWER TO HEAL

Amanda Cochrane and Karena Callen

DOLPHINS
AND THEIR POWER TO HEAL

BLOOMSBURY

First published in Great Britain 1992
Bloomsbury Publishing Limited, 2 Soho Square, London W1V 5DE

Copyright © 1992 by Amanda Cochrane and Karena Callen
The moral right of the authors has been asserted

A CIP catalogue record for this book
is available from the British Library

ISBN 0-7475-1160-8

10 9 8 7 6 5 4 3 2 1

Typeset by Hewer Text Composition Services, Edinburgh
Printed by Butler and Tanner, Frome and London

PHOTO SOURCES
Kathie Atkinson/Oxford Scientific Films: pages 22–3
Jen and Des Bartlett/Bruce Coleman Limited: page 15 *top right*
C. Anthony Binder: page 6
S. C. Bisserot, F.R.P.S./Nature Photographers Limited: page 27 *top right*
Dr Clive Bromshall: page 23 *top right*
Alain Compost/Bruce Coleman Limited: pages 4–5
Gerald Davis/Colorific!: pages 8–9
Dr Horace E. Dobbs/International Dolphin Watch: page 7
Francisco Erize/Bruce Coleman Limited: page 12 *top left*
Patrick Fagot/NHPA: page 25
Jack Stein Grove/Bruce Coleman Limited: page 16
John Hayward/NHPA: page 24
Hodson/Greenpeace: page 32
Gérard Lacz/NHPA: pages 3, 30
Frans Lanting/Bruce Coleman Limited: pages 17, 18 *top left*
Luiz Claudio Marigo/Bruce Coleman Limited: pages 12–13
Stan Minasion/Frank Lane Picture Agency: page 11 *bottom right*
Doug Perrine/Planet Earth Pictures: pages 1, 2, 26–7, 28–9
Rowlands/Greenpeace: page 31
Edward Schallenberger/Frank Lane Picture Agency: pages 10–11
Paul Sterry/Nature Photographers Limited: page 21
Mike Valentine/Oxford Scientific Films: pages 18–19
R. Van Nostrand/Frank Lane Picture Agency: page 20
James D. Watt/Planet Earth pictures: pages 14–15

*To my parents and to Claire for their love and support, to
Marty for his patience and for believing in me, and to our
beautiful baby, Shannon Emerald Georgia.*

KC

*To my mother, my father and my sister Susan Mary for
their unerring love and faith in me, and to my close friends
for their encouragement and patience. Special thanks to Vicci
for her moral support and guidance. To my much missed
companions Fred and Flory.*

And to all the dolphins, for their inspiration . . .

AC

ACKNOWLEDGEMENTS

A special thank you must go to the following people for sharing their precious time and knowledge with us: Ric and Lincoln O'Barry for their hospitality and for access to their resources; Dr Peter Evans; Dr Horace Dobbs; Doug Cartlidge; Dr Betsy Smith; Dr David Nathanson; Dr Richard Ferraro; 'Captain' Ron Canning; Elaine Morgan; Dr Michel Odent; Bob Morris; Dr Peter Guy Manners; Denise Herzing; Sam LaBudde at the Earth Island Institute; Roger Mugford; Dr John Lilly; Tony Bassett; Dr Margaret Klinowska; Graham Timmins; Nick Davies at the Whale and Dolphin Conservation Society; Richard Green at Sea Shepherd; and Martin Radford for allowing us access to his extensive library.

And for their faith, encouragement and help, thank you to all of the following: Dasha Shenkman; David Reynolds and all at Bloomsbury; Margaux Dodds; Liz Sandeman; Lucy Maiden; John Hunt, Judy Keil and everyone at The Dolphin Circle; Alex Templeton; Stevie Hughes; Sarita Montrose.

....

CONTENTS

FOREWORD

These creatures bring a blessing with them. No day in which they have played a part is like any other.
From *Mani: Travels in the Southern Peloponnese*, by Patrick Leigh Fermor.

As the sun emerged from below the horizon, the sailing boat slipped silently out of the harbour. A gentle breeze fluttering in the sails sped us towards the turquoise waters of the open sea. We had heard reports of dolphins being sighted off the coast, but there was no guarantee they would grace us with their presence. However, the sea was calm that day – always a promising sign – so we scanned the surface intently. As the hours swept by we began to give up any hope of spotting these elusive creatures. Then, just as the boat turned to head for home, they appeared. To begin with, we could see just two fins in the distance, occasionally breaking the surface, but soon others emerged from out of the blue. The dolphins drew closer, and suddenly we were surrounded by countless sleek and silvery forms slipping through the water. Some took up position beside the bows and we could see them twisting and spinning in the slip stream. The desire to be amongst them was so overwhelming that we overcame our apprehensiveness about being in deep, open water and slipped over the side of the boat. Now fully immersed, we could hear ourselves being bombarded with high-pitched squeaks, clicks and creaking sounds. The dolphins knew that two alien creatures were in their midst, yet to our delight they did not flee. From a safe distance, they circled us, nodding their heads quizzically. Their curiosity quenched, all but two moved off to resume fishing just a few feet away. The remaining pair ventured closer. In perfect synchronicity they dived deep, spun around, then spiralled up towards us, passing so close that they almost touched us. As our gaze met theirs, we were struck by the near-human quality of their glance. In an attempt to hold their attention, we dived underwater and spun around, mimicking their aquatic prowess as best we could. Intrigued, and possibly even amused, they lingered for a while, then with a flick of their flukes, they vanished, leaving us breathlessly bobbing in the water. We were moved to tears of joy.

The extraordinary experience of swimming with wild dolphins fired a fascination which turned into a near obsession for us both. Although we experienced our very first dolphin encounters independently, we discovered that we both shared the same sensations. We had been mesmerized by the dolphins' beauty, grace and serenity, exhilarated by their vitality and *joie de vivre*, and deeply touched by their unconditional acceptance. From then on, these smiling creatures would creep into our waking consciousness and even into our dreams.

Many people have highlighted the dolphins' unfathomed intelligence as a source of awe and wonder, but this does not explain the potent influence they exert on the psyche. According to folklore, myths and legends from around the world, dolphins have enchanted and fascinated man since time immemorial and were held in the highest esteem by some of the most sophisticated civilizations. The Minoans reputedly dedicated temples of devotion to dolphins. Stories of dolphins seeking human companionship and forming special bonds of friendship abound in classical Greek literature, suggesting that this phenomenon is not just some 'New Age' fad. Could it be, we wondered, that at some stage in our evolutionary past our pathways crossed and that the memory of this affinity lives on in the recesses of our subconscious? Certainly, many so-called primitive tribes living close to nature seem to have a special rapport with dolphins. Were dolphins in some way responsible for putting us back in touch with a more 'natural' way of life? We examined ancient healing philosophies and religions from all over the world, and discovered they shared a common core: we can only enjoy true happiness, inner peace and good health when we live in harmony with nature. Altruistic and compassionate by nature, the dolphin is an embodiment of such beliefs and thus an inspiration for humankind.

Our quest to fathom, and if possible elucidate, the healing power of dolphins took us to Africa, Bali, the Bahamas, the Florida Keys, Turks and Caicos Islands and Greece, to the less hospitable and chillier south-west coast of Ireland and to Northumbria, where we encountered pods of wild dolphins, lone friendly dolphins and dolphins held in captivity. During our travels we met and spoke to a number of cetacean experts, researchers, animal welfarists, dolphin trainers and self-confessed dolphin lovers. Those people who had had the good fortune to enjoy close contact with dolphins in the wild invariably agreed that the experience was profoundly uplifting, all absorbing and even spiritual, and that these close encounters left a long-lasting impression. Many people reported feeling in some way 'changed for the better' by their encounter. We heard accounts of dolphins alleviating cases of chronic depression, enhancing recovery from life-threatening illnesses such as cancer, speeding up the learning potential of handicapped children and helping therapists to break through into the world of autism. We became convinced that the 'dolphin-effect' was real, not something that we had imagined. These animals had the power to affect people deeply on a psychological and perhaps even a physiological level.

Sadly, whilst such interactions may benefit us, they do not always bode well for the dolphins. After visiting various enterprises where these creatures are held captive, we came away feeling deeply saddened rather than elated. Denying the dolphins the freedom of the seas and the natural way of life that is their birthright is, to our minds, inherently wrong. More alarming, perhaps, was discovering to what extent man's activities threaten dolphin lives. Every year thousands of dolphins perish in nets deliberately set on them to catch tuna, as well as in vast drift nets which currently stripmine the oceans. And in some parts of the world dolphins are blatantly hunted. Meanwhile, our wastes are insidiously poisoning the seas, putting the future of these remarkable creatures at risk. It is to our detriment that we destroy the precious gifts nature has to offer.

Until he extends his circle of compassion to all living things, man will not himself find peace.
Albert Schweitzer.

Amanda Cochrane and Karena Callen, 1991.

Part One

THE HEALING DOLPHIN

Chapter One
....

THE POWER TO HEAL?

INTRODUCTION

Dolphins seem to possess the extraordinary ability to trigger the healing process within people. Our interest was initially captured by reports back in the 1970s that several people suffering from psychological disturbances such as acute depression had made remarkable and apparently permanent recoveries after swimming with friendly wild dolphins. At the time it seemed barely credible, but since then countless people who have swum with such dolphins have said that the experience has had a powerful impact on their lives. This idea has been further reinforced by our own experiences of swimming with both a pod of wild dolphins in Bali and friendly solitary ones in Ireland and England.

It would appear to be much more than mere coincidence, and we were intrigued by how and why dolphins exert their healing influence. There is no doubt that, symbolizing freedom, vitality, joy, *joie de vivre*, grace and serenity, they have a remarkable power to uplift the spirit. Simply being in their presence seems to arouse feelings of profound inner peace and happiness and often induces a state of euphoria. Although acknowledged in the past, in our own time the health-enhancing and restorative powers of such positive states of mind are only just coming to light. Yet the dolphin's healing potential reaches beyond the limits of pure positive thinking. Our research suggests that the effects may be physiological as well as psychological. For dolphins seem to emit special energy and sound vibrations which can have a potent influence on body, mind and spirit. Above all, dolphins teach us that only by living in harmony with the natural environment can we truly experience real happiness, inner peace and good health.

HEALING – AN ANCIENT WISDOM

With the realization that modern medicine has its limitations has come a revolution in how we perceive and treat illness. Drugs and surgery may help to alleviate the symptoms of disease, but they do little to promote a sense of total wellbeing in both mind and body. In their blinkered quest for increasingly sophisticated 'cures', scientists have often overlooked some of the simplest yet most effective tools for rekindling feelings of vibrant health and happiness. An examination of any ancient healing tradition uncovers the same underlying theme: that nature holds a cure for man's ills. In the light of this knowledge, the idea that dolphins possess healing qualities is not as extraordinary as it may first appear. Yet we cannot expect dolphins alone to heal us. Rather, they are an inspiration that helps us to explore our own self-healing potential. There is something in that old adage 'Physician heal thyself' – real healing can come only from within ourselves.

In the 20th century, we have come to regard good health as the absence of disease. But total wellbeing lies beyond this limited concept. It is a state encompassing such qualities as contentment, peace of mind, vital energy and a sense of deep security. Wise men living thousands of years ago believed that this paradisiacal state was characterized by the complete integration of mind, body and spirit. Such wholeness was possible only when man lived in peace and harmony with the natural world. The early physicians were ahead of their time in many ways. They viewed illness as a sign that the body had strayed in some way from a state of equilibrium. Physical symptoms were merely the expression of an imbalance that was also present on mental, emotional and spiritual levels. The ancient healing traditions aimed to restore the integrity of mind, body and spirit, and nature played a vital part in all forms of healing.

Today, we live an increasingly artificial existence. Cocooned in concrete cities, it is easy to feel entirely separate from and superior to the natural environment. Yet in severing the bond with Mother Nature, we lose touch with the very essence of our being and are easy prey for all kinds of emotional and physical disturbances. Dolphins symbolize the kind of qualities that the ancient philosophers most admired. Living in complete harmony with its natural environment, the dolphin enjoys the kind of freedom and joy to which most humans aspire. Gentle, peaceful and compassionate, it exudes pure happiness and vitality, which suggests a being in perfect mental, physical and spiritual balance. Dolphins are often described as possessing a sense of spirituality, a quality that the ancient Greeks called divine, and those people who have enjoyed close encounters with dolphins remember the experience as 'magical', 'transcendental' and 'out of this world'. Such a sense of oneness with nature is the very essence of the transcendental experience which Freud aptly described as the 'oceanic feeling'. If we have a lesson to learn about living, then surely dolphins can be our teachers: they seem more than willing to share their 'knowledge' with us.

Yet what we have to learn from the dolphin is hardly a new concept. Some 5,000 years ago, sages living in the mountains of India expressed their healing philosophies in the famous Vedic texts. The principles of *Ayurveda*, Sanskrit for 'the science of life', have been introduced to the 20th century by Maharishi Mahesh Yogi, the founder of Transcendental Meditation. Fundamental to Ayurvedic thinking is the notion that the natural state is one of perfect health and happiness. When the forces within us are in harmony and balance with the natural environment, we are immune to physical and emotional disturbances. In *Ayurveda*, the state of mind assumes tremendous importance, for good health springs from being happy and at peace with ourselves. When we lose contact with the source of happiness, we lose touch with the source of everything in nature, ourselves included. Maharishi suggests that these principles are borne out by modern physics, since, according to quantum theory, all matter stems from energy, and all forms of energy are constantly interacting with one another. The essence of Ayurvedic healing is that only when we are at one with nature do energies harmonize, giving rise to the experience of true bliss.

The same underlying principles are found in the ancient Chinese philosophy of Taoism. Back in the third millennium BC, the Yellow Emperor Hwang Ti expressed his thoughts in one of the oldest known medical books, the *Nei Ching*. These ideas were embellished and further articulated, first by the great philosopher, Lao Tzu, who lived during the sixth century BC, and subsequently by Chuang Tzu, another philosopher, some two hundred years later.

Taoists perceive the universe as a living organism infused and permeated with the life force, a rhythmic, vibrational energy which they refer to as 'Chi' or 'Qi'. Taoists teach that if man lives in harmony with the laws of nature, his whole system will be balanced physically, mentally, emotionally and spiritually. This allows Qi to flow freely and evenly through the body, passing smoothly along invisible energy channels known as meridians. But problems arise when we consider ourselves separate from and superior to nature, for Qi then becomes stifled. When this happens, we experience emotional troubles, such as anxiety, irritability, anger, frustration, fear and depression. These in turn disrupt the healthy functioning of the physical body, giving rise to all manner of discomfort and even disease.

Nowadays, urban life, with its chemical pollution, excessive time pressures, refined and pesticide-laden food and lack of regular physical activity serves to distance us from nature. In Chinese medicine, healing is aimed at restoring the free flow of Qi through the body in order to redress physical, mental and spiritual imbalances. The technique of acupuncture, for example, employs needles inserted at key points on the meridians to release blockages. Taoism is also a philosophy for living which promotes and restores peace of mind and good health. According to Lao Tzu, the goal should be to become like a newborn baby, for in the first throes of life we are completely flexible and open to new experiences. In this state, every aspect of the self is in harmony. When we grow up, we become unnaturally sophisticated as a way of coping with life's pressures, and develop a more rigid and unyielding nature which creates tension between the physical, emotional and spiritual aspects of our being. The way back to our original state of balance and harmony lies in developing a peaceful mind and attitude towards life.

According to the philosopher Chuang Tzu, yearnings for wealth and materialistic gain are largely responsible for disrupting peace of mind. When we are born, we have very few essential requirements, apart from the need to eat, drink, sleep, play and satisfy our natural curiosity. But the more sophisticated and apparently civilized we become, the more 'needs' we develop. In his book *Perfect Happiness* Chuang Tzu observed that striving for riches, honours, security and an abundance of good food inevitably brings disappointment. While some desires may be fulfilled, others remain unsatisfied and become a source of worry and confusion. This leads to negative thoughts and emotions which shatter our happiness and undermine our health. Only by letting go of these obsessive desires can we hope to attain real peace of mind.

The civilized Greeks living in classical times also perceived that materialistic gain alone did not bring happiness, and they, too, appreciated the link between nature and the harmonious integration of body, mind and spirit. The ancient Greeks had a great reverence for the natural world, as is well illustrated in their myths, and placed great faith in the body's ability to heal itself given a conducive environment. This they identified as the *vis medicatrix naturea* – the healing power of nature.

Their temples were built in places of extraordinary natural beauty. At the sanctuary of Asklepios, near Epidauros, the most important healing centre in mainland Greece, Apollo was worshipped as the god of medicine. In Greek mythology, Apollo sometimes took the form of Delphinius, the dolphin, which suggests that perhaps the ancient Greeks may have recognized and even harnessed the healing power of the dolphin. Such speculation apart, we do know that healing methods used at the sanctuary often involved faith healing and auto-suggestion. Ahead of their time, the early Greek physicians knew of the power of positive thinking and stressed the importance of *mens sana in corpore sano* – a healthy mind in a healthy body. The drive to achieve balance between mind, body and spirit also had the support of the Greek culture and education system. In the words of Plato, 'Good education is that which tends most to the improvement of mind and body. My belief is not that the good body by any bodily excellence improves the soul, but on the contrary, that the good soul by her excellence improves the body so far as may be possible.'

The native American Indians maintained that by coming into harmony with the flow of nature, a person is able to attain equilibrium of their physical, emotional, mental, sexual and spiritual aspects. Naturally, kinship with all creatures of the earth, sky and water was of paramount importance to this philosophy. The Indians used animal totems as part of their healing culture and each animal represented a particular quality. The dolphin symbolized manna, or life force, to the Indians. According to Indian teaching, the dolphin was the keeper of the sacred breath of life and was a healing totem used to release emotional tension.

THE ELEMENTS OF HEALING

The Healing Power of Joy

As a result of our own experiences and those of the many people we have encountered through our research for this book, we believe that dolphins can heal people in several ways. The most obvious is by virtue of their happy, tranquil and compassionate nature. Anyone who has been fortunate enough to swim with a dolphin, particularly one living wild and free, invariably describes the experience as euphoric. The incident has such significance that it is indelibly committed to memory, and whenever the dolphin encounter comes to mind, a feeling of intense pleasure wells up inside. Indeed, even just watching dolphins leaping and cavorting for sheer joy cannot help but bring a smile to the lips.

The sages of old recognized the healing power of happiness: Vedic literature, for example, states that to be happy is to be healthy. Such views were echoed by Theophrastus Bombastus von Honeheim, better known as Paracelsus, who lived in the 16th century and may be dubbed the father of psychosomatic medicine. He estimated that the mind, will, imagination, emotions and perceptions had a vital role to play in the promotion of health and the prevention of disease. 'The spirit is master, the imagination is the instrument, the body is the plastic material. The moral atmosphere surrounding the patient can have a strong influence on the course of his disease,' he wrote. Paracelsus believed that virtue was the most potent of all the healing forces, and felt that we must acknowledge a spiritual dimension to the healing process.

In recent years, scientific investigation into the influence of the emotions on physical well-being has been lending strong support to this ancient wisdom. Increasingly, the individual's state of mind is being viewed as a vital component of any diseased state, and it is thought that rekindling feelings of contentment plays an important part in recovery. Researchers working in the relatively new field of psychoneuroimmunology, more commonly known as PNI, are convinced of a link between negative emotions and various disease states, and are coming even closer to explaining this phenomenon in scientific terms. PNI is the study of how psychological and emotional states influence disease resistance via interactions with the nervous, endocrine and immune systems. There now seems little doubt that the body's immunity against infections, foreign bodies and malignant cells is under the ultimate jurisdiction of the brain, with control possibly being exercised in an exceedingly complex fashion through intermediary changes in the nervous system, neurochemical and hormonal output. According to Dr Novera Herbert Spector of the National Institute of Neurological Diseases at the National Institute of Health in the United States, 'Interactions between the brain and the immune system are now the subject of research, not only by psychologists and psychiatrists, but also by physiologists, immunologists, cell biologists and molecular biologists from all branches of the biomedical sciences.'

The brain is not only a complex computer, but an endocrine organ — one that releases internal secretions known as hormones and neurotransmitters. Scientists have discovered that it produces a pharmacy of chemicals that are associated with sleep, anxiety, aggression, concentration, learning, fear and pleasure — to name but a few emotional states. Dr David Baltimore, winner of the Nobel Prize for Medicine and Physiology, believes that there is a quantifiable link between mind and matter, spirit and body, imagination and reality. 'Realizing that states of mind (neurotransmitters) and the long-lasting chemical actions that control slow processes such as growth and reproduction (hormones) are almost one and the same, gives us some knowledge of the mind/body problem. It says quite clearly that processes within the brain that trigger a hormone release can cause enormous effects on the body.'

Substances called neurotransmitters play a key role in the physical manifestation of emotions. We now know that the state of euphoria or intense pleasure is accompanied by a surge of natural substances known as endorphins. Chemically akin to morphine, these substances act as potent pain-killers. It is not only endorphins that are released. Another neurotransmitter, serontonin, which is linked to feelings of serenity and tranquillity, is produced in a similar way. The receptors of these substances are found not just in the brain, but in all body tissues, and it seems that they may actively promote and restore good health. Similarly, a sense of exhilaration has been found to trigger the production of some of the most potent anti-cancer chemicals, the leucotrienes and interferon.

It is clear that Andrew Taylor Still, the founder of osteopathy, was onto something when he suggested that all the pharmaceutical agents required for the maintenance of health are manufactured in the human body. However, reasons for unhappiness are of course personal, and it would be almost impossible to pinpoint one common source of melancholy. Some people have an inherent tendency to look on the gloomy side of life; and the philosophers of the past would no doubt attribute much present-day discontent to the severing of our ties with nature.

In Western society, stress is largely responsible for many negative emotional states. Anxiety, bitterness, fear, anger, frustration and irritability often stem from unfulfilled desires and ambitions – from striving too hard and wanting too much. Left unchecked over a long period of time, such emotions can cause a breakdown in physical health and hinder any attempts at recovery. Dr Ari Kiev, one of America's leading authorities on depression, is the director of the Social Psychiatry Research Institute, New York, and a clinical associate professor of psychiatry at Cornell University Medical College. He conducted his own research into the curative capacity of dolphins. In an article that was published in the *Medical Tribune*, Kiev suggested that 'swimming with dolphins facilitates the reduction of psychological defences and negative self-concepts, and creates an experimental domain in which people can move beyond ego and identify with a collective consciousness characterized by energy, love, compassion, reverence and awe'. Kiev maintains that dolphins enable us to 'let go' of stereotypical ways of thinking about ourselves, so that we can experience the here and now. 'The dolphin brings us to the now and teaches us to live beyond the boundaries of compulsion. It nurtures our capacity for surrender and trust, for love and serenity, and facilitates a level of consciousness that has an untapped therapeutic potential for humankind.'

It is this altered state of consciousness that we believe to be so important in the healing process. Numerous people suffering from serious illness, ranging from depression to AIDS, have reported dramatic changes in their emotional state. For many, dolphins help them to release their feelings, to experience true happiness and live in the present, if only for a moment. The international fashion photographer Stevie Hughes, who has had full-blown AIDS for two years, believes that his encounter with wild dolphins, just off the Bahamas, has not only contributed to his acceptance of the fact that he has AIDS, but has also revitalized his life and given him a new sense of perspective. Having spent a week waiting to see wild dolphins in very poor weather conditions, Hughes was just about to give up hope of having any encounter with the animals when on the last day a pod of dolphins encircled the research boat that he was on.

'I was scared at first, but looking into their eyes I felt that I had been reborn. I could literally feel them scanning me, the sound was so loud. My heartbeat increased and I lost all sense of self and of time. It no longer mattered who I was, that I had AIDS, that I might die. I felt completely humbled in their presence and grateful for the experience.'

Hughes stayed in the water for over an hour before he had to get out to warm up and rest. Having also experienced an encounter with captive dolphins, Hughes believes that that bears no comparison to swimming with them in the wild. 'It was a meaningless experience and quite upsetting. You pay $10 to get your hands on a dolphin – I suppose it's convenient. But when they come to you in the wild, it's like a miracle, an amazing gift.' Although he is very aware that the dolphins did not cure him, he is no longer scared of dying and feels that he can live his life to the full. 'Because they love you unconditionally, no strings attached, it is the purest experience you can have.'

Peace of mind and feelings of contentment go hand in hand, and there is no doubt that we cannot help but feel soothed and uplifted by the gentle and joyful nature of dolphins. Modern research has also shown that when the mind is calm, it triggers the release of chemicals called benzodiasopenes, a natural form of Valium or Librium, by cells all over the body. Although, as yet, no one has measured the release of these chemicals following an encounter with a dolphin, we know from our own experiences that simply being in water can actually precipitate their release.

The idea that dolphins have extraordinary uplifting powers was noted by Dr Horace Dobbs, a British researcher, back in the mid-1970s. Two incidents convinced him that dolphins had a special therapeutic influence on the human mind and spirit. In the first, Geoff Bold, a lifeboat mechanic who was close to nervous breakdown, swam with a friendly dolphin called Donald. After this encounter, Bold's depression miraculously lifted. Secondly, a few years later, when Dr Dobbs took a group of people out to see Simo, a friendly bottlenose dolphin living in Wales, Dr Dobbs was intrigued to see that the dolphin spent most time with one man, Bill Bowell. Then aged 54, Bowell had previously suffered both a heart attack and nervous breakdown and had slipped into a state of deep depression. The meeting with Simo was a remarkable turning-point for him. He described his dolphin encounter as more therapeutic than all the anti-depressant drugs he had been taking. After subsequent swims, Bowell started to change from being apprehensive, withdrawn and nervous into an altogether more confident and outgoing person. As a result of observing a dramatic change in not only these, but several other people suffering from psychological disturbances, Horace Dobbs set up Operation Sunflower, which aims to study the therapeutic powers of dolphins and make them available to as many people as possible.

The suggestion that dolphins can alleviate depression and promote a healing response remains somewhat controversial and, according to many dolphin scientists, is without any real scientific basis. None the less, whale and dolphin expert Dr Peter Evans, a research population geneticist at the University of Oxford and founder of the Cetacean Group of the UK Mammal Society, takes an open-minded view. As a scientist, Evans has no time for any mystical or 'New Age' theories about dolphins, but he does believe that encounters with dolphins can have a therapeutic value because of the powerful effect that they have on our emotions. Evans has a particular interest in the relationships formed between humans and friendly wild dolphins, and he is fascinated by both man's need to interact with the dolphin and the dolphin's need to bond with man. 'Like dolphins, humans are social beings and quite often they don't fit in to social groups. Because of this, they get depressed and feel isolated. They can be uplifted by dolphins because dolphins appear to be genuinely interested in them and don't make any demands on them – something which other human beings do. Dolphins don't cover up their feelings, so there is a genuine relationship and interchange of emotions.' In other words, because dolphins are wild creatures with a natural curiosity and a love of fun and games, we find it flattering and delightful when they turn their attention to us. Evans himself has been deeply affected emotionally when in close contact with wild dolphins: 'I think dolphins can have a therapeutic effect simply through the response that a human has to receiving attention from another animal – perhaps attention that is being received for the first time. Because the psychological element plays a very important role in healing, I think it is possible that they do contribute to the healing process.'

The Love of a Dolphin

Dolphins are compassionate by nature: it has often been reported that if a dolphin is drowning, other members of its pod will come to its aid. Supporting the ailing dolphin under its fins with their bodies, they will carry it for miles with its blow-hole above the surface of the water so that it can breathe. And dolphins exhibit such compassion not only towards members of their own species, but also towards humans. There are innumerable stories of dolphins saving people from drowning. Furthermore, researchers investigating the healing power of dolphins have noted that when dolphins are in the water with human companions, the creatures seem to direct their attention towards those people who are weak and ailing, or, in other words, to those who are in distress. According to Dr David Nathanson, a researcher who has been working for several years on human/dolphin encounters and therapy, 'Being highly sensitive, dolphins have the ability to home in on those who seem to need help. For those people who cannot cope with the loss of a familiar person, the contact of dolphins can have a deeply positive effect, more so because it is coming from something other than the human form. Unlike many other animals, dolphins don't give up on people who are unresponsive to them. They continue to exude compassion.'

The fact that the affection or love that dolphins appear to exude is unconditional is also important. The power of such love is not a new or revolutionary idea: some 2,500 years ago, the Buddha Siddhartha Gautama, having attained the state of enlightenment, realized that we are all looking for love in life. But in relationships, we often start off loving someone and later discover that we are not receiving the same kind of love in return, so we feel cheated. This is not 'pure' love, for it is based on greed, insecurity and fear of rejection. Only by learning to give and receive love unconditionally can we grow spiritually to find our own source of happiness and inner peace.

In this regard, Jemima Biggs, who suffers from manic depression and anorexia nervosa, claims that her experience with Fungie, a wild dolphin in Dingle Bay, County Kerry in Ireland, has changed her life. Biggs' depression started when she was only nine, and by the time she was twenty-five she was overcome by morbid and what she describes as 'catastrophic fears'. 'When a person is depressed, she avoids eye contact even with those who care the most. One shuts out other people and one's own feelings too. When Fungie looked in at my personal anguish, he was seeing me as not even I had been able to see myself. But I did not feel afraid. I could trust him.' Although Biggs is by no means cured of her illness, she believes that her encounter with the dolphin has altered the way in which she thinks about herself and has enabled her to deal with reality. 'Sometimes I think the power of swimming with Fungie lay in his acceptance of me in the water in a physical sense – it did not matter what I looked like, whether I was fat or thin. The experience was one of mutual and unconditional love and trust which perhaps only another intelligent species like the dolphin can provide. We must be humble enough to learn.'

Some progressive-thinking physicians are convinced that unconditional love has extraordinary healing powers. Dr Bernie Siegel, surgeon and author of *Love, Medicine and Miracles*, suggests that all healing is related to the ability to give and accept this form of love. He believes that all disease is ultimately related to a lack of love or to experiencing only love that is conditional. In his view, the exhaustion and depression of the immune system that such love creates lead to physical vulnerability. The common denominator in all depression is a lack of love or a loss of meaning in life, at least as it is perceived from the point of view of the depressed person. Illness often functions as an escape from a routine that has become meaningless. One of the most common precursors of cancer is traumatic loss of love and a feeling of emptiness in life. Siegel suggests that many people, particularly cancer patients, grow up believing that there is a terrible flaw at the centre of their being, a defect which they must hide if they are to have a chance of love. Feeling unlovable and condemned to loneliness if their true selves become known, such individuals set up defences against sharing their innermost feelings with anyone. They feel that their inability to love is shrivelling them up, which leads to further despair. Because such people experience a sense of profound internal emptiness, they come to see all relationships and transactions in terms of getting something to fill the vaguely-understood void within. They therefore give love on the condition that they get something in return, whether this be comfort, security, praise, or a comparable kind of love. Such 'if' love is exhausting and prevents the expression of the authentic self.

Siegel further suggests that unconditional love is the most powerful known stimulant of the immune system and that it boosts levels of immunoglobins and T killer cells. If this is so, it is no wonder, then, that dolphins appear to be able to help people recover from life-threatening diseases. Some inconclusive but interesting evidence that this may be the case is illustrated by what happened to one woman at the Dolphin Research Center in Grassy Key, Florida, who was suffering from breast cancer which had also spread to her lymph glands. Given eight to twelve months to live, Marilyn Rivest came to the centre to swim with the dolphins. A few days after her first swim, she reported that the tumour in her breast had suddenly shrunk. Sadly, to date, her physical remission has not lasted, but Rivest has none the less found a new vitality and serenity in her life that have amazed both doctors and researchers alike. There are a number of other centres in the United States which offer dolphin encounters, and many of these establishments claim that such interactions have therapeutic benefits. The Dolphins Plus Center in Key Largo, Florida, which is run by the Borguss family, has now opened its doors to mentally and physically handicapped people, and has also become of great interest to people with life-threatening diseases such as cancer and AIDS, although Dolphins Plus does not advertise or promote swim therapy for those with serious illness. The projects at both Dolphins Plus and the Dolphin Research Center in Grassy Key are discussed in more detail in Chapter Three.

Emotional Release

Although encounters with dolphins can ultimately help people to achieve greater serenity, ironically, dolphins tend to elicit extreme emotional reactions in us. In addition to feeling intense joy, many people burst into tears when they come into close contact with dolphins, and even watching and hearing dolphins on video and cassette tapes can be sufficient to induce crying. Our own experiences and those of others who have had encounters with these animals suggest that the dolphin triggers the release of pent-up emotions and deep-seated feelings that have been trapped inside us.

Claire Holt, for example, was deeply affected by her encounter with Freddie, a friendly wild dolphin, off the coast of Northumbria. 'Every morning I woke up in tears and I felt very emotional. Much of the emotional release is to do with the fact that you are not communicating with any form of language, but on a basic, spiritual level that reaches your very core. That's why you behave in a very childlike, uninhibited way — there are no complicated layers. I'm sure that dolphins trigger sensations that we have lost but can recognize in these creatures.'

Dolphins seem to possess the power to make an impression on, or reawaken, our emotional centre, which resides in the limbic system, one of the most primitive regions of the brain. Feelings of both pleasure and pain can be triggered by stimulation of this area.

Many people who have entered into a state of depression because they are unable to cope with life, suffer from an emotional anaesthesia which effectively prevents them from feeling either pleasure or pain, as they have lost sight of the emotional side of their lives. A similar suppression of emotion is also characteristic of many cancer patients. They have poorer outlets for emotional discharge. A clinical psychotherapist, Dr Lawrence LeShan, has been studying the relationship between personality and illness. His investigations have revealed an inextricable link between despair and the onset of cancer. LeShan believes that those who suppress their emotions, whether these be of anger, sorrow, pleasure or frustration, are more likely to develop certain forms of cancer. His research has been backed up by Dr A. H. Schmale and Dr H. Iker at the University of Rochester in New York State, USA. Studies also reveal that negative mental attitudes suppress the immune system, thereby leaving the body open to attack from disease.

While it may be possible to use drugs to numb pain or artificially reproduce feelings of pleasure, the effects of such substances are shortlived and can bring on much worse symptoms of withdrawal. Our experiences with dolphins suggest that by contrast, whether the animals bring on feelings of euphoria or tears, they are exerting an essentially natural, safe and positive therapeutic influence.

The Energy Connection

It is our belief that dolphins exert their healing influence on people on a subtle energetic level, and researchers working at the forefront of dolphin healing are beginning to substantiate this notion. All creatures have energy fields that extend beyond their physical body. These force fields are explained in scientific terms by the fact that the brain and the associated nervous system are run by electrical signals. Whenever electrical energy flows, it generates an electrical field. It was Harold Saxton Burr, an American researcher and

Professor of Anatomy at Yale University Medical School, who discovered overall body fields in men and women as well as in animals, trees, plants and raw protoplasm when investigating the electrical phenomenon in the 1940s. He called these fields bio-electrical or electrodynamic L fields – the fields of life. He theorized that the organization of a living thing, its pattern, is established by an electrodynamic field, which determines the arrangement of the components of the organism and is in turn determined by them. Like a finger print, this electrical field is characteristic of a particular living thing. Burr believed that the L field is the shaping influence that keeps us as we are, despite the fact that our bodily tissues are constantly being broken down and renewed. The L field is susceptible to fluctuations: for instance, in women, during the menstrual cycle there is a voltage change in the field at the time of ovulation. The L field also seems to be altered by disease. Unusual changes have been noted in cancer patients, and it has been suggested that the L field has potential as a diagnostic tool. Certain techniques can be used to measure it, the best-known ones being Kirlian photography and the more recent electronography developed by the Romanian medical doctor and electronics expert Ion Dumitrescu.

Burr spent some time working with Yale University psychiatrist Dr Leonard Ravitz, and proved without a doubt that emotions affect our life fields. The strength and quality of the field appear to be influenced by the electrical activity of the brain, or, in other words, by mental states. This helps to explain the potent influence of the mind on the health of the physical body. Burr and his colleagues also found that emotional instability is marked by a high L field. This discovery is borne out by the fact that brain wave frequencies are also higher in manic states, which in turn lends credence to the Chinese idea that an energy imbalance showed that mind, body and soul were not in harmony and was an early warning sign that disease was imminent.

Just because we cannot actually see or touch these force fields does not mean that we do not sense them. Clearly, some people are more sensitive than others, and such people often make excellent healers, for they can detect and work on areas of subtle energy imbalance in others. In the animal kingdom, an awareness of this energy vibration seems almost second nature. The 'sixth sense', for example, is an instinct that warns of danger.

There seems little doubt that dolphins are highly sensitive to subtle energy vibrations. Their sophisticated sonar reflects vibrations which give them detailed information about their environment, their fellow dolphins and objects around them. The fact that they can apparently distinguish when a woman is menstruating, even though they have no sense of smell to speak of, bears this out. Although there is no single explanation as to how dolphins can distinguish when a woman is menstruating, there are several schools of thought. Some scientists have suggested that they may be able to 'taste' the hormones that are being released during menstruation. Others believe that dolphins can use their ultrasound to scan the lining of the womb in order to determine the stages of the menstrual cycle. Another theory relates to the dolphin's ability to pick up on subtle energy changes in our bioelectrical or electrodynamic L field. There is a change in the voltage of the L field during menstruation, and because dolphins are sensitive to these electrical variations, they are able to distinguish menstruation from ovulation. Dolphins' ability to sense changes in the L field also helps to explain how they can differentiate between people who are ill, both emotionally and physically, and those who are in good health.

This capacity to sense a person's emotional state has led many a dolphin trainer and researcher to suggest that dolphins are 'telepathic', and at least one such researcher, the neuroscientist Dr John Lilly, who has worked with dolphins for over 20 years, is convinced of this. Certainly, dolphins seem to be much more intuitive than most people, which is hardly surprising, since in so-called 'civilized' societies, most people are left-brain dominant. That is to say, the logical, analytical hemisphere of the brain is more active than the intuitive, imaginative right hemisphere. In fact, we may all possess the potential to be 'telepathic' if we gain access to our right-brain and pay attention to our instinctive feelings. Indeed, in various supposedly 'primitive' cultures, telepathy and an inherent ability to 'tune in' to the vibrations of other people and of nature have been part of the way of life. The Australian Aborigines spoke of 'learning on the wind', and the African bushmen described in Laurens van der Post's *The Lost World of Kalahari* communicated at a distance using telepathy. This is also true of the Maoris, the American Indians and many other societies.

If dolphins can sense imbalances in the bio-field, can they possibly help to rebalance it in the same way that traditional healers work? We know that the bio-energy field of the body can be affected by sympathetic resonance with similar force fields. This phenomenon is known as bio-entrainment. Living with someone else's aura creates a knock-on effect as each person's vibrations become attuned to the other's. So, while we are usually glad to be uplifted by 'good' vibrations, we instinctively tend to shy away from the drag of negative ones. A person who is inwardly truly happy will make other people feel encouraged just by his or her presence, and the stronger the personality, the more influential it will be. The dolphin bio-energy field is unique. By virtue of its peaceful, content and compassionate nature, the dolphin has an energy vibration which exerts a powerful and positive influence on humans. Depressives and the emotionally unstable appear to be particularly responsive and receptive to these subtle energies.

Entrainment of brain as well as body functions can also occur from this electrical force field. John Lilly suggests that the dolphin's brain waves equate with those in the alpha and theta regions — that is, with those waves that, in humans, accompany the meditative state. This may explain why people who spend some time in the water with dolphins describe the experience as transcendental. Could it be that their brain waves start to resonate with those of the dolphin? Tony Bassett, a sound engineer, has suggested the possibility that dolphins may silently pulse ultrasonic frequencies of around 6Hz that attune human brain waves to a theta state — a theory which could explain why many people, including ourselves, who have swum with dolphins enter a meditative state where they become totally oblivious to anything else around themselves other than the presence of the dolphins.

The Healing Power of Water

When considering the potential healing effect of human and dolphin interaction, we cannot ignore that there is a powerful medium involved – water. Many proponents of the healing dolphin theory believe that water is just as important in the healing process as the dolphins themselves. The restorative powers of water have been extolled throughout the ages. The ancient Greek dramatist Euripides waxed lyrical about the healing properties of the sea and claimed that it held a cure for all man's ills. And in our own time, the French obstetrician, Michel Odent, author of *Water and Sexuality*, a book based on man's affinity to water, its therapeutic properties and the benefits of water birth, is certain that we are drawn to water as a result of our phylogenetic memory: in other words, because of our aquatic past (see Chapter Four).

Human life begins in water when we spend the first nine months of our existence in the womb, floating in a carefully controlled environment which is both safe and sound. The constant sensation of water around us and on our skin, known as 'primal skin feelings', gives us our first sense of our own bodies and of our immediate environment. It is little wonder then that in later life, many of us actively seek to recreate this watery haven by taking the plunge when we feel under stress or insecure. Throughout our evolution, too, we have always lived near a source of water. In many cultures, water is also a symbol of femininity, of the mother. In the ancient Indian Hindu Veda, water is called *matritamah* – the 'most maternal'.

There are many theories as to why water has such potent therapeutic qualities. Excluding our natural affinity with water, and the 'aquatic ape' theory, scientists have been able to pinpoint certain physiological changes that occur when we are immersed in water.

Freedom from Gravity
The ancient Greeks were the first to recognize the physiological benefits of being in water. The mathematician and inventor, Archimedes, discovered the physical law of buoyancy – the Archimedes Principle – which concluded than any body which is completely or partially submerged in a fluid at rest is acted upon by an upward or buoyant force. The freedom from gravity that we experience in water produces physiological changes within the body. On land, our brains are occupied with calculating and computing the effects of gravity, and organizing ways of keeping the body upright in spite of the constant downward pull of the gravitational field. Moshe Feldenkrais, a postural expert, believed that many of the stimuli received by the nervous system were generated by muscular activity resulting from the influence of gravity, which decreases our sensitivity to and

awareness of both external and internal reality. By contrast, being buoyant frees our brain and nervous system from much of this gravitational stress, thereby allowing our sensory perception to expand. Although water does not completely eliminate the influence of gravity, it does permit us to experience the greatest freedom from the gravitational pull that is attainable without going into space.

It is perhaps no coincidence that the creator of flotation tanks, fast becoming the Valium of the 1990s, was none other than Dr John Lilly, who initiated much of the research into human/dolphin interaction. Lilly devised the flotation or sensory deprivation tank in order to study areas of neurophysiology. His aim was to record the electrical activity of the brain and the simultaneous changes in the emotional state, in an attempt to establish a link between the brain and the emotions. Lilly believes that flotation reduces the effect of muscular tension, thereby allowing blood to flow and circulate more freely, and blood pressure and pulse rate to drop, and hence producing similar physiological effects to deep meditation. In Lilly's opinion this is due to the fact that flotation also appears to induce a theta state – a condition in which the brain produces waves of between 4Hz and 7Hz. Everyone generates such waves naturally, at least twice a day, in fleeting moments when we drift from a conscious drowsy state into sleep and again when we awaken from sleep into consciousness. The theta state is associated with dreamlike but vivid mental images, often perceived in conjunction with intense childhood memories. In this state, we have access to our subconscious creative side, which is conducive to insight, inspiration and enlightenment.

Researchers have also suggested that swimming with dolphins may trigger Alpha brain waves, which are generated at around 8Hz–12Hz. When in the Alpha state, the brain is unfocused but still alert. Alpha waves are linked to feelings of relaxation and serenity.

Water or hydrotherapy is also beneficial for those with illnesses such as arthritis and bursitis, because it reduces the physical stress on the body's structure. Hydrotherapy is now used in hospitals throughout the world to rehabilitate those with broken bones, torn tendons and ligaments, spinal injuries, as well as people with severe physical handicaps such as spina bifida and cerebral palsy. Dr David Nathanson, a psychologist who works with dolphins in conjunction with neurologically impaired children, believes that water plays a significant role in the therapeutic effect which dolphins appear to have on his patients: 'There has been a lot of research and literature which has reported the benefits of hydrotherapy, and this kind of therapy has been used successfully for treating people with brain damage and spinal injuries. Introducing water and thereby allowing people to experience a relaxation response is very important in the healing process. The combination of dolphins and water made an interesting proposition. In 1979 I went up to Oceanworld in Fort Lauderdale and did some pilot work with a group of Down's Syndrome and autistic children, to see if the idea held any real merit. The results were far more dramatic than I expected.'

Nathanson's study involved five children, of whom he noted that those with Down's Syndrome responded much better than those with autism. His views are controversial, because he uses the dolphins as a 'tool' or 'medium' to aid the learning process. The dolphins were deployed as part of a simple behavioural modification stimulus and reinforcement (see Chapter Three). Similar work is being carried out by Denis Brousse, a Professor of Biology and Physical Education, who has started a project in Lyons, France, using hydrotherapy to treat handicapped and autistic children. The difference between the work of Nathanson and Brousse is that the latter uses only water, believing that water alone has powerful therapeutic benefits. Hermione Swinford heard about Brousse's work through Michel Odent and decided to take her two-year-old daughter, Athene, who suffers from a neuromuscular disorder similar to cerebral palsy, to Lyons to work with Brousse. She states that 'Brousse initially taught me not to be afraid of the water, so that I would be confident. This then would be transmitted to Athene, who was actually afraid of water.' Brousse taught Swinford to enter the water in a physically and mentally positive way. He then showed her some fish-like swimming movements to boost her confidence and to encourage her to 'feel at one' with the water. Parents are also taught to let the child go in the water, so that he or she can experience release both from gravity and from any physical restraint. According to Swinford, 'Even children who have severe physical disabilities begin to unfold in the water. They slowly lose their fear and begin to move about, as if they are in a familiar, soothing environment.' Brousse also uses sound vibrations similar to those chanted by Tibetan monks. Parents are trained to make the sounds underwater next to the child, and to tap the soles of his or her feet to create a 'primal environment' similar to that of the womb. The success of Brousse's work raises many questions, including the possibility that water alone can be used as a therapy for handicapped children without the need for dolphin interaction.

The Chemical Factor
Research into the effects of flotation and immersion in water has shown that they have a significant impact on the release of brain chemicals. The neuroendocrinologist Dr John Turner and psychologist Dr Thomas Fine of the Medical College of Ohio in the United States have discovered that floating lowers levels of norepinephrine (adrenalin), cortisol and ACTH, all of which chemicals are directly linked to high levels of stress and stress-related illness. Raised levels of cortisol, for example, were found in people with 'Type A' personalities – those who were aggressive and hyperactive, and who were susceptible to heart disease and attacks – whereas 'Type B' personalities, who tended to be relaxed and almost immune to heart disease, had much lower levels (sometimes as much as 40 times lower). High levels of cortisol also depress the immune system, making us more vulnerable to auto-immune diseases such as Multiple Sclerosis, ulcerative colitis and even certain forms of cancer.

In addition to these discoveries, we can be almost certain that the combined physiological effect of water and the uplifting stimulus of the dolphin creates happiness. Researchers believe that water triggers the release of endorphins, the body's natural supply of opiates or pain-killers. It appears that being in water 'switches off' the production of certain chemicals linked to stress and illness, whilst increasing those which are beneficial, such as endorphins. Philip Applewhite, a biochemist at Yale University, believes that levels of endorphins make a huge difference to the way that we perceive our environment. In his view, 'Those with more endorphins released during certain activities may be happier about any given situation or event in their lives than those with fewer endorphins. That is, doing the same thing may be more pleasurable to one person than another because for that person, more endorphin molecules are released in the brain. Happiness, then, lies not outside the body, but within. Happiness is not an illusion; it is real and has a molecular basis.'

Dolphin Sound Effects: The Healing Power of Sound

The newest and perhaps most controversial theory that has been advanced to explain the dolphin's ability to trigger our healing mechanism is now gaining scientific corroboration. A person who is in water with dolphins can actually feel him- or herself being 'scanned', and hear the various echo-locative clicks being directed at him or her. Sometimes, it feels as if the sound is almost by-passing one's ears and going straight to the brain, as one can feel the clicks vibrating in one's skull. Ric O'Barry, the dolphin expert who trained the famous Flipper, asserts: 'Being in the water with dolphins makes a person feel very good. A lot of it is physical. You can feel the animals scanning you; you can hear a "ping" or a "click" like the creaking of a door and feel a not unpleasant sensual something go all through your body.'

The healing potential of sound was known to ancient civilizations, and yet we are only now beginning to understand how sonic vibrations can affect both our physical and mental wellbeing. Humans share with dolphins an emotional response to sounds – they have the power to move us. Dolphins also convey their emotional state by means of the quality of their sounds, in much the same way as we do, and seem to enjoy certain kinds of music. Back in the first century AD, Pliny wrote: 'The dolphin is an animal that is not only friendly to mankind, but is also a lover of music, and it can be charmed by singing in harmony, but particularly by the sound of the water organ.' The water organ was a musical instrument invented by an Egyptian in about 300 BC, which was used at festive occasions near the sea. The high notes would have given out ultrasonic vibrations which the dolphins could hear. Many classical Greek writers also tell of dolphins being attracted by the music of flutes.

When we talk about sound, we are referring to a form of energy vibration that we can actually hear. Vibrations travel through space in the form of waves, and the speed at which the wave completes a cycle is known as the frequency, expressed as cycles per seconds or Hertz (Hz). Humans' sonic range (that is, the range of our hearing) extends from 20Hz to 20,000Hz, or cycles per second, while dolphins' covers from 100 to 150,000Hz. Below the level of 20Hz, sounds are inaudible to us, and beyond 20,000Hz the vibrations are known as ultrasound. Sound has a dramatic impact on our senses. According to the psychiatrist Dr John Diamond, while some sounds and rhythms have a positive and uplifting effect, others can be draining and weakening. Diamond believes that rock music, for example, can be detrimental to the human body if the latter is exposed to such sounds for long periods of time. Furthermore, he maintains that the anapestic stopped beat of some forms of rock music results in loss of symmetry between the two cerebral hemispheres of the brain, resulting in subtle perceptual difficulties and a host of stress-related symptoms.

Another aspect of sound is the difference between the rate of body vibration and the impact of incoming frequencies. Dr Steve Halpern, an American pianist and musicologist, has discovered that body cells rarely vibrate at more than 1,000Hz, whereas our range of sound perception extends to 20,000Hz. The body therefore has to filter a broad range of incoming sounds, acting like a vibratory transformer, which can create stress. Sounds like the 'hum' of a television, which resonates at 15,750Hz, can have a very draining effect.

The ancient Greeks developed the theory that sound in the form of music or tone could have a healing effect: Aristotle, for example, reported that flute music could stimulate our emotions and release pent-up tension. The Greeks often had zithers playing as they dined, as these were thought to aid digestion. Casiodorus believed that the Aeolian form of music could treat mental disorders and help to induce sleep, whilst the Lydian mode was suitable for children and could 'soothe the soul when oppressed, with excessive care'. Pythagoras developed the concept of healing through melodic intervals and rhythms, although we have unfortunately no idea what the music sounded like. The writer Iamblichus, a noted mystic, wrote in great depth about Pythagoras' work at Crotona. He reported that Pythagoras had established a strong connection between the senses and music and that sound contributed 'greatly to health, if used in an appropriate manner'. By using various contraptions and apparatus, the precise form of which Iamblichus fails to explain, Pythagoras combined 'diatonic, chromatic and enharmonic melodies' which he believed had a direct effect upon negative emotions, particularly sorrow, rage, pity, pride and anger. According to Iamblichus, Pythagoras was able to correct these negative feelings by using the positive force of certain melodies that he had composed.

It is our belief that the whistles and squeaks that the dolphin emits may contribute to the healing phenomenon, by virtue of their influence on our emotions, in a similar way to both ancient and modern music therapy. The Viennese neuroscientist, engineer and musician Dr Manfred Clynes, who is head of the Research Centre at the New South Wales Conservatorium of Music, has shown that emotions exist in their own right as potential patterns in the nervous system and can be triggered by sound and music in a general way, independently of associations with people or events. In his opinion, certain passages of music, depending on the shape of the musical phrases in their structure, can generate such responses as joy, sadness, love or reverence. The musical expression of such emotions requires not only a certain spacing in time and pitch, but also that the amplitudes in the music follow an appropriate essentic form which 'can touch the heart as directly as a physical touch'. Clynes believes that these essentic forms have a therapeutic application. He has defined the Standard Cycle of Emotions, which consists of seven feelings – anger, grief, love, sex, joy and reverence. Each of these emotions, by Clynes' reckoning, has a span of expression ranging from 4.8 seconds (anger) to 9.8 seconds (reverence).

But how does all this relate to dolphins? According to the British doctor Peter Guy Manners, who has been investigating the therapeutic use of sound for 20 years, every part of the human anatomy produces a sound or vibration. When there is an illness or dysfunction in an organ or gland, there are measurable changes in its vibratory or resonant characteristics. To 'rebalance' the organ, Manners created cymatic therapy – now widely established throughout the world – in which controlled computed harmonics are used to treat the relevant organ. Manners maintains that the brain's energy levels play a very important role in sustaining overall energy levels of the body. When energy in the brain is low, or when the left and right hemispheres of the brain are unbalanced, it cannot function efficiently. However, if you can restore this balance, you can go on to treat areas of disease in the rest of the body. He suggests that because energy flow is audible and magnetic in nature, it can be rebalanced by magnetic cymatic or sound energy. Could it be that dolphins have the ability to 'tune into' disharmonies in the human body? Manners observes that 'When swimming with dolphins, they come alongside, as if investigating, sounding us out. Investigation shows that dolphins do have a therapeutic effect on humans. For example, people with paraplegia or mental depression tend to feel better when they interact with dolphins. I believe that it is possible that dolphins can vary their sonar to pick up vibrational form and can detect any imbalances of sound. In the water they are in the best possible position to pick up the force field of a human being. Of course, at present these are all only theories. As yet we have no substantial proof, but it would appear to make perfect sense on a scientific level.' And could dolphins be doing with sound what is being done with cymatics? As far as Manners is concerned, 'Their sonic systems are far more efficient than our technology. I feel certain that they have this ability.'

Many people will of course view these ideas with great scepticism, but cymatics is very similar in principle to many ancient Eastern healing techniques. Eastern practitioners believe that there are seven main energy power centres, or *chakras*, within the 'subtle' body – that is, the body just beyond our physical body. According to ancient texts from Indian yogic literature, *chakras* act like energy transformers, converting energy of one form and frequency to another. Illness can stem from energy blockages within the body, and only by unblocking these energy channels can the correct energy balance be restored and optimum health achieved. Acupuncture, reflexology and certain forms of chanting are all used to restore the free flow of energy, using a similar underlying theory to that of Manners' cymatics, which in essence uses one form of energy to stimulate the flow of energy in the physical body.

The sounds that dolphins emit are in the region of 1,000Hz to 80,000Hz, whereas our communication range is lower and narrower, lying between 300Hz and 3,000Hz. As previously mentioned, the sounds audible to us lie between 20Hz and 20,000Hz, which means that we can only actually hear the noises dolphins make between 1,000Hz and 20,000Hz. This does not mean, however, that we do not sense or respond to those of an ultrasonic nature.

For the past 20 years, Tony Bassett, an electronics engineer, has been studying the effect of certain sound vibrations on brain waves. He has found that those frequencies in the region of 2,000Hz appear to trigger the production of endorphins, natural pleasure-inducing chemicals, and he has been using this therapy, with remarkable success, for easing the pain of withdrawal from heroin addiction. Such frequencies are within the dolphin's sonic emission range, which may help to explain why contact with dolphins can evoke feelings of euphoria.

It is also interesting to note that in Ayurvedic medicine, certain 'primordial' sounds are thought to have the power to inhibit the proliferation of cancer cells. Furthermore, recent studies have revealed that canaries deprived of each other's songs suffer from a retardation of brain growth – their singing, in other words, seems to promote and stimulate the growth of brain cells.

Some forms of ultrasound, too, are now being used as an alternative to invasive therapy, to destroy cataracts, kidney and gallstones, and even some kinds of tumour. Is it possible that the dolphin's ultrasonic frequencies work in a similar way, hence the numerous accounts of tumours shrinking and cancers regressing in patients who have swum with dolphins? The obstetrician Michel Odent has no doubts that ultrasound has a biological effect on us. 'We know that ultrasound has a biological effect – it is not neutral. It may well be that certain frequencies trigger the production of certain enzymes or neurochemicals.'

The ultrasound frequencies used in medicine are much higher than those emitted by the dolphin: ultrasonic scans that are used to enable an examination of the unborn fetus, for example, operate on 3.5 million Hz, and frequencies of up to 10 million Hz are used in surgery to break down certain forms of tumour and kidney stones. The dolphin's range stops at 80,000Hz, but, as we have seen, sound expert Tony Bassett believes that even low frequencies – from 2,000Hz up – can have a positive biological influence. As yet, there is little scientific proof that the dolphin's ultrasound is powerful enough either to scan our bodies in any detail or to induce a physiotherapeutic effect. There have been many anecdotal reports, however, that suggest that ultrasound may play a part in the healing

Wild dolphins exude an energy and a vitality that have uplifted man since time immemorial.

Wild Atlantic spotted dolphins (Stenella frontalis) interacting with a diver in the Bahamas.

The bottlenose dolphin (Tursiops truncatus) is one of the species most familiar to man.

Mother and baby dolphin bond closely for up to six years before the young dolphin joins its contemporaries.

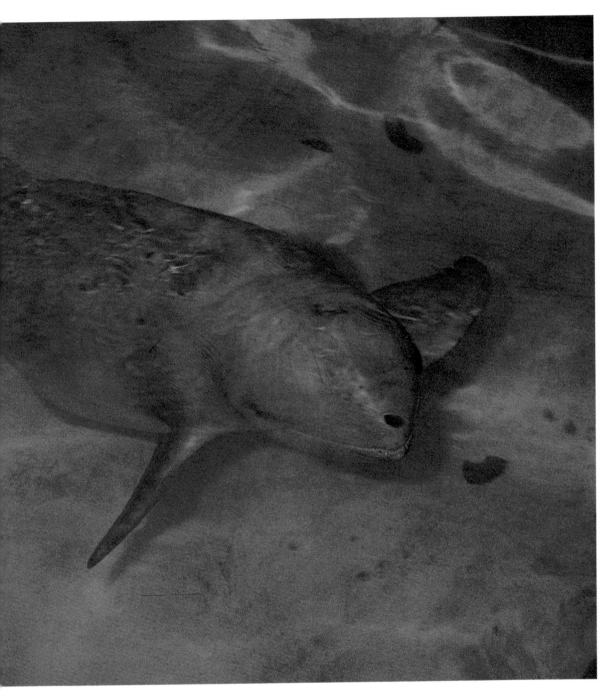

A rare Irrawaddy dolphin (Oraella brevirostris), found in the Makaham River, East Borneo.

The dolphin receives deflected sonic vibrations through its mandibular nerve, located just below the lower jaw.

Like humans, dolphins communicate not only through sound but with body language. Dolphins will mimic a human's body posture in the water.

Therapist Dr David Nathanson at the Dolphin Research Center, Florida, USA, with one of the dolphin 'teachers'.

At the Dolphin Research Center, semi-captive dolphins are employed to facilitate the learning process in children suffering from Down's Syndrome, neurological disorders and physical handicaps.

A family of Hawaiian spinner dolphins. Dolphins live in close-knit communities called pods. Highly social creatures, they have a complex code of behaviour which enables them to live in harmony with both their environment and one another.

The freshwater Amazon river dolphin (Inia geoffrensis) is in great danger of becoming extinct.

Commerson's dolphin (Cephalorhynchus commersonii), one of the most distinctly marked ocean-dwelling dolphins.

*The pantropical spinner dolphin (*Stenella longirostris*) is one of the most aquadynamic dolphin species.*

Spotted dolphins in the Bahamas.

A pod of dusky dolphins (Lagenorhynchus obscurus) in their natural habitat — the shallow waters of islands and coastal regions.

Southern right whale dolphins (Lissodelphis peronii) *off the Chilean coast.*

interaction that takes place between man and dolphin. One instance was noted by researchers at a dolphin swim programme in the United States. According to their report, a female swimmer who was participating in the daily dolphin swim was rammed in the ribs by a normally docile dolphin. Somewhat upset and shocked by the incident, she was taken to a nearby hospital to be X-rayed. When the doctor in charge of her case received the X-ray results, he reported that he had found a tumour in her lung, just beneath the ribs where the dolphin had bruised her. Had the dolphin spotted the tumour, or was the episode mere coincidence?

Dr Richard Ferraro, who has been working with diagnostic ultrasound for 15 years, and who is now studying dolphin communication using ultrasonic devices, agrees that dolphins are able to scan us using echo location – audible sound frequencies – and that it is possible they could see inside the human body and detect physiological abnormalities. However, he is very doubtful that dolphins could actually use their ultrasound to kill tumours or effect any biological changes: 'I've been working with diagnostic ultrasound for many years, and I don't think it is possible that dolphins can use their ultrasound for any therapeutic purpose. The power to heal, however, is something we know very little about. Who knows if it's possible for dolphins to evoke a healing response in humans?'

DOLPHIN THERAPY

We now turn to the issue of how we can experience the healing power of dolphins without compromising their freedom. We have no doubt that the most powerful therapeutic benefits stem from close encounters with wild dolphins. However, at present, encounters with solitary wild dolphins are, inevitably, few and far between. There are a number of centres throughout the world which operate swim programmes, but sadly dolphins held in captive situations respond differently to us because the encounter is forced, arising not because the dolphins choose our company but because they are held captive and often rewarded with fish for paying us any kind of attention. In highlighting the healing potential of dolphins, the last thing that we want to encourage is captive dolphins in every institution and hospital, or an increase in the number of dolphins taken from the wild. Currently, there are a number of dolphinariums, obviously keen to improve their credibility at a time when public opinion is welling up against them, which are urging the sick and handicapped to come and visit their whales and dolphins, and we have heard of a couple of instances which we found quite ridiculous and which illustrate the fact that the healing potential of dolphins can be misinterpreted. Windsor Safari Park in the United Kingdom, for example, has taken to allowing paraplegics in wheelchairs to watch dolphins in their pens before the shows. Quite what the therapeutic benefits of such encounters might be, we have no idea, but it is a prime example of lack of understanding. We have also heard about a young girl with a brain tumour who was allowed to swim with the dolphins at

Flamingoland in Scarborough. Again, this illustrates the misinterpretation and misuse of the dolphin's healing potential: ideally, the only way that dolphin interaction should take place is in the wild, on the animals' terms. Fortunately, there are also a growing number of wild dolphin projects which enable people to see and encounter dolphins in the creatures' natural habitat, so allowing the dolphins the freedom to choose or avoid human company.

But what we should really be aiming to do is to learn from the dolphin and explore how best to use synthesized versions of 'dolphin technology' to elicit a healing response. There is growing evidence that even watching videos and films of dolphins, and listening to recordings of their sounds, can help to trigger similar emotions to those experienced when one is actually in the presence of dolphins – although the effect is of course diluted. We have no doubt that many people could benefit enormously if dolphin therapy was used in this way too.

There is already a plethora of audio 'healing' tapes that involve dolphin sounds, and many of these tapes also incorporate visualization techniques that help the listener to conjure up dolphin images and encounters. Dr Horace Dobbs, known for his work with depressives and dolphins, and founder of Operation Sunflower, a project which studies the effects of human/dolphin interaction, is fronting a project called Dolphin Dreamtime. This originates in Australia and combines auto-suggestion with music that comprises dolphin sounds based on Aboriginal telepathic links with the dolphin. Dobbs, who refers to this form of therapy as the 'audio pill', is studying the effects of the Dolphin Dreamtime tape on a number of volunteers. He claims that the response to the tape has been very positive and that a wide variety of people, some suffering from depression and mental illness, have noted therapeutic benefits. Dr Dobbs is simultaneously working on another project which aims to simulate the healing effect of a dolphin encounter. He plans to develop, design and construct the world's first Dolphin Therapy Pool, by combining dolphin images, perhaps in the form of holograms, with the soothing effect of water and dolphin sounds. Dobbs feels that in this way, many people could benefit from the healing power of dolphin interaction without having to exploit live dolphins.

At the Bretforton Hall Clinic in Worcestershire in the United Kingdom, Dr Peter Guy Manners, the creator of cymatic sound therapy, has devised a therapy he calls Aqua Sonics, which he uses to treat patients with a variety of ailments. 'We are experimenting with playing dolphin sounds underwater to see if they have an effect, although as yet, we do not know specifically which frequencies to use. However, results show that the dolphin sounds seem to have a relaxing and calming effect on patients, even though they are inaudible to the human ear.'

In both the United States and the United Kingdom, various organizations have been set up to promote the benefits of watching all kinds of animals in their natural environment and to study the healing potential of encounters with animals (see Chapter Three). The

Latham Foundation for the Promotion of Humane Education, in the United States, founded by Milton and Edith Latham in 1918, promotes the wellbeing of people, animals and their mutual environment. The Foundation provides an educational service which can supply videos and films that investigate the physical and mental benefits of the 'Human/ Companion Animal Bond' – the interaction between animals and humans. The underlying philosophy of the Foundation is 'respect for all life through education', an idea which sits well with the spirit of the dolphin. Another organization, the Delta Society, also in the United States, is geared to encouraging partnerships between humans and animals and to educating and inspiring people by means of videos and films. The Society offers a wide range of films of both wild and domestic animals, which it sends to schools, hospitals and old people's homes to encourage interaction with animals and to inspire those who have no access to pets themselves. In the United Kingdom, The Society for Companion Animal Studies (SCAS) was set up in 1979 by a group of psychiatrists, psychologists, social workers and veterinary surgeons from Britain and the United States to promote interest and education in relationships between humans and companion animals. Since then it has organized major conferences, initiated much research into the therapeutic benefits of interaction with animals, and provided a full information service for the general public.

Being shut away in hospital environments is not conducive to the healing process. By contrast, anything which recreates a feeling of being at one with nature, be it videos of wild dolphins, or tapes of natural sounds, could play an enormous part in healing. This, surely, is the medicine of the future.

....

Chapter Two

DOLPHIN MIDWIVES

INTRODUCTION

Dolphins and humans share a common approach to birth and child-rearing. In both dolphin and human society, birth is a very female event, and as far as human birth is concerned, it is only relatively recently that men have begun to get involved in the processes of labour and delivery. Dolphins give birth in the presence of experienced female 'midwives', with the mother being supported throughout her labour by these aquatic attendants. Meanwhile, the male dolphins distance themselves from the labouring female and guard the territory to keep predators at bay. An examination of human society also reveals that men act as the protectors and hunters, whilst women disappear into a private domain to give birth either amongst other women or in isolation. The renowned French obstetrician, Michel Odent, one of the pioneers of the water birth movement, has pointed out that, in his experience, women are often better off on their own during labour and really only need help in the second stage, just as the baby is about to emerge. Perhaps we have strayed too far from our natural behaviour by including men in the total birthing event, and we may have much to learn from the dolphin's approach.

Like most female mammals, the mother dolphin carries her unborn infant in her body until it is ready to be born. In the case of dolphins, the gestation period is almost a year, and the baby is connected to the mother by an umbilical cord which supplies nutrients and oxygen. Like some pregnant women, the expectant dolphin engages in what appears to be antenatal exercise in readiness for the birth. She may flex and bend her tail and head, arching her body and tensing her muscles, as if preparing for contractions during labour. Dolphins in captivity have been observed exercising in this manner for up to an hour each day in the weeks preceding the onset of labour. After the birth, the close bond between mother and baby is maintained and, like a human child, the dolphin infant is completely dependent on its mother for many months. When it is born, it swims up to the surface within moments to take its first breath, assisted by the mother and sometimes by a dolphin midwife which may nudge it gently upwards. Then, within twenty-four hours of its birth, the baby begins to suckle, and from this point onwards stays close by its mother's side. This intimate bonding between mother and baby is of paramount importance to the development and survival of the dolphin, just as it is for the human child.

WATER BABIES

In human society, the idea of water birth is not new. Although in our own time, water births have only recently come into the limelight, they were practised by the ancient Egyptians, the ancient Greeks – Aphrodite was apparently born from the foam of waves – the Maoris, Panamanian Indians, Japanese women living by the sea, coastal Aborigines and some Pygmy tribes. In Polynesia, some women still give birth in the warm waters of coral reef lagoons. This attraction to water is not surprising. A primal environment, water not only links back with our evolutionary aquatic past, but also offers a comforting reminder of our first nine months of life, spent bobbing around in the soothing environment of the amniotic fluid.

Furthermore, modern research into the use of water during labour has shown that water is beneficial and supportive, and helps to relieve pain. Studies into the use of water in childbirth have revealed that being in water can change our perception of pain. Nerve fibres carry electrical impulses from pain receptors at any site of painful stimulus to the dorsal horn of the spinal cord, and from there they are transmitted to the cerebral cortex in the brain. In the 1970s, two researchers, Wall and Melzack, created the 'gate theory' of pain. They discovered that painful sensations can be modified or partially 'gated out' by sensations of warmth and touch on the skin. (This is also why massage can help to reduce pain.) Because pain impulses are transmitted more slowly than sensations of warmth and touch, it is thought that water can work to reduce pain: immersion in water appears to stimulate touch and temperature nerve receptors throughout the body, which in turn send pleasure signals to the brain. Michel Odent also believes that water has specific pain-relieving qualities: 'From my experience, water appears to reduce the woman's neocortical control, thereby helping to dull painful sensations.'

In the 1960s, the concept of water birth was pioneered in Russia by Igor Tjarkovsky, a swimming instructor, male midwife and researcher. Tjarkovsky observed that many mammals could be trained to give birth in water and to nurture their young in an aquatic environment. His research seemed to show that water not only facilitated a gentler, easier and less painful birth, but also appeared to influence the development of the newborn animal. He transferred his theories from animals to humans when his daughter, Veta, who was born prematurely, was introduced to water shortly after her birth. Tjarkovsky noted that the aquatic environment apparently speeded up her growth and development – it was as if the water acted like a synthetic womb.

He then took his work a step further, and installed a glass tank in his bathroom in which he helped many women give birth. From this research, he observed that children born underwater have a better start in life. In deliveries which take place on dry land, it appears that the sudden exposure, at birth, to the force of gravity after months of weightlessness in the womb, coupled with the equally sudden exposure to a huge amount of oxygen, may have a detrimental effect on the baby's brain function. By contrast, Tjarkovsky asserted that in water births, 'We are not confronting the child with anything new. We are simply prolonging the uterine conditions so beneficial to development. Living in water is totally natural for a newborn. He's never done anything else.' Although many adversaries of this theory argue that water birth is potentially hazardous, and suggest that there is a high risk the babies might drown, Tjarkovsky and Odent say in defence of the method that there is no more likelihood of the baby drowning in the birthing pool than of it drowning in its own amniotic fluid. 'The reflex to breathe is stimulated by contact with cold air, not by emergence from the birthing canal,' points out Michel Odent.

When Odent first encountered the phenomenon of women wanting to give birth in water, at Pithiviers hospital in France, he was unaware of the impact it would have on attitudes to childbirth. He believes that because water tends to reduce adrenalin, the hormone associated with fear and anxiety, and reduces the force of gravity and creates a soothing, womb-like environment, it helps to induce a physiological state called the 'relaxation response'. In labour, this helps the woman to deal with contractions and allows her to be completely absorbed in her own body and the experience of the birth.

DOLPHINS AND BIRTH

It seems likely that there has always been a connection between dolphins and child birth: perhaps it is more than mere coincidence that the Greek words for 'dolphin' and 'womb' are so similar, being 'delphis' and 'delphys' respectively. According to many delphinologists, dolphins hold a fascination for pregnant human mothers. Bizarre as this may sound, there have been many reports by women who, during pregnancy, have swum with dolphins, that the animals hone in on the unborn fetus and pay it special attention. One possible explanation for this is that the dolphin's extraordinary echo-locative powers enable it to 'scan' the abdomen of a pregnant woman and detect the presence of the baby. Although the ultrasonic frequency that dolphins beam out stops at around 80,000Hz, while the scanning machines in hospitals use 3.5 million Hz, the sound engineer, Tony Bassett, has no doubts that the dolphins can still 'scan' us, although they will not get such a refined 'picture'.

There are other, more mystical explanations offered as to why dolphins should have an affinity with pregnant women. One theory proposed by Igor Tjarkovsky is that the dolphin and the unborn child 'share the same non-specific language', or, in other words, can communicate telepathically with one another. Far-fetched as this may seem, there are nevertheless many stories in both American Native Indian and Aboriginal culture that endorse this notion of telepathic communication. For example, one tribe of Aborigines from the coast of northern Australia are called the Dolphin People and are supposedly able to communicate with dolphins 'mind to mind'.

Aside from this theory, Tjarkovsky and fellow researcher Dr Igor Smirnov have been involved in many experiments in which dolphins were present at human births. Smirnov was engaged in one particularly interesting experiment in which he worked with a pregnant woman who went into labour in the water of the Black Sea whilst in the presence of dolphins. As her labour progressed, the dolphins encircled her protectively. Smirnov described the incident thus: 'It was magical. The minute the dolphins appeared, all of the mother's fears and anxieties were diminished; a very serene and tranquil birth took place.'

Since 1979, Tjarkovsky, too, has been studying the relationship between pregnant women, babies, young children and dolphins. During the summer of that year, he and several other researchers from the All-Union Scientific Research Institute for Physical Culture, Moscow, together with a number of female athletes, women in various stages of pregnancy, mothers and their children, made an expedition to a dolphin research station on the Black Sea. There Tjarkovsky and his team carried out a number of experiments with the dolphins. Many of the trials had to be undertaken at night whilst the station researchers slept. Although the latter were worried that it was dangerous to let newborn babies swim in the water with the dolphins, none the less, the staff allowed Tjarkovsky to carry out his studies undeterred. The results were remarkable. The dolphins appeared very aware of the needs of the tiny babies and children, swimming gently beside them and moving slowly at the childrens' pace. And the creatures seemed quite happy to indulge them in their games. Even the youngest children were not afraid to ride on the dolphins, using the various saddles that Tjarkovsky and the other scientists had constructed. Some of the babies were also quite happy to hold onto the dolphins as the animals dived under the water to search for food. The dolphins always surfaced when the children needed a breath of air.

Tjarkovsky believes that the dolphin's bio-field — its electromagnetic or energy force field — has a very powerful effect on human beings of all ages, especially babies and young children. This would explain why, in his experiments, the dolphins seemed to eliminate any fears of the water, giving the swimmers a great sense of security, peace and deep contentment.

Tjarkovsky's other controversial work with children involves plunging babies with certain health conditions, such as a weak heart, asthma or poor circulation, into cold water, often head first, so that they have to learn quickly to control their breath. He believes that this helps to strengthen the baby both physically and psychologically, by triggering the immune system and certain neuro-chemicals, and by stimulating muscular contractions. During one of his sessions, involving a baby in the Black Sea, an incident occurred which made him realize just how developed the dolphin's powers of communication were and how sensitive the animals were to human suffering. 'I remember this incident very clearly,' he recounts. 'I was working with a one-month-old baby girl underwater, counting the seconds as usual to see when it would be time to swim up. Suddenly two dolphins came swimming at me at top speed. At first I thought that they were angry. I grew frightened when they shoved me aside and pushed the child up to the surface. But they only wanted to give her air. When I came to the surface several seconds later, I realized that I hadn't been sufficiently attentive. I had stayed underwater a little too long. The dolphins seemed to have noticed this before I did, and perhaps to have sensed a signal that I wasn't aware of from the child.'

HOMO DELPHINUS

It was the legendary free diver, Jacques Mayol, who first conceived the idea of a species he called *Homo delphinus* – 'dolphin man'. Having witnessed the work of both Michel Odent and Igor Tjarkovsky, Mayol was inspired to write a book entitled *Homo delphinus* which investigated the relationship between man, dolphin and water. The book's description of the emergence of a so-called new race or species of human babies born in water who exhibit dolphin traits, such as incredible prowess in the water and an ability to dive to great depths and hold their breath for up to three or four minutes, has led to much debate.

Proponents of water-birthed babies and infants who spend much time in the water immediately after birth and during their formative years, suggest that the children are physically stronger, more intelligent, happier and better adjusted than most others. They also suggest that aquatic babies are more intuitive and appear to feel a strong link with dolphins, even if they have not been born in their presence. In 1971, an Australian swimming instructor and midwife, Cookie Harkin, started work on developing 'Babyswim' programmes which encouraged parents to teach their newborn infants and young children to swim. Harkin also set up pre- and post-natal swimming programmes to strengthen the body for childbirth and to create a close bond between mother and child after delivery. More recently, she has taken her work a step further and has started a project which involves taking her 'water babies' to swim in the open sea and to encounter dolphins. Harkin believes, like Tjarkovsky, that both the fetus and the newborn baby have brain waves that are attuned to those of whales and dolphins, thereby facilitating telepathic contact.

Estelle Myers, a dolphin researcher who is also Australian, has become renowned for her work with dolphins and water birth. Myers suggests that we have much to learn from cetacea, especially dolphins. She believes that babies 'born from the water of the womb into the water of the world have a potential to dive 200 feet on a breath of 16 minutes', are more likely to be non-aggressive, and are predisposed to living in harmony and peace with each other and the environment.

Despite the appeal of such ideologies, one must question whether the mere fact of being born into water can really create a new race of aquatic humans. Be that as it may, perhaps by watching these 'water babies' develop and grow up, we can in some way learn more about the dolphin.

Chapter Three
....

DOLPHIN TEACHERS

INTRODUCTION

During the course of our investigation into the dolphin's healing powers, another aspect of human/dolphin interaction that came to our attention was that of handicapped children and dolphins. Since the 1970s, several research programmes have centred their attentions on the dolphin's ability to help unlock the secret world of the autistic child and to assist in teaching the mentally handicapped. Our curiosity about these matters was tempered with some scepticism and also with certain reservations, as the programmes operate in conjunction with captive rather than wild dolphins. Nevertheless, we decided that this facet of the dolphin's power to assist our own healing potential was an important one.

PET THERAPY – A NEW SCIENCE

Doctors and scientists have known for many years that animals can play a vital role in maintaining the equilibrium of the human mind and body. In the 1960s, Dr Boris Levinson, a renowned New York psychiatrist, found that the presence of a pet during psychiatric sessions greatly improved his contact with his patients, particularly those who were withdrawn. Since then, many of Levinson's theories have been backed up by modern research. A recent study by the National Institute of Health in the United States reported findings from a number of researchers who had studied the effects of household pets on the owners' physical wellbeing. The heart rates and blood pressure of those who spent time each day with their pets, stroking them and talking to them, were significantly lower. Some researchers reported that the results were also similar to those obtained in studies involving people who meditated regularly. Scientists are now investigating the possible health benefits that can be derived from interactions between humans and animals. This field of work is known as zootherapy, animal-facilitated therapy, or pet therapy. At the Ohio State University, for example, companion animals have been used in the rehabilitation of severely withdrawn psychiatric patients, while researchers at the Universities of Maryland and Pennsylvania have shown that animals can improve the survival rate of patients who have suffered heart attacks.

Animals, be they dogs, cats, horses or dolphins, can also play a vital role in communication with children who suffer from a variety of handicaps. Horseriding for children with physical disabilities was initially considered simply a novelty, yet several years of studies revealed that in fact it gave such children a new sense of freedom and achievement which they then carried over into their everyday lives. Many parents of children who had been involved in such projects noted positive behavioural and mood changes in their offspring – children were less difficult, were able to assimilate information more easily, and their learning capacity increased.

During our own research quest, we were lucky enough to spend time with Dr Betsy Smith, Ph.D., an educational anthropologist and associate professor in the School of Public Affairs and Services at Florida International University, Miami. She has explored the benefits of pet therapy and has turned to dolphins in order to help autistic children. Autism is a developmental disability which usually manifests itself in the first three years of life. Occurring in approximately five out of every 10,000 births, it is four times more common in boys than in girls. Autism has been observed throughout the world and appears to affect children from all racial, ethnic and social backgrounds. In most cases, the cause is not known, although researchers have suggested that the condition is due to physical rather than psychological factors and that it could be linked to nutritional abnormalities – specifically zinc deficiency and high levels of lead – or to exposure of the fetus to electromagnetic radiation whilst in utero. There are several types of autism, each linked to neurological impairment. The symptoms include slow development or lack of physical, social and learning skills; immature speech patterns, or limited understanding of ideas and use of words without attaching the usual meaning to them; abnormal responses to sensation; abnormal ways of relating to people, objects and events (for instance, in many cases of autism, the child often does not use toys in the way they are intended to be used). Dr Smith observes that 'autistic children also appear to suffer from anxiety, which in turn blocks them from learning. They need to be content and relaxed to learn.' From her research, Smith suggests that dolphins help to create these essential positive emotions, freeing the children from anxiety and stress.

She started her work with autistic children and dolphin therapy in the early 1970s, when the World Dolphin Foundation established a programme called The Dolphin Project, at Mashta Island on Key Biscayne in Florida. Bottlenose dolphins were kept in a one-and-a-half-acre lagoon to provide a free-swimming environment where they could behave very much as they do in the wild, without having to perform tricks. Together with the president and director of scientific research for the Foundation, Dr Henry Truby, and Nancy Phillips, a consultant to the South Florida Society for Autistic Children, Dr Smith noted that neurologically impaired children appeared to respond positively to close contact with these free-swimming dolphins. In particular, Dr Smith recorded the case of David, a retarded adult and one of the dolphins, Liberty, who normally exhibited aggressive and unruly behaviour. 'The dolphin became gentle, patient and attentive when

David entered the water and initiated contact,' noted Smith. David, who was usually very cautious near water, and slow to adapt to new stimuli, entered the water almost immediately and began talking to Liberty, reaching out to stroke the animal. The results of the initial studies also showed clearly that dolphins could increase autistics' communication skills and encourage such people to relate to the real world whilst improving their learning abilities.

From this preliminary study, Dr Smith and her colleagues set up Project Inreach in 1978. The aim of the project was to investigate the possibility that specific dolphins and autistic children could elicit unprecedented communicatory demonstrations and that the dolphins could provide a therapeutic benefit for the children and their parents. As before, the project was set up on Key Biscayne in conjunction with Wometco Miami Seaquarium, which provided three Atlantic bottlenose dolphins and several dolphin trainers. The dolphins – Dawn, which had a patient and gentle personality, Holly, which had lost her baby, and Sharkey, a gregarious and energetic male – were accustomed to human interaction and had been specially selected. Eight children between the ages of 10 and 17, all of whom could communicate in some way using expressions and gestures, but could not speak, were volunteered by the South Florida Society for Autistic Children. In order to study the interactions carefully, the researchers taped and video-recorded six encounter sessions lasting from four to six hours. A spectograph was used to measure the human and animal signals made during the encounters. All forms of communication, both verbal and non-verbal, were noted by researchers. In one particular instance, it was clear that the dolphin and the human had made a significant connection. Michael Williams, an 18-year-old who from the age of six had been diagnosed as 'a non-verbal autistic child' (that is, one unable to produce human sounds), was of particular interest to the researchers. At the second session, he began to make a 'clicking' sound, similar to that made by the dolphins, to attract Sharkey to participate in playing with a ball. On tape, the researchers found it difficult to differentiate between the dolphin's click and Michael's clicking, although there was more of a difference between his and the female dolphins' clicks. Michael continued to make the clicking sound whenever he saw images of dolphins. Richard Prager, Michael's teacher, observed: 'After the first couple of sessions, I noticed that Michael was happier. He was easier to work with, more relaxed and more enthusiastic in class.' The other parents, teachers and investigators also noticed that all the children were more approachable, calmer and seemed to be happier as a result of contact with the dolphins. These effects appeared to last for up to a fortnight after each encounter.

After the success of this project, Smith went on to instigate a second research programme in 1981 – the Dolphins Plus Study. Incorporating the information from Project Inreach, the Study was designed to encourage autistic children to communicate by using dolphin interaction. The Dolphins Plus Marine Mammal Center, at Key Largo in Florida, where specially acclimatized dolphins and people who feel at ease in the water can make contact in as natural an environment as possible, was chosen by Smith for the study. At Dolphins Plus, unlike some of the centres where interactions take place, the dolphins are not on a food-reinforcement reward system. Smith feels strongly that the dolphins should interact of their own free will with the children and that the encounters should not be forced. From our own observations, the dolphins seemed to enjoy participating in the project and did not need the promise of a fish reward to maintain interest in the children. Furthermore, the animals began to recognize the children and showed obvious pleasure at the prospect of another encounter (see Part III, pp. 97–131).

Using younger children than in her previous study, Smith's objectives were to investigate further any non-verbal interactions between dolphins and autistic children. The project also continued to chart the progress of Michael Williams, who showed significant signs of improvement during the four-year period since his initial involvement in Project Inreach in 1978. From the results of the Dolphins Plus Study, Smith concluded that the Atlantic bottlenose dolphin could stimulate uncharacteristic spontaneous behaviour in an autistic person. She asserts: 'I believe that the explanation of this phenomenon involves the role of play and play therapy.' Smith also believes that dolphins enable greater therapeutic benefits to be achieved than do other domestic pets. 'Dogs, cats and doves have been used in therapeutic programmes with children, but these animals do not have the natural spontaneous play repertory of the dolphin. Nor do they have the intelligence of the dolphin, and that is the key. A dog will return a thrown stick in a stereotypical manner to an autistic child as long as he [the dog] is rewarded. The dolphin, however, will continuously change the game. If the child gets tired of being towed, then the dolphin will come up and push the child playfully around.' Dr Smith further maintains that the supportive nature of the dolphin's environment, and the fact that the dolphin is an animal which has exhibited a natural affinity with human beings since time immemorial, are key factors in explaining the success of dolphin-facilitated therapy.

Smith is very concerned that neither the dolphins nor the handicapped children should be exploited, and she is careful to point out that although she herself is certain that dolphin therapy works better than interaction with dogs or cats, there is no real proof of this in scientific terms. There is one thing however of which she is sure – that dolphins do affect humans at a very deep level. 'When you swim with dolphins you experience similar physiological changes to those experienced in deep meditation. Dolphins are totally absorbing – they are the ultimate Zen experience if you like.' Although Smith's work has been with dolphins in captive and semi-captive environments, she believes that the ultimate accomplishments will be achieved by people who are working with dolphins in the wild. In her view, such researchers 'are the ones who can make those kind of breakthroughs. In captivity we are only learning bits and pieces about the dolphin. To truly understand how the dolphin functions, we need to make more contact in the wild.'

Zootherapy and Down's Syndrome

At the Dolphin Research Center in Grassy Key, Florida, Dr David Nathanson, a psychologist, researcher and professor at the Florida International University, recently received international acclaim for his successful study entitled *Using the Atlantic Bottlenose Dolphin to Increase the Cognition of Mentally Retarded Children*. Nathanson's theory is that the deficiency of a mentally handicapped child lies not in his or her cognitive abilities, but in his or her ability to focus his or her attention. Nathanson's research into pet therapy had alerted him to the fact that there were two things to which handicapped children responded best – music and animals. Experts had noted that handicapped children in classroom settings are generally easily bored and have short attention spans, of between five and 10 minutes. But if such a child is given a puppy or a kitten, the child pays attention for a longer period, of about 20 to 25 minutes. Researchers observed a similar response to music. Once the child's attention is captured, the teacher can then begin to teach. Nathanson was interested in finding ways of increasing the childrens' attention span more significantly, thereby improving their ability to learn and decreasing the time that it takes to teach them. He initially developed a programme which used dolphins as part of a simple behavioural modification – as a stimulus and reinforcement. Using picture boards of words the children had to learn, Nathanson and the dolphins' trainers taught the dolphins to push the board towards the children. If the latter responded correctly, they got a 'reward' or reinforcement, consisting of being allowed to feed or touch the dolphins. Nathanson chose dolphins because of their gentle disposition and intelligence, and because it was clear that children would enjoy kissing, petting and swimming with them in exchange for giving correct responses. The idea of using dolphins in this manner, rather like giving a child a sweet, is unacceptable to many dolphin activists, but when one actually witnesses the dolphins, Nathanson and the children in action, it is difficult not to see the value of this form of interaction.

Although this aspect of his work is controversial, none the less the results have been startling. Nathanson found that the learning abilities of some of the children involved in the project increased by as much as 500 per cent. Although he has no precise explanation as to why dolphins are successful 'teachers', he believes that it is due to a combination of factors: 'Being able to pet and swim with a dolphin is a much more stimulating reward for effort than the "very good" the children get in a classroom. Obviously, they're much more motivated to respond to teaching. The presence of the dolphins has a very potent stress-reducing effect on the children. The dolphins are so beautiful and so graceful, so pleasant to touch. It puts the children in such a deeply relaxed state that they become much more receptive to teaching.'

Nathanson next tried working with the children on a one-to-one basis, with their mothers taking the place of the dolphins. He claims: 'The kids, especially those with

Down's Syndrome, did better with the dolphins.' (Down's Syndrome, once referred to as Mongolism, is the most common genetic cause of retardation. There are different types, but the most common is caused by the presence of an extra 'piece' of chromosome on the twenty-first pair.)

Having carried out these preliminary studies at Ocean World, in 1988 Nathanson set up a project at the Dolphin Research Center. This involves six children with various handicaps, ranging from Down's Syndrome to cerebral palsy, with whom Nathanson spends two days a week working in conjunction with dolphins. Although many people have argued that he is merely using the dolphins as a 'tool', exploiting their good nature, playfulness and sensitivity, both children and parents alike seem to benefit greatly from Nathanson's work. We observed several sessions – with Dean-Paul Anderson, a five-year-old boy suffering from Down's Syndrome; Armando Parra, an eight-year-old boy with hydrocephalus; and Billy Rainer, a three-year-old boy also with Down's Syndrome. Dr Nathanson, known to his patients as 'Dr Dave', came to life in the water with the children, encouraging them to enjoy both it and the dolphins' attention, whilst helping them to learn new words and invent stories. The three children have been coming to the centre for over two years and according to their parents, have made remarkable progress. Dean-Paul was barely able to speak or do anything for himself when he initially visited the centre for a two-week session. His mother, Cathy, believes that both the dolphins and Dr Dave have effected significant changes in her son, the main benefit being that he is happy and content. Nathanson believes that the most therapeutic element is the fact that the children are in a different and challenging environment. As he points out: 'On the whole, hospital environments are not the best places for people with neurological disorders or handicaps. They are alien, clinical, unfamiliar, and not very stimulating for children. I believe that dolphin therapy works because of a combination of factors – the dolphins play a role, but so does the water and the fact that the children are in a new and exciting environment.'

Other Projects

Projects to encourage the interaction between handicapped children and dolphins are now being launched throughout the world. Although many animal rights campaigners believe that there is very little validity in such schemes, especially in those set up in conjunction with dolphinariums that appear to be using the programmes to gain credibility, there is no doubt that parents and children alike can gain much from involvement in this kind of project. In Australia, handicapped children from the Keebra Park Special School are taken to swim once a week at Sea World in Queensland. The principal of the school, Kevin Hansen, believes that the encounters have brought many of his pupils out of their silent world: 'None of our children has language, but they all start making noises directed towards the dolphins. Autistic children, especially, come out of their own private world to explore the animals. It is important therapy for the children in many ways. Two-thirds of our children are in wheelchairs and have trouble moving their limbs, but once in the water they become weightless and start reaching out to touch the dolphins.'

No doubt these examples of dolphin therapy are just the first of many, yet the question remains – can we really condone keeping dolphins in captivity? Even though it is impossible to create controlled encounters – an essential requirement when dealing with those with physical and mental handicaps – with dolphins in the wild, can the existence of centres like Dolphins Plus and the Dolphin Research Center ever be justified? The researchers themselves are unable to answer this question, which presents the familiar dilemma of whether to put the interests of humans or animals first.

....

Part Two

THE CHEMISTRY OF ATTRACTION

Chapter Four

THE EVOLUTIONARY AND MYTHOLOGICAL EVIDENCE

IN THE BEGINNING

In the hope of tracing the origins of the special attraction between man and dolphin, we turn now to the evolution of our respective species. Is it possible that at some period in the distant past, our evolutionary paths once crossed, and dolphins lived in close contact with people? Does such a memory still linger in the recesses of some primitive region of the brain? In seeking answers to such questions, we have to go back to the beginning.

The Evolution of the Dolphin

Some 500 million years ago, life was evolving in the sea. As some creatures developed lungs and the ability to breathe air, they gradually moved out of the ocean and on to dry land. These terrestrial animals evolved a backbone and warm blood. They carried their young in their bodies and, once the babies were born, suckled them with milk. In short, they became mammals.

Then, between 50 and 60 million years ago, during an era known as the Eocene, something strange may have occurred. Certain small, possibly otter-like creatures apparently returned to the sea. They appear to have been related to Artiodactyla, the ancestors of modern ungulates (hoofed mammals such as cows and deer). Although the reason for this move still eludes explanation, experts believe it took place in the western branch of the ancient Tethys Sea, in a region which now comprises the Mediterranean Sea and Asian subcontinent. The animals in question started to settle down in the swamps and coastal fringes which had previously been inhabited by large marine reptiles like the plesiosaur and Ichthyosaurus before they disappeared, along with the dinosaurs, at the end of the Cretaceous period (about 65 million years ago). In this swampy environment, the Archaeoceti, the most primitive ancestors of modern dolphins and whales, began readapting to life in the water once again. To survive and thrive in their new home meant modifying almost every part of their bodies. They had to be able to swim, rather than walk, and also to surface to breathe. In addition, they needed to develop new methods for detecting and catching their prey. Gradually their torso became increasingly streamlined and torpedo-shaped to allow swifter movement through the water. Their skin became smoother as they slowly shed body hair, although they probably kept their whiskers. Their nostrils, originally in a snout-like position at the front of their face, slowly migrated back and up towards the present position of the blow-hole. They also developed structures to seal them against water. The creatures' front legs became paddle-shaped for steering, while their back legs steadily receded. For better propulsion, the animals gained a flat tail fluke and a point of flexion in the tail vertebrae which enabled it to beat up and down. The earliest Archaeoceti fossils found in India, Pakistan and North Africa suggest that, despite becoming progressively better suited to an aquatic existence, these primitive creatures retained four recognizable limbs for millions of years. So they may have enjoyed the best of both worlds. While spending most of their time in the water, they could still climb back on to the land, maybe to graze on vegetation and give birth to their young. Though their ancestors were undoubtedly ruminants, these creatures now had heterodont teeth for cutting and grasping, suggesting the animals were also catching and eating fish.

The Archaeoceti dominated the Eocene era, slowly venturing away from their original home in the Tethys Sea and moving out into other oceans. By the end of this era, however, they were less abundant and disappeared off the fossil map altogether around 38 million years ago. At the dawn of the Oligocene period (38–25 million years ago) they had been succeeded by two sub-orders of cetaceans, Odontoceti (toothed whales) and Mysticeti (baleen whales). Ancestors of present-day dolphins, the Odontoceti were grouped into several different families. Experts suggest that the earliest species were already using a basic kind of echo location to find their way around the seas. Although similar in body form and lifestyle to some of today's species – the shark-toothed dolphins (squalodontidae) that emerged in the late Oligocene and early Miocene eras may have lived rather like modern killer whales – in many ways, however, the Odontoceti were quite different. The Odontoceti appear to have been larger than modern-day dolphins, with more elongated, telescoped heads, sharp, pointed teeth and possibly flexible necks. It has been suggested that today's river dolphins may bear the closest resemblance to these prehistoric ancestors.

They were superseded by Rhabdosteidae, short-snouted primitive dolphins about three metres long. Fossil evidence suggests that these creatures were very abundant in the early to mid-Miocene period (about 15 million years ago). At about this time, or perhaps even earlier, the river dolphins that presently inhabit the Amazon in South America, the Yangtze in China, the Indus in Pakistan and the Ganges in India were also evolving. With their elongated snouts, paddle- or fan-shaped flippers, and small dorsal fins, they are generally regarded as the most prehistoric-looking of all the dolphins. By the end of the Miocene epoch, some five million years ago, most of the modern species of cetaceans, including the oceanic dolphins, were fully evolved and swimming in the sea just as they do today.

When we think of dolphins, we tend to visualize the 'Flipper' variety, or bottlenose dolphins (*Tursiops truncatus*). There are, however, some 26 species of cetaceans belonging to the family Delphinidae. Their classification (see the chart opposite) can be somewhat confusing, for many taxonomists consider the small whales, like the beluga (white whale), narwhal and pilot whale to belong to this family, and indeed their behaviour and lifestyle are remarkably similar to those of dolphins. Furthermore, although, technically, porpoises (six species, including the harbour porpoise and Dall's porpoise) belong to a separate sub-group, they are often mistaken for dolphins. As a rule of thumb, species over three metres in length are usually called whales, and smaller species, dolphins, while porpoises are usually no longer than 2.2 metres. However, overlaps do exist.

Different kinds of dolphins have developed in particular ways to suit their ecological niche. Common dolphins (*Delphinus delphis*), spotted dolphins (*Stenella attenuata*), spinner dolphins (*Stenella longirostris*) and hourglass dolphins (*Lagenorhynchus cruciger*) tend to live in the deep waters of the oceans and are often seen riding the bow-waves of boats. Bottlenose dolphins (*Tursiops truncatus*), dusky dolphins (*Lagenorhynchus obscurus*), and Hector's dolphins (*Cephalorhynchus hectori*), by contrast, usually stay in the shallower waters of coastal regions and may be spotted swimming off islands. Some dolphins have adapted to living in warm, tropical waters, while others seem perfectly content in the chillier seas of the northern hemisphere. Bottlenose dolphins may live in both, but if one that was born and raised in, for example, the Gulf of Mexico, were suddenly moved to cold British waters, it would be unlikely to survive the shock of such a temperature change.

While on the subject of dolphin species, it is worth noting that the dolphins that appear in the folklore and art of classical Greece were probably the distinctively marked common dolphins that are found in abundance in the Mediterranean Sea. They are recognizable by a cloak of dark colour on their backs, and eyes that are strikingly ringed in black and white. The Ancient Greeks were probably also familiar with the striped or Euphrosyne dolphin. Significantly, its name translates as 'joyfulness', one of the three graces in Greek poetry.

CLASSIFICATION OF DOLPHINS

OCEAN-DWELLING DOLPHINS (*Delphinidae*)	RIVER DOLPHINS (*Platanistoidea*)	PORPOISES (*Phocoenidae*)
Bottlenose dolphin (*Tursiops truncatus*)	Amazon river dolphin (Boto) (*Inia geoffrensis*)	Harbour porpoise (*Phocoena phocoena*)
Striped dolphin (*Stenella coeruleoalba*)	Chinese river dolphin (Baiji) (*Lipotes vexillifer*)	Spectacled porpoise (*Australophocoena dioptrica*)
Spinner dolphin (*Stenella longirostris*)	Ganges river dolphin (*Platanista gangetica*)	Burmeister's porpoise (*Phocoena spinipinnis*)
Common dolphin (*Delphinus delphis*)	Indus river dolphin (*Platanista minor*)	Finless porpoise (*Neophocoena phocoenoides*)
Pantropical spotted dolphin (*Stenella attenuata*)	Franciscana (*Pontoporia blainvillei*)	Dall's porpoise (*Phocoenoides dalli*)

Atlantic spotted dolphin
  (*Stenella frontalis*)
Clymene dolphin
  (*Stenella clymene*)
White-beaked dolphin
  (*Lagenorhynchus albirostris*)
Atlantic white-sided dolphin
  (*Lagenorhynchus acutus*)
Pacific white-sided dolphin
  (*Lagenorhynchus obliquidens*)
Dusky dolphin
  (*Lagenorhynchus obscurus*)
Hourglass dolphin
  (*Lagenorhynchus cruciger*)
Fraser's dolphin
  (*Lagenodelphis hosei*)
Commerson's dolphin
  (*Cephalorhynchus commersonii*)
Peale's dolphin
  (*Lagenorhynchus australis*)
Heaviside's dolphin
  (*Cephalorhynchus heavisidii*)
Northern right whale dolphin
  (*Lissodelphis borealis*)
Southern right whale dolphin
  (*Lissodelphis peronii*)
Humpback dolphins
  (*Sousa chinensis; Sousa teuszii; Sousa plumbea*)
Rough-toothed dolphin
  (*Steno bredanensis*)
Risso's dolphin
  (*Grampus griseus*)
Tucuxi
  (*Sotalia fluviatilis*)
Hector's dolphin
  (*Cephalorhynchus hectori*)
Chilean dolphin
  (*Cephalorhynchus eutropia*)

Irrawaddy dolphin
  (*Oraella brevirostris*)

Vaquita
  (*Phocoena sinus*)

The Evolution of Man

Although, on the face of it, the evolution of dolphins seems pretty straightforward, there are many gaps in our knowledge and much of the story is speculative. Man arrived too late on the scene to see the majority of ancient cetacean species, as they had already been and gone. None the less, expert opinion suggests that the whales and dolphins of today were already in existence at a time when man was still a long way, in evolutionary terms, from achieving his present state of development.

The story of the emergence of *Homo sapiens* or modern man is still something of a mystery. Numerous questions remain unanswered, the most pertinent being when and how we became so different from the primates, who are generally accepted as being our closest cousins. One possible explanation is that at some time in the past, like the early Archaeoceti, our primitive ancestors dwelt along and on the banks of estuaries and spent much of their time in the water. The 'aquatic ape' theory was put forward by Alister Hardy, Professor of Zoology at Oxford University, in a paper published in the *New Scientist* back in 1960.

Hardy suggested that many of the characteristics which separate man from the apes could be accounted for if he had passed through a semi-aquatic phase a long time ago. This idea was then taken up by the television journalist Elaine Morgan in her first book, *The Descent of Woman*, published in 1972, which became an international bestseller. In subsequent books, *The Aquatic Ape* and *The Scars of Evolution* (Souvenir Press), she puts forward a convincing case for the aquatic ape theory. While many mainstream anthropologists still dismiss it out of hand, others are starting to consider it more seriously. After an international conference – held at Valkenburg in the Netherlands in 1987 – to discuss the pros and cons of the aquatic ape theory, a number of scientists are now prepared to endorse it as a tenable hypothesis.

Personally, we were drawn to the idea of man's ancestors being semi-aquatic, because it seemed to make sense of human beings' love of the sea. It also helps to explain the therapeutic power of water and provides clues as to why humans have an affinity with dolphins. For, if Elaine Morgan is correct, our aquatic phase would have taken place between nine and three million years ago, at a time which corresponds with the emergence of the dolphins of today. Let us now examine some of the evidence to support the suggestion that man did indeed go through such an evolutionary phase.

It is now widely accepted that the human story began in Africa. Twenty million years ago, during the Miocene period, a population of all ape types, ranging in size from a small gibbon to a large gorilla, was living in Kenya. At this time the weather was mild, the rainfall heavier than today, and forests were flourishing. The apes appeared to be doing well, for Dr Louis Leakey has dug up their bones in abundance in the region of Lake Victoria.

It now seems possible that our earliest 'hominid' ancestor was the Australopithecus, who lived some three million years ago. The most famous is 'Lucy', whose complete skeleton was found at the northern end of the Rift valley in Ethiopia. Along with others of her kind, whose bones were buried in the Afar peninsula and Olduvai Gorge, Lucy walked on two legs and used crude pebble tools.

So, between three and nine million years ago, something must have enticed her into standing upright and taking the first major step towards becoming human-like. But what? Traditionalists suggest that when our ancestral primates came down from the trees on to the open savannah, they needed to stand upright to survey the horizon while looking for game and to leave their hands free for carrying weapons and tools.

Proponents of the aquatic ape theory are not convinced. Bipedal posture, they argue, is violently unnatural for apes, and they would have needed a pretty good incentive for standing on two legs. Did hunting really provide it? And why, unlike other apes, did man lose his hair, develop a layer of subcutaneous fat, start making love face to face, begin talking, and become so adept at swimming? The aquatic ape theory suggests that, amongst those morphological and physiological features regarded as being unique to man, a surprising number are not peculiar at all, but occur also in those mammals which left the land and returned to the water. Let us consider these features one by one.

Standing Upright
The aquatic ape theory suggests that the first impulse to stand upright came when our ancestral primates waded into the sea. To keep their heads above water, it would be only natural to rise up on two legs. Although most primates fear water, crab-eating macaques have overcome this instinctive hurdle in order to feed, and will wade up to their waists in the sea. When aquatic apes ventured out of their depth, they would tread water to keep vertical and hold their heads above the surface. Seals, dugongs and manatees adopt a similar position when something arouses their attention. The aquatic primate, after a few million years of wading, and subsequently floating and swimming, would have returned to land endowed with a more flexible spine and better balance, making erect posture easier to sustain.

Swimming and Diving
Although, among apes, the aversion to water is rarely overcome, by contrast, many humans enjoy being in the water, even if it is just to bathe and splash about. For a significant number, swimming seems to be second nature, and in recent years it has been found that human babies are able to swim before they can crawl. In the first year of life they seem as happy with their heads underwater as above it. In such circumstances they behave placidly, gazing around with eyes wide open. They also have remarkable breath control, and an inborn reflex which stops them breathing during short spells below the surface, so that water cannot get into their lungs. Like baby dolphins (and unlike baby

chimps), the human babies' extra fatty tissue endows them with natural buoyancy, which they lose as they start to crawl or walk.

Man also shares with aquatic animals a 'diving reflex'. His heartbeat and oxygen consumption drop quite markedly, though not to the same degree as most marine mammals. However, pearl and sponge divers have been known to dive to 175 feet, as deep as some species of dolphins and porpoises. The famous freestyle diver Jacques Mayol was able to plunge to a depth of over 100 metres during a single held breath. Mayol believes that dolphins were a source of inspiration to him. One particularly meaningful relationship with a captive dolphin called Clown fuelled Mayol's desire to go beyond the limits of human achievement (Luc Besson's cult film, *The Big Blue*, is based upon his story).

The Naked Ape

Nakedness is the most striking difference between man and apes. We do have hairs all over our bodies, but the hairs are shorter, finer and less conspicuous. The traditionalists suggest that we shed our hair to keep cool in the heat of the savannah. So why, Elaine Morgan asks, did the hunting male, who was likely to overheat in the course of the chase, retain more hair than the slower-moving female waiting back home?

The aquatic ape theory points out that virtually all hairless mammals are either aquatic or wallowers. The longer an animal has been in the water, the more complete the hair loss. Dolphins still retain a few vestigial bristles around their snout, but otherwise their silken skin is entirely naked. Most pinnipeds (seals and sealions) have water-resistant hair, possibly because they return to land to breed and rear their young, thereby often spending weeks on cold, windswept beaches. But for an African ape, chilliness was not a problem. However, looking after infants in the water would have been tricky. How do you carry a child when you are not entirely at ease in the water yourself? A study of Aboriginal behaviour in Tierra del Fuego may provide a clue. It reports that 'the women spend long periods in the water, with the children hanging on to their hair'. If we subscribe to the aquatic ape theory, this detail may explain why humans kept the hair on their heads, and perhaps even also why women are less likely than men to lose their locks.

Growing Fatter

Marine mammals that have shed their fur have a layer of fat laid down under the skin as an alternative form of insulation. This fatty tissue provides protection from the cold, makes their bodies more buoyant, stores energy, and gives their figure a more streamlined outline.

In some dolphins such tissue accounts for up to 50 per cent of their body weight. Plumpness also distinguishes *Homo sapiens* from the other primates, a fact that provoked Professor Hardy into thinking that humans may be ex-aquatics. On average, fat accounts for 15 per cent of total body mass in man and 27 per cent in women. Monkeys rarely have more than five per cent. Like other land mammals, they only store a small amount of fat under the skin, just enough to keep it supple; the rest is laid down around the internal organs. It is interesting to note that the discovery of Venus de la Corna, carved by a Palaeolithic sculptor in France some 30,000 years ago, may provide an insight into the natural female human form at that time. To judge from this sculpture, her thighs were heavy, her waist generous, her bottom ample and her bosom substantial, although her arms, shoulders and calves were quite slim.

Sweat and Tears

On returning to land, extra subcutaneous fat may have created problems of temperature control, so humans started to perspire. Providing they stayed close to rivers and streams, replenishing lost fluids did not pose any problems. The tears we shed may also have originally served the purpose of excreting salt from sea water. Most mammals have tear glands, whether they weep or not, which secrete small amounts of saline solution to protect and lubricate the surface of the eyeball. But very few shed tears in response to emotional agitation, and those that do, tend to inhabit the sea. Man is the only weeping primate. Proteins found in tears suggest that maybe they later took on the additional role of ridding the body of the waste products of stress.

Sex

Like dolphins, humans make love face to face and are orgasmic. Yet compared to the other primates, we are the exception to the rule. Behaviourists suggest that our distant ancestors started having sex in this way to help cement the pair-bond. Looking into each other's eyes makes the whole affair less impersonal and therefore more conducive to monogamy.

But, as is common knowledge, satisfying sex does not necessarily mean a man stays faithful to a woman and vice versa. The most successful pair-bonders among the apes are not humans, but the gibbons. They live in small family groups and mate for life, but, like the other apes, they do not copulate face to face. However, viewed as aquatics, we are no longer the 'odd man out'. For dolphins, sex appears to be an enjoyable pastime, not merely a method of reproduction. It is also a way of establishing and reaffirming relationships within pods (see Chapter Five). If, for a moment, we abandon our preconditioned ideas of what is 'socially acceptable' behaviour, perhaps we will discover that we have more in common with dolphins than we care to admit.

Talking Sense

Communication is a complex affair. In primates, visual signals have developed to the highest degree. Gestures, postures, movements and facial expressions convey a tremendous amount of information about the ape's feelings, wishes, intentions and social relationships. So what induced humans to start speaking as well?

Elaine Morgan suggests that when moving from land to water, our normal modes of communication were disrupted. Scent signals were no longer of any use, and facial expressions were difficult to read underwater. Among aquatic animals, sound communication is of paramount importance. Whales and dolphins have such acute auditory perception, that they rely on it to a far greater degree than sight. Like us, they seem to have developed a complex language. Of course, primates can also make sounds, and grunt and chatter. But the difference is that we have acquired apparently far greater conscious control over the kind of noises we emit. This achievement goes hand in hand with conscious control of breathing, which is also a feature of all aquatic animals. If, through swimming and diving, a pre-hominid learnt to control his breathing and vocalization, on returning to land, he would have been well-adapted to starting to speak.

Big Brain
Another feature we have in common with dolphins is a large and complex brain. Among the primates, there has been a steady, adaptive increase in brain size throughout the evolutionary period. Yet the development of the human brain does not follow this trend. It takes an unprecedented leap forward. Man's brain now deviates from the mammalian norm to an extent shared only by the bottlenose dolphin. Again, Elaine Morgan finds an answer in the aquatic ape theory. She points out that moving from land to water requires a new locomotive repertoire as limb movements come under conscious control and adjustment. This requires a lot of brain power. If, having acquired the ability to swim and dive, the aquatic ape then returned to land, he would have needed to perfect yet another kind of locomotive skill – namely, walking upright on dry land. These evolutionary 'shocks' may have provided the stimulation required for the brain to burgeon in size.

In his book *The Driving Force* (co-written by David Marsh), the respected nutritionist Michael Crawford suggests that the aquatic explanation for man's big brain makes sense from a physiological point of view. He points out that special kinds of lipids, known as the essential fatty acids, are the building blocks for brain tissue. These acids belong to two families: the omega 6 fatty acids, which come from leafy green, seed-bearing plants, and the omega 3 fatty acids, which derive from marine phytoplankton and algae. Crawford's laboratory work shows that our brains use a consistent balance of 1:1 of both the omega 3 and omega 6 fatty acids. Studies of dolphins accidentally caught in tuna fishing reveal their brains to have exactly the same ratio, whereas in fish tissues, it is 1:40 in favour of the marine-derived fatty acids. So, biochemically, dolphins are still land mammals living in a marine environment. By contrast, in land mammals, the balance is tipped the other way. They have three to six times more omega 6 than omega 3 fatty acids. Crawford suggests that the dolphin could have maintained its brain capacity because the necessary omega 3 fatty acids were available in the sea. So what about man? Had he stayed on the plains, like the other savannah species, he would have found it difficult to obtain enough omega 3 fatty acids to supply the needs of his brain and visual system. But, if he settled down in a vacant niche between land and water, things would have been different. He would have got his omega 6 fatty acids from leafy vegetation, nuts, seeds, and small terrestrial mammals, whilst obtaining substantial amounts of omega 3 lipids from freshwater foods, coastal sea foods and marine mammals.

So much for the characteristics common to both man and aquatic mammals. Is there any other evidence to suggest that during some period in our evolutionary history we could have spent our days splashing about in the sea – an existence which may have brought us in close contact with other marine mammals, including dolphins? Elaine Morgan thinks man's aquatic phase may have occurred sometime between three and nine million years ago. She puts forward the view that in parts of Africa at this period, drastic environmental changes were taking place. The sea came in and flooded vast areas in the north of the continent; parts of forested areas were cut off from the mainland, forming islands and sea marshes. Populations of apes marooned on such islands may have found that their usual food resources were dwindling, and turned to the sea surrounding them to augment their diet. If this were so, to extract flesh from shellfish they may have learned to smash them open with pebbles or small stones. Could this be how tool use began?

Leon P. LaLumiere Jr, a palaeontologist from the University of Maryland in the United States, discovered an area in the northern and central Afar triangle, in the region of the Danakil Alps, which was effectively cut off from the rest of Africa by the sea between the late Miocene and late Pliocene. This has been substantiated by geological data. He believes that when the Danakil region was rejoined to the mainland, the likeliest route that the hominids would have taken was southward along the African Rift valley. When Donald Johanson unearthed 'Lucy's' skeleton, he also found the remains of crocodile and turtle eggs, and crab claws. In fact it would appear that all the fossil sites in the Rift valley which are now desert or near-desert were then green and lush tropical forests laced with lakes and winding rivers.

Elaine Morgan visualizes our early ancestors reclining under shady trees at the water's edge, perhaps living on fruit, greenery and fish, rather than as shaggy creatures trekking through parched grass and turning to scavenging and hunting to supplement their diet. But if this is so, having adjusted to a semi-aquatic existence, why did these hominids give it up? Morgan proposes that instead of them leaving the sea, it was probably rather the sea that receded. The primitive ancestors of man may therefore have moved back up the estuaries and rivers, settling close to the water which is where they felt most comfortable.

Perhaps even today we carry this memory with us. The notion that certain kinds of behaviour, emotions and feelings are not learnt but inherited is one that has long fascinated scientists. It suggests certain instinctive reactions or responses are actually coded in DNA, the genetic material. There is no telling how ancient some of these responses may be. The most famous experiment to prove the existence of such a phylogenetic memory was carried out by the scientist Niko Tinbergen on birds that are preyed upon by hawks. He took newborn chicks that had been deprived of parental contact and flew the outline of a hawk above their heads. All exhibited abject terror, a reaction that was purely instinctive – that is, not taught by their parents. Scientists have also isolated an area of the monkey's brain where the memory of the fear of snakes resides, and have managed to destroy it.

Could the attraction between man and dolphins stem from a memory of a time when our primitive ancestors lived in close contact with these creatures? It is a fact that although, personally, neither of us feels particularly comfortable in deep water, on spotting wild dolphins for the first time we both overcame our inhibitions and leapt in. At the time, the voice of reason screamed 'You must be mad.' But our initial unease was overwhelmed by an instinctive trust that the dolphins would not harm us. And although it is hard to put into words, being in the presence of dolphins also evokes a sense of familiarity or recognition, particularly if one makes eye contact with them. It is just as if a distant memory is being revived.

THE EVIDENCE OF MYTH

In search for clues as to our ancient ancestors' relationship with dolphins, we shall now turn to so-called 'primitive' peoples like the Aborigines, Maoris, Polynesians and American Indians, for the essence of their culture and belief systems has changed little in thousands of years.

The Australian Aborigines are particularly fascinating, for they represent possibly the oldest existing human lineage. Anthropologists generally regard them as direct descendants of the Neanderthals who lived in Europe some 200,000 years ago, a pure race that is quite separate from others. The Aborigines are inherently peaceful people who think of the Earth as their mother and live close to nature. Their culture is one of the most ancient known today, for it dates back some 40,000–50,000 years. The origins of various animals, plants and earth sites, along with their cultural affiliations with humans, are described in Aboriginal fairy-tale or mythology. Aborigines believe that during the mythical past, or 'dream-time', their ancestors, who were human although they often possessed supernatural powers, emerged from the ground to wander over the land. At 'story-places' – often water-holes and sites along the 'dream path' (now sacred spots and totemic centres) – they created plant and animal species, modified the landscape and established ceremonies for their descendants to follow. At such ceremonies, the mythological history is ritually re-enacted through the use of myths, songs, painting and mini-dramas. This ensures that the spiritual and emotional bonds that exist between the people, their ancestors and the land are kept alive.

The natives of Groote Eylandt, an island in the Gulf of Carpentaria in northern Australia, regard themselves as the direct descendants of dolphins. At their traditional ceremonies to celebrate the mythical past, the tribal elders decorate themselves with painted dolphin images. They then chant and dance themselves into a trance-like state in which they are able to step into the 'dream-time'. This story of the dolphin dream-time illustrates how, in Aboriginal culture, men and dolphins are perceived as being closely linked.

In the very early days, the Earth was inhabited by spirit beings who took the form of animals, birds and fishes. Some of these first ancestors were called the Indjebena, the dolphins. They were smaller than the dolphins we know today, and led a happy, carefree life, spending most of their day in play. In those days the wisest creatures in the ocean were the yakuna, the bailer shells. They possessed exquisite shells and spent most of their time creeping slowly along the ocean floor looking for tiny creatures to feed on.

Dinginjabana, leader of all the dolphins, was very strong, bold and agile. His mate, Ganadja, in contrast was a cautious yet curious creature. Rather than sporting with her kind, she preferred to visit the yakuna. They learnt to trust her and taught her about the ways of the ocean, so that she too grew wise and knowledgeable.

Dinginjabana scorned the yakuna because they could not move swiftly through the waves. He became jealous of the time his mate spent with them, and told her to stay away. But Ganadja enjoyed her visits and ignored his warnings. This made him angry. Dinginjabana began to tease the yakuna, swimming up to them fast and swishing his powerful flukes to create a current that sent them spinning over the sand.

Although the yakuna also loved Ganadja, they did not trust the other dolphins. The next time the Indjebena began to tease the yakuna, Baringgwa, the leader of the yakuna, told the dolphins: 'All I have to do is shout and Mana, the tiger shark, will come to my rescue.'

Large, sleek and with row upon row of sharp teeth, Mana was the dolphins' worst enemy. He would lie quietly on the coral, waiting for an unsuspecting dolphin to swim close, then rush forward slashing and cutting with his teeth until the water ran red with blood. The first time Baringgwa threatened them in this way, all the dolphins forgot their game and swam away, but when they realized the yakuna had not called Mana, they returned to their sporting. Another day, while frisking in and out of the waves, the dolphins once again became tired of their play. Dinginjabana suggested going to find the yakuna. 'Let's get Baringgwa and toss him in the air, catching him as he falls back in the water,' he cried, and all the other dolphins agreed it would be good fun. Ganadja objected strongly, but her words simply made Dinginjabana more determined and he swam off straight away to look for Baringgwa.

Having found him, Dinginjabana dislodged the yakuna leader from the sand and carried him to the surface. The dolphins then took it in turn to toss Baringgwa into the air, catch him and toss him again – young and old, male and female, all joining in the game. Baringgwa warned them that the yakuna would call the sharks to protect him, but the dolphins laughed. As they played on, black shadows appeared in the deep water beneath the dolphins, who were too preoccupied to notice. Suddenly, the shadows darted to the surface. As the slaughter began, the sea turned scarlet with dolphin blood. Dinginjabana himself was sliced in half as he tried to swim away. Ganadja, hiding on the yakuna bed, screamed in terror as she saw her husband's head float down next to her. One of the sharks heard her and swam down to find her. Realizing that the shark would certainly find Ganadja, the yakuna cried, 'Come press your body right to the bottom. Then we can cover you with our shells!' The shark swam past without noticing her, and Ganadja was saved. She was the only member of the Indjebena tribe to escape the massacre. After several months of desperate loneliness, she gave birth to a fine son which she named Dinginjabana after his father. He grew much larger than the other dolphins, so he did not fear the sight of Mana, the tiger shark. He was the first of the silver tribe of dolphins that we see today.

The souls of the dolphins who were slaughtered became very hard and dry. After much time had passed, they were reborn on dry land, where they became the first human beings. Never again would their spirits swim swiftly through the waves. One night, long after her son had grown up, Ganadja was swimming near the shore when she saw her husband, Dinginjabana, who was now a two-legged man. Thrusting her body up onto the shore, she heaved herself over the sand by her flippers. When Dinginjabana recognized his wife, Ganadja gave a joyful cry and suddenly took the shape of a human being. In time, the human Dinginjabana and Ganadja had many children, who became the people of Groote Island. They are the only ones who remember that dolphins are ancestors of the entire human race. However, all the dolphins swimming in the ocean are the offspring of mother Ganadja, so they have never forgotten that the two-legged people on land are their cousins. This is why, even today, dolphins seek out their human kin to play as they did in the days of the dream-time.

Similarly, another Aborigine tribe, living off Mornington Island, which is also in the Gulf of Carpentaria, still believe that their fortune and happiness depend on keeping in contact with the dolphins, and aptly call themselves the 'Dolphin People'. As young boys in the community grow up, they undergo a series of tests or initiations to cultivate their sensitivity and intuition. The most sensitive youth will become the tribal shaman or medicine man. He possesses the ability to speak directly to the spirits of animals, plants, trees and even stones, and can keep open the channels of communication between people and dolphins. The Dolphin People believe their shaman is in fact a dolphin that has chosen to reincarnate as a human being. He knows a complex combination of whistles that signal to the dolphins to venture close to shore. The whistling becomes increasingly animated before stopping altogether. At this point, the shaman explains, he speaks to the dolphins telepathically – mind to mind.

Despite their geographical proximity to the Australian Aborigines, the New Zealand Maoris are actually related to the Pacific Polynesians. Their common ancestors are thought to have migrated from Indonesia some 2,000–2,500 years ago. Yet, like the Aborigines, they also once regarded dolphins as being some kind of god or influence that guided them to understand the things that they wanted to know. Waipu Pita, a contemporary Maori elder living in New Zealand, describes the dolphin thus: 'To me, it is a human being in the sea. We only call the dolphins when we need help in a rough sea or are in difficulty, or if there is something we would like to know about relatives at a distance over the ocean. If a relative is sick when the dolphin appears, it will give a sign whether or not that person will recover or has already recovered. We can tell from the way it leaps.'

The Polynesian people of the Gilbert Islands (now known as Kiribati) also used to call the dolphins. In a ritual practised up until the last decade or so, the Kahuna (the shaman) would enter a dream-like state in which his spirit left his body and sought the dolphin folk in their home. He invited them to a dance with feasting in the village, and if his words were spoken correctly, the dolphins would come swimming into the bay. Rushing to greet them, the Gilbert Islanders would wade into the water, and drive, then haul, the dolphins up onto the shore. Sadly, in this ceremony, the dolphins ended up as the main delicacy of the feast.

Polynesian folklore has been compared, on an intellectual level, with the mythology of ancient Greece in the days when stories were told by wandering bards. Interestingly, many of the Polynesian tales concerning dolphins saving humans and repaying acts of kindness are remarkably similar to those appearing in classical Greek literature. However, the ancient Greeks would have considered it sacrilege to harm, let alone kill a dolphin. For they regarded dolphins with a special reverence. There is even evidence to suggest that they believed the animals were divine beings, worthy of worship:

Diviner than the dolphin is nothing yet created, for indeed they were aforetime men and lived in cities along with mortals, but by the devising of Dionysus, they exchanged the land for the sea, and put on the form of fishes: but even now, the righteous spirit of men in them preserves human thought and human deeds.

(Oppian, *Halieutica*.)

The legend of how dolphins came into being also shows that the Greeks knew that there was something different about dolphins. Although the creatures lived in the sea, they were not the same as fish, for they exhibited many human-like characteristics.

According to Greek mythology, Dionysus, the god of wine and frenzy, on finding his ship was unseaworthy, hired another from some Tyrrhenian sailors who claimed to be bound for Naxos. But they proved to be pirates and, unaware of his immortality, steered for Asia to sell him as a slave. When he realized what they were planning, he became furious and called upon his magical powers. He made a vine grow from the deck and twine itself around the mast and rigging, covering the ship with leafy garlands. Then he filled the vessel with wine and the sound of flutes, turned the oars into serpents and conjured up a ferocious bear. Turning himself into a lion, Dionysus leapt upon the ship's master. In terror, the pirates leapt overboard into the sparkling sea, where they were changed into dolphins.

Before that time, according to Greek myth, there were no dolphins. After it, they symbolized benevolence and honour in the sea. Another myth indicates that the first Greek god to appreciate the usefulness of dolphins was, not surprisingly, Poseidon, lord of the ocean. Desiring a wife who would be at home in the sea depths, Poseidon courted Thetis, the Nereid. She was the daughter of Nereus, the wise man of the sea, and his wife, Doris. (In Greek mythology there were usually fifty Nereids, possibly moon goddesses, who often rode on the backs of dolphins.) However, when it was prophesied that any son born to Thetis would be greater than his father, Poseidon allowed her to marry a mortal named Peleus. Poseidon next approached the dark-eyed Amphitrite, another Nereid, but she fled from his embraces and hid in the Atlas mountains. Poseidon sent messengers after her, amongst them a dolphin which carried the god upon its back. The dolphin pleaded Poseidon's cause so persuasively that Amphitrite emerged from her hiding-place and consented to become Queen of the Sea. To show his gratitude, Poseidon set the dolphin's image in the sky. The constellation Delphinus comprises four bright stars in the shape of a miniature diamond forming the dolphin's body, with a fifth representing its tail. Delphinus lies on the edge of the Milky Way, just east of Aquila in the northern Hemisphere.

While myths were obviously a figment of the imagination, they usually contained a truth or moral. In principle, Greek myths told of the importance of loving and respecting the natural world, and taught that abuse of nature would result in divine retribution. Many of these stories illustrate the kindly, cooperative nature of the dolphin, and suggest that it held a special place in the heart of the divine gods. Those who showed love and respect for the dolphin were rewarded, whereas those who treated it with contempt and malevolence were sure to experience the wrath of the gods.

Who invented these myths? Greek mythology seems to have taken root and flourished under the Mycenaeans during the so-called 'Golden Age' of Greece, which lasted from about 1600 to 1100 BC. By design, this mythology brought the divine down to earth and minimized the differences between mortals and men. While the gods dwelt on Mount Olympus, they willingly came down to earth, mingled with man and also took on the human form. But although the Mycenaeans built lavish temples and shrines to their gods, these immortals were never articles of faith imposed on people with religious authority. Instead, mythology was open to individual interpretation and belief.

The Mycenaeans themselves were direct descendants of a primitive Indo-European people who came from the north into Greece, eventually reaching as far south as Crete. Here they encountered the amazingly civilized Minoans – so named after their legendary King, Minos – who were living an immensely rich and cultured existence. Parallels can be drawn between these people and the ancient Egyptians. Various aspects of Cretan thinking and culture were adopted by the Mycenaeans, including perhaps an appreciation of dolphins. Frescoes decorating the ancient Minoan palaces at Knossos and Phaestos depict dolphins gambolling in the waves, as does local pottery dating from around 2000 BC. Dolphins also feature in the art of Thera (Santorini) from around 1500 BC, and are still the national symbol of Santorini. According to Greek mythology, the sun god, Apollo, transformed himself into a dolphin and asked to be worshipped in this form. Did the Minoans and, following their example, the Mycenaeans, regard dolphins as divine beings? The legend of how Apollo came to establish the famous oracle at Delphi sugggests this is possible.

The son of Zeus, Apollo was one of the greatest gods in the Hellenic Pantheon. Political as well as spiritual life was dominated by his personality, and music, poetry, philosophy, astronomy, medicine and science all came under his control. It was said that Apollo's wanderings brought him to a tranquil glade on the southern slope of the snow-capped Mount Parnassus. Here he decided to build a glorious temple. But first, he had to slay Python, the dragon guarding a shrine to the Earth Mother on his chosen site. This accomplished, Apollo turned his attention to finding ministers to serve at his oracle. While pondering upon this, he became aware of a ship carrying Cretans from the palace of Knossos across the seas to Pylos. Taking the form of a dolphin, Apollo leapt into the sea and steered the ship off its course towards the sea shore at Crisa, a place in the vicinity of his temple. Then he revealed his true identity to the bemused sailors, ordered them to make an altar, and pray to him as Apollo Delphinius – the dolphin. According to Hesiod's 'Hymn to Apollo', which dates from the seventh century BC, Apollo declared: 'And inasmuch as that first on the hazy sea I sprang upon the swift form of a dolphin, pray to me as Apollo Delphinius; also the altar itself shall be called Delphinius.'

This, then, was how Delphi acquired its name. Inscriptions reveal there was also a temple to Apollo Delphinius at Knossos and a Cretan month bearing the same name, hinting at links between Delphi and Crete, and at the possible existence of a dolphin cult in classical times.

The oracle at Delphi was famous during this period. Its early reputation was built on some spectacular successes in sheer clairvoyance. People journeyed from far and wide in quest of enlightened answers to all manner of problems, both public and private. Cryptic responses were uttered by the Pythia, a simple peasant woman who went into trances, rather like a medium. Her answers were then interpreted by priests serving at the temple. The original archaic temple, probably made of painted wood and terracotta, was burnt down in 548 BC and replaced by another of stone, sheathed in a splendid marble façade. The stone ruins are still etched with the inscription 'Know thyself'. We would like to posit the purely speculative but not unreasonable notion that the temple was adorned with frescoes and statues of dolphins, which may have been connected with spiritual guidance and divine inspiration. For to our mind, the freedom dolphins symbolize also represents our own quest for self-knowledge and implies the independence that springs from conquering the passions and fears which block the path to spiritual growth.

Amongst those who made their pilgrimage to Delphi during the classical era were the historian Herodotus and the philosopher Plato. The Greek writer Plutarch was a close friend of Clea, the Delphic priestess of his day, and in later life, he too became a priest at Delphi. In his philosophical work *Moralia* he writes: 'Its [the dolphin's] affection for man renders it dear to the gods, for it is the only creature who loves man for his own sake . . . To the dolphin alone, nature has granted what the best philosophers seek . . . friendship for no advantage. Though it has no need at all for any man, yet it is a genial friend to all and has helped many.'

Arguably the most cultured people of their era, these Grecian dolphin-lovers were fascinated by man's existence, his behaviour and relationship to the universe. The Greeks saw a 'divineness' in the world and lived at one with nature. They probably had a better understanding of the art of living than most civilizations in existence before or since. Realizing that material wealth alone could not bring happiness, they placed greater value on nourishing the spirit through music, poetry, art and the simple beauty of nature. In dolphins they recognized the qualities they prized most highly: grace, intelligence, strength, vitality, humour and unconditional love. To the Greeks, dolphins also represent the nurturing feminine principle, as can be observed from the assonance between *delphis* (dolphin) and *delphys* (womb). The very word dolphin, written in Greek, is an enchanting representation of the animal's twisting motion through water. An appreciation of the dolphin's beauty and grace is also reflected in classical Greek art. Statues of dolphins, sometimes straddled by young boys, may have been commonplace, for the Greek traveller Pausinias reports seeing them on his journeys. In some Greek cities, even the coins were embellished with dolphin motifs.

As we have mentioned, the works of many classical Greek scholars, such as the historians Plutarch and Herodotus, the poets Pindar and Oppian, and the naturalists Aristotle and Theophrastus also reveal a genuine admiration and fascination for dolphins. Such writings tell tales of dolphins saving men from drowning, steering ships to safety, befriending young boys, repaying acts of kindness and helping fishermen to make their catch. Perhaps dolphins were aware of the Greeks' affection, for they seemed to respond with amazing acts of friendship (see Chapter Eight) which until recently were regarded as quite unbelievable. One such friendship may have occurred over 2,200 years ago, for it is recorded by Duris (340–260 BC), a pupil of Theophrastus. The incident is reputed to have taken place at Iasus, not far from Miletus in Karia (present-day Turkey) and concerns a boy called Dionysius. Along with other boys from his wrestling school, Dionysius played at the sea shore. One day a lone dolphin came up to him and, lifting the boy onto his back, swam out to sea. Then, sensing the boy's fear, the dolphin took him back to the safety of the shore. This happened time and time again, the friendship between boy and dolphin growing stronger each time. One day, in its eagerness to follow Dionysius ashore, the dolphin became grounded on the sand and died. On hearing this tale, Alexander the Great summoned the boy. Interpreting the dolphin's affection as a sign of the deity's favour, he made Dionysius head of the priesthood of Poseidon at Babylon.

THE BOND BREAKS

Greek culture had a profound influence on other peoples living at that time. It was the Greeks' respect for dolphins which probably encouraged the Romans to take an interest in these creatures too. The Romans, however, were far less impressed with the beauty of nature, regarding it as something extraneous to spiritual wellbeing. Indeed, anthropo-centrism, the notion that everything revolves around and is there to serve ourselves, took root and flourished under the Romans. Theirs was a male-dominated society which seemed to fear the femininity of ancient 'Mother Earth' that inspired such reverence in the Minoans and classical Greeks. It is perhaps not surprising, then, that Roman tales of friendly dolphins tended to have tragic endings. When the expense involved in entertaining officials who came to see the dolphin that played with people at Hippo became too great, the townspeople simply decided to do away with their 'problem' and slaughtered the dolphin (see Chapter Eight).

Although Christianity, too, perpetuates the notion that man is superior to the 'beasts of the field', it has also absorbed many pagan ideals. When the early Christians started to bring their teachings to the Mediterranean, they were undoubtedly impressed by Greek thought, for in the early Christian church, the dolphin was upheld as a symbol of swiftness, diligence and love. In fact, Christ, as saviour of souls, is often represented by a dolphin. If pierced by a trident or anchor, the dolphin also symbolizes Christ on the Cross.

Over the last 2,000 years or so in the 'civilized' West, the bond between humans and dolphins seems to have been almost totally severed, but times are changing. As we enter the so-called New Age, interest in dolphins is undergoing a revival. With the dawning of the 'age of Aquarius', many people are once again turning to ancient religions and philosophies to increase their understanding of the nature of our existence and relationship to the planet. Above all, this seems to be a time for spiritual growth. We believe it is no mere coincidence that dolphins, with their qualities of joy, compassion and unconditional love, are finding their way into our hearts and consciousness at this particular point in history.

For, since the Second World War, western society has seen some radical changes. The disintegration of small 'village' communities has spawned a plethora of social problems. Deprived of any real sense of 'belonging', many people now suffer from feelings of isolation, insecurity, and uselessness. In an increasingly competitive environment, true friendship characterized by compassion and unconditional love can be hard to find. Little wonder then that some people are now turning to dolphins in the hope of rediscovering amongst them some of the finer qualities of human nature.

Chapter Five

THE LIFE OF A DOLPHIN

INTRODUCTION

Flipper, eponymous star of the well-known 1960s television series, has helped to create in our minds a rather Disney-like portrait of the dolphin. We tend to think that all dolphins, like him, are jolly, friendly creatures which seem all too eager to interact with us. While in some respects this is true, it is by no means the entire story. Although dolphins possess certain endearing qualities, such as inquisitiveness, compassion, and a sense of fun, it is important not to judge them by our own standards.

Dolphins are free-spirited, wild animals that generally speaking far prefer the company of their own kind. They live in remarkably elaborate, sophisticated societies which appear in many ways to resemble our own.

In this chapter we will examine the life and habits of the wild dolphin, since it is only by knowing a little about its behaviour and existence in the open seas that we can hope to understand and appreciate its true nature.

> What a marvel shalt thou contemplate in thy heart and what sweet delight, when on a voyage watching when the wind is fair and the sea is calm, thou shalt see the beautiful herds of dolphins, the desire of the sea; the young go before in a troop like youths unwed, even and if they were going through the changing circle of a mazy dance; behind and not aloof their children come the parents great and splendid, a guardian host even as in Spring the Shepherds attend the tender lambs at pasture.
>
> Oppian, *Halieutica*.

THE FABRIC OF DOLPHIN SOCIETY

Dolphins are highly social creatures which live together in pods or communities. These vary considerably in size. They can comprise as few as five or six dolphins or as many as 100 or more. On the whole, dolphins of a certain species tend to stick together. However, bottlenose dolphins are certainly known to mingle with spotted dolphins off the coast of Grand Bahama Island.

Having dedicated some 25 years of his life to studying dolphins, Dr Kenneth Norris, Professor of Natural History at the University of California, Santa Cruz, has no doubts that dolphin society is on a par with our own. 'Dolphins are a high order of animals with a more complex social structure than a simple set of family ties; one that functions more like our own, where we have friendships and associations beyond the family,' he writes. 'The more we know about dolphins, the more we care for them.'

Dolphins do not set up families consisting of father, mother and offspring, in the accepted sense. Their society is much more fluid. Individuals will form bonds of friendship and associate on a fairly regular basis with other members of the community to which they are not necessarily related.

The cetacean researcher and conservation biologist Dr Randall Wells has contributed a great deal to our knowledge of the way dolphins interact and relate to one another in the wild. Although based at the Chicago Zoological Society, Wells actually spends most of his time at Sarasota, Florida, where he has been observing a community of around 100 bottlenose dolphins living in the bay since 1970. The Sarasota dolphins have set up permanent residence in the shallow, inshore waters to the east of the barrier island chain. Their extensive home covers an area of some 100 km sq. (35−40 miles), and the dolphins rarely stray from this region. The 'home' range seems to be determined largely by food availability. If fish are plentiful, the dolphins will not need to forage as far afield as when food is in short supply. Some dolphin groups appear to migrate to other homes as the seasons change, possibly to enjoy warmer waters and a better food supply.

Within a community, dolphins of the same sex and of roughly the same age seem to spend most time with one another. Young immature males (less than 10 years of age) are often seen swimming together in pairs and occasionally trios, establishing what appear to be strong attachments. The same is true of adult males. Wells suggests that the male pairs may protect each other from predators such as sharks, and cooperate in hunting for fish.

Likewise, young females without calves, in other words females which are usually under seven years old, tend to spend their days in each others' company. In a feature entitled 'High Society', Dr Wells writes: 'Nat and The Kid . . . were born into the same adult female band and have been together for most of their lives. Now, even though they have reached sexual maturity, they are nearly inseparable.'

The older males carry the most responsibility for the welfare of the whole community. If something disturbs or threatens the pod the biggest male seems to take on the role of leader. He gives the signal for the dolphins to huddle together, males on the outside, mothers and young in the middle, and then decides what course of action to take.

While genuine friendships appear to exist between the younger dolphins, the strongest bonds are formed between mothers and calves. From observations of dolphins in captivity, the mothers appear to show what can only be described as real devotion to their offspring. At one dolphinarium, a mother was seen trying to lift her stillborn calf from the bottom of the pool, by taking its flipper in her mouth and trying to grasp its body between her own flippers. On another occasion, an infant dolphin died during the night. The next morning the mother was found still supporting its body at the surface, presumably in the hope that it might start breathing again.

Almost 2,000 years ago, the Roman scholar Aelian recounted a touching story in his works on animals which suggests that mother dolphins are even willing to sacrifice their own lives for the sake of their calves.

> The female dolphin far surpasses all creatures in its devotion to its offspring. When a fisherman either wounds a young dolphin with his harpoon or strikes it with his barb, the mother is not scared by what has occurred, not restrained by fear, but by a mysterious instinct follows her yearning for her child . . . though one confront her with terrors never so great, she is still undismayed and will not endure to desert her young one which has come to a bloody end; it is even possible to strike her with the hand, so close does she come to the hunters, as though she would beat them off.
>
> And so it comes about that she is caught along with her offspring, though she could save herself and escape. But if both her offspring are by her and she realizes one has been wounded and is being hauled in, she pursues the one that is unscathed and drives it away lashing her tail and biting her little one with her mouth . . . making a blowing sound as best she can, she gives the signal to flee which saves it. So the young dolphin escapes while the mother remains until she is caught and dies along with the captive.

In the Sarasota dolphin community studied by Dr Wells, about five calves are usually born each year, and the death rates are low, perhaps because mothers receive help in caring for their offspring from other dolphins. Dr Wells has observed that in the wild, mothers with calves often form 'play-pens' around the youngsters, allowing them to interact within a protected enclave. Sometimes a female dolphin may 'baby-sit' for a mother while she goes off to look for food. Such dolphins are known as 'aunts', because they are often related to the calves they are caring for. When the mother returns, she is often greeted by her baby with a high-pitched whistle of excitement, and all three dolphins may swim off together. Adult females with calves apparently form bands that may include three generations – grandmother, mother and babies – as well as unrelated females.

In the wild, calves remain with their mothers for between three and six years, even though they are no longer suckling. The reason for this seems to be a form of schooling. During the time a calf is with its mother it learns patterns of social interaction, group foraging and feeding techniques. It starts to recognize members of the community and dolphins belonging to neighbouring groups, as well as natural predators, and the features and limits of its home range. This story, told by Wells, shows that such information starts to be gleaned at an early age. 'One day Merrily, Granny's nine-month-old daughter, got tangled in a fishing net near the northern extreme of the range. We removed and held her, hoping that Granny would come looking for her, but a thunderstorm forced us to send her back on her own. Hours later we found the young dolphin in her mother's familiar waters, four miles to the south, and by the next day she and Granny were together again.'

Having been initiated into the ways of the 'dolphin' world, calves leave their mothers to join groups of other adolescent dolphins. No one is sure precisely what form the impetus for this separation takes. For even if the mother becomes pregnant again, her first calf still stays with her for up to six years, and in the Sarasota group, one undersized dolphin called Wee Willy has been with his mother, Mrs March, for 10 years, possibly because he needs her protection from predators such as sharks. In any event, once young females have matured and given birth themselves, they rejoin their mother's band once again.

To determine such relationship patterns, Randall Wells' research involves catching, tagging and releasing the individual dolphins. The team of captors include 12 biologists, a marine mammal vet, a commercial fisherman who sets the net, and volunteers from Earthwatch. From blood samples, Wells is hoping to find out whether male dolphins which associate with one another are actually related. This is made possible by DNA fingerprinting and chromosome band analysis, carried out by Debbie Duffield of Portland State University in Oregon. By counting growth rings in the dolphins' teeth, cetacean experts can estimate their age.

Wells has found that the oldest dolphin in the community is a 44-year-old female. Like humans, female dolphins tend to outlive the males, and survive well into their mid- to late forties. The oldest males tend to be in their late thirties. The lifespan of dolphins also seems to vary between species, with the largest animals living the longest. The average lifespan of common, bottlenose and Ganges river dolphins tends to be 20 years, while narwhals and spotted dolphins may live to be 40–50 years old.

There is no doubt that Wells' work is providing an insight into the structure of dolphin society, but some say that this is at a price. For any dolphin, capture is inevitably highly stressful, and some are likely to sustain injuries as they are lifted out of the water. Non-invasive study methods are, for animal welfarists, a more acceptable option. Such methods centre on identifying individual dolphins by their specific markings, especially nicks on their dorsal fins, and by dedicated observation of the animals' movements and behaviour patterns. With the help of a team of dolphin-watchers, the cetacean expert Dr Peter Evans is currently conducting a long-term study of a considerably smaller population of bottlenose dolphins living in the Moray Firth in Scotland. His findings confirm those of Wells: 'Individual [dolphins] will associate with each other over many years, but they also spend a lot of time away from that partner, socializing with dolphins in other groups. This gives rise to a very fluid situation similar to human society in the west. Dolphin society has the potential to be as sophisticated as our own, but there is a danger in drawing parallels and of putting human values on dolphin behaviour. We should consider dolphins on their own terms.'

THE NATURE OF DOLPHINS

In dolphins, the desire to care for one another, especially in times of trouble, seems to be instinctive. Such compassionate behaviour may, in some respects, have evolved from their need to breathe to stay alive. For dolphins, being mammals, survival hinges on being able to come to the surface of the water for air. If an individual is unable to do this, others will come to its aid.

Members of the Living Sea Gulfarium at Fort William Beach in Florida witnessed this behaviour at first-hand when they noticed an underwater explosion had injured a bottlenose dolphin in the bay. The animal rose to the surface in distress and then sank. Immediately, two other dolphins came to his assistance. They positioned themselves on either side of their wounded companion, putting their heads under his flippers, and carried him to the surface for air. In this position they were unable to breath through their blow-holes, so they had to let go of their casualty from time to time to catch a breath themselves. But they always returned to their first-aid stations straight afterwards.

Dolphins in trouble appear to communicate this to others using a certain 'distress' whistle. Being highly sensitive, it is possible that the animals may sense this emotional state in one another too. The story of Pauline suggests that even dolphins which are complete strangers will help each other in times of trouble. Pauline was a female dolphin who was caught for display. As soon as her captors slipped her into a tank they realized that she was suffering from acute shock. She could not swim and kept sinking to the bottom. To keep her alive, they built a float and slid her onto it. For two days she drifted, now able to breathe, but refusing food. From time to time she whistled, as if crying for help.

The next day her captors caught yet another dolphin, a healthy male. Now Pauline's distress calls were answered. The new dolphin immediately swam to her side and nudged her head gently. She responded by beating her tail flukes weakly up and down. Realizing that she might be trying to swim, the dolphinarium staff took away the float. Very slowly, Pauline began to move. If she started to sink in the water, her new companion would swim down and push her back to the surface. From then on the dolphins never left each other's side. Sadly, Pauline died from an abscess that developed where she had been caught with a fishing line. As if grieving for her, the male dolphin floated listlessly around the pool, refusing to eat, until he, too, died.

Dolphins also appear to extend their altruistic behaviour to humans: there are countless stories of dolphins coming to the aid of people in distress. Do the animals recognize in us the need to breathe air to survive, and is this why they have been known to lift people up to the surface of the sea to save them from drowning? The ancient Greeks apparently believed this to be the case. One of their most popular tales was the story of Arion's rescue, which crops up time and time again in the classical texts. The event supposedly took place during the reign of Periander, the tyrant of Corinth, in the sixth century BC. It was first written down by the Greek historian Herodotus, who heard it from the people of Corinth and Lesbos, and was subsequently related several centuries later by Plutarch, Aelian and Oppian.

Arion of Methymna in Lesbos was reputedly the most gifted lyre-player of his day. His talent took him to Periander's court, where he composed and performed for the king. Whilst there, he decided to travel to Italy and Sicily to earn some money. Reluctantly the king agreed, but not without first stipulating a date for his return.

Having amassed a small fortune abroad, Arion made plans to return to Corinth. Trusting the Corinthian men, he hired one of their ships to carry him from Taras to Italy. Once at sea, however the crew plotted to throw Arion overboard and steal his money. On discovering their despicable plan, Arion beseeched the sailors to spare his life in exchange for all his money. But, thinking that he would betray them, the sailors insisted that he either kill himself or jump into the sea.

Noting their determination, Arion asked them to let him sing one last song. Pleased by the prospect of hearing this famous musician perform, the crew agreed to his proposal. So Arion donned his singing robes, took up his lyre and sang the 'Shrill Strain' – a high-pitched, apparently well-known song in honour of Apollo. Then he threw himself into the ocean. The crew sailed on to Corinth, believing that they had seen the last of Arion. But a dolphin, so the story goes, rescued Arion, and, lifting the musician onto its back, took him to shore at Taenarus. From there Arion made his way to Corinth to tell his tale. Thinking it too far-fetched, Periander kept Arion under close watch and waited for the sailors' return. When they arrived, he asked what news they brought of Arion. They replied that he was safe and well in Tara. But when confronted with Arion, still in his singing robes, they were forced to confess their evil deed.

It is interesting to note that this tale involves the use of a high-pitched song. Is it possible that there is some truth in the story, and that dolphins could have been drawn to the ship by the sound of Arion's singing and playing, and lifted him out of the water and took him to shore?

More recent accounts of dolphins helping people to shore certainly suggest that such ancient fables are not just fairy stories. In 1943 an attorney's wife was bathing from a private beach off the coast of Florida when a strong undertow pulled her under, and she started to swallow water. She recounts that all of a sudden she was given a tremendous shove from behind, and landed on shore gasping for breath. On looking around to see who had done this, all she saw was a dolphin leaping around in the waves, and, just beyond it, what appeared to be another. A man who saw the incident from the shore reported that when he first saw the woman, she looked like a dead body. Then the dolphin came up and pushed her from behind. The animal beyond was in fact not a dolphin, but a shark.

Cynics say that dolphins have also been sighted diligently carrying an old mattress to the surface of the sea, and that we therefore flatter ourselves in thinking that they are singling us out as worthy of rescue. Other people, however, are not so sure. Even if dolphins do show an innate tendency to carry drifting objects, it still does not explain why dolphins habitually carry human subjects to the nearest shore rather than out to sea.

In his book *Follow a Wild Dolphin* Horace Dobbs recounts an incident which suggests that dolphins can even tell the difference between real and faked distress. A group of divers were practising a life-saving drill off Penzance. Donald, a friendly dolphin who had established his home in these waters, was enjoying their activities. He would push his nose mischievously between the 'victim' and the 'rescuer', nudging them in opposite directions. Later that afternoon, a young student teacher named Keith Monery was struggling in the water, this time for real. Donald swam straight for him, and onlookers were concerned that the dolphin might think the struggle was all part of the same game. But when rescuers arrived on the scene they found Donald gently supporting Keith from underneath. The animal then appeared to help them tow the distressed young man back to the boat. Dobbs posits that perhaps Donald sensed that Keith's distress vibrations were genuine, whereas those in the morning were faked. Sharks certainly have the ability to sense distress, so there is no reason why dolphins should not also be able to.

Although sharks are one of their few predators, dolphins can kill them in self-defence by ramming them in the gills with their snouts. Maybe dolphins also see sharks as a threat to humans, for stories of dolphins herding sharks away from swimmers in the water are also quite common. A long-distance swimmer, John Koorey, reports for example that while crossing the channel between the north and south islands of New Zealand, he was joined by a school of dolphins. Having accompanied him for some time, they suddenly swam off for no apparent reason. Shortly afterwards, they returned again and gambolled around him as if nothing had happened. He was later told by people on the boats following him across Wellington Sound that the dolphins had been seen driving away a group of sharks swimming nearby.

A few years ago a remarkable event took place on the Black Sea. A small Russian fishing boat was suddenly surrounded by several dolphins who began to push the vessel towards a buoy. There the fisherman were amazed to discover a young dolphin trapped in the buoy's anchor line. When the men freed the baby dolphin, the rest of the school started whistling joyfully. They then escorted the fishing boat all the way back to port.

Although such stories and anecdotes give us some insight into the nature of dolphins, there is still much to learn about their behaviour in the wild.

Reading the Signs

In an attempt to understand dolphins better, since 1985 the behavioural biologist Denise Herzing has been 'eavesdropping' on a population of about 50 wild spotted dolphins living off Grand Bahama Island. Her research is purely observational. Using a catamaran as a floating field station, she is able to approach the pod without disturbing the dolphins unduly. During the time she has been studying them, a bond of trust has formed which allows her to enter into their private world. She has been able to record their interactions, on video and acoustically, and her work is shedding new light on the true nature of wild dolphins.

Herzing explains that certain body postures and movements provide information about dolphins' relationships with one another as well as about their mood state, but to interpret these poses and movements properly you also have to consider them in context. 'Dolphins are incredibly tactile creatures. They use their fins, not just to steer and manoeuvre themselves, but also to stroke and touch one another. This physical contact helps establish bonds of trust. Dolphin "friends" may swim along face to face touching flippers, as if holding hands.'

For male dolphins, the penis also serves as a tactile organ and they use it as we do our hands. We may interpret this kind of 'feeling' as being of a sexual nature, although it is often purely exploratory. Dolphins also enjoy the sensation of having their skin rubbed, the expression in their eyes revealing what can only be described as bliss. But despite their inquisitive nature, dolphins are shy, highly sensitive creatures, and will only let people they know and trust touch them. Grabbing at a dolphin is akin to invading its 'personal space' and, if free to do so, the animal will simply swim away. When a dolphin touches a person of its free will, it is expressing the ultimate gesture of trust.

Dolphins that appear to be closely bonded may swim in synchrony: they twist, turn, dive and spin in perfect harmony with one another. Dolphins also mimic humans, although the reason for this remains unclear. Denise Herzing tells of an incident when a human mother entered the water with her baby. One particular dolphin watched closely as this happened, then swam off. Minutes later the dolphin returned with a calf too.

Dolphins are often depicted as gentle, good-natured creatures, possessing the tolerance and patience of saints. This is largely true, but when provoked, dolphins may also behave quite aggressively. Herzing asserts: 'When two dolphins face each other head on and clap their jaws together, it is like deer clashing antlers.' Such behavioural displays may be a sign that dolphins are establishing some kind of hierarchy amongst themselves.

Dolphins often open their mouths when in an aggressive mood, and if they start nodding their head, too, it shows that tension is mounting. Violent jaw-clapping is at the top end of the scale of aggressive behaviour. A male dolphin may clap its jaws at another male that approaches when it is attempting to seduce a female. Dolphin trainers often encourage dolphins to open their mouths while squeaking and shake their heads, because this gives us the impression that the creatures are 'talking' and nodding in agreement. Taken in a real-life context, however, what this actually means is that the dolphin is exceedingly angry.

According to Herzing, 'Tail-slapping is often a warning sign that a dolphin is annoyed or irritated. Mother dolphins slap their tails to get the attention of their offspring or to "tick them off". A young female may do this during courtship to tell a male she's had enough of his advances. Even distinctive breathing can sometimes be read as a threat signal.' In dolphin shows, this tail-slapping is invariably wrongly portrayed as a friendly 'waving goodbye'.

Dolphins also rake each other with their teeth. In the wild, it tends to be the younger individuals that have the most scars, indicating that they may be inflicted when one dolphin is attempting to dominate another. However, dolphins also get tooth-rake marks during mating, so perhaps these are not always aggression-linked. It is even possible that they might sometimes be 'love bites'.

Denise Herzing suggests that aggressive behaviour in dolphins may be species-related. 'Bottlenose dolphins seem to have many more tooth-rakes, signifying more clashes and aggressive confrontations. The spotted dolphins seem to be more passive and peaceful; I think of them as the Tibetans of the dolphin world. They also behave differently towards people. In the wild, spotted dolphins are very tolerant, perhaps because they have had little adverse interaction with humans. In this region, bottlenose dolphins are often caught for display in dolphinariums. They seem to be more wary and will stay away from humans, suggesting they do communicate fear to one another.'

Randall Wells has witnessed the Sarasota bottlenose dolphins behaving aggressively towards dolphins from other groups. On one occasion a 600-lb male who has lived in the bay for more than 20 years did a full body-slam on top of two dolphins from Tampa Bay. In the dolphin's defence, it seems possible that aggressive behaviour is often kindled by stressful situations. Nowadays the Sarasota dolphins are fighting to survive in a changing and inhospitable environment. It is small wonder that they should wish to protect their precious home and food resources.

'The stress of being confined in small, concrete tanks also encourages dolphins to behave out of character,' writes William Johnson, the animal welfare consultant to the Geneva-based Bellerive Foundation, in his book *The Rose-Tinted Menagerie*. 'It reduces the highly evolved dolphin society into a primitive pecking order with the stronger, more aggressive animals not only fighting each other for supremacy, but also hounding the weaker ones into submission, illness or death.

'In an oceanarium in Florida it was observed how several bottlenose dolphins persistently chased away one of their ailing companions to prevent it feeding, even going so far as to pull the fish from its mouth. This anti-social behaviour continued even after the "thieves" had gorged themselves to excess. In the wild dolphins hunt cooperatively in schools, herding the fish and sharing the reward.'

It may be that social stresses and pressures will make the normally placid, compassionate and good-natured dolphin behave in an uncharacteristically selfish and aggressive way. In this respect, dolphins show a remarkable similarity to human beings.

It is important to consider that to generalize about dolphin behaviour may be taking a rather narrow perspective. For there is little doubt that dolphins have their own unique personalities, as anyone who has worked closely with captive dolphins will agree. Some dolphins are more tolerant and eager to please than others. In his book *Behind the Dolphin Smile*, Ric O'Barry recounts his experiences of working with Flipper. There were actually about six different dolphins which played the part, one of whom was called Patty. O'Barry describes her as a particularly belligerent dolphin which would rush at actors and other people in the water, slapping her tail and giving the clear signal that she expected more out of life than this. One day O'Barry decided to teach her a lesson. As she swam past, he thumped her on the back next to her dorsal fin. She slowly swam towards the other end of the tank, turned, and then went for him like a torpedo. The next thing he knew, he was coming round from concussion at Mercy Hospital.

However, something that has clearly emerged from Denise Herzing's underwater observations is the innate inquisitiveness of dolphins. If something attracts their attention, they show interest and will cautiously explore it. This curiosity helps explain why dolphins seem eager to interact with people. Their obvious fascination with the various happenings in their environment gives the impression that dolphins lead busy and active lifestyles. We will now examine their way of life in more detail.

THE DOLPHIN'S LIFESTYLE

Playing

Dolphins appear to devote much of their time to playing and generally having fun. Seeing them leaping and gambolling in the waves, it is hard to imagine that they are having anything other than a good time. But as Dr Peter Evans points out in his book *The Natural History of Whales and Dolphins*, when young animals play, they are often learning important actions. Dolphins have frequently been seen repeatedly practising aerial leaps and flips, fin and head slaps. Such activities may have a greater purpose than pure pleasure. When dolphins leap clean out of the water, it is often to see whether seabirds are gathering on the surface to feed on fish. Noisy splashing jumps may serve to scare fish into a tight cluster for an easier catch. The complex aerial displays that take place after feeding may be jumps for joy, but they may also serve a social function, such as establishing the bonding that comes from shared pleasure.

However, it is also true that dolphins sometimes play just for fun. Young dolphins will occupy themselves in what seems like an exuberant game of 'tag', and even the more sedate elderly male dolphins can be seen romping around from time to time. For dolphins seem to be natural hedonists. Whether surfing on the huge breakers off the coast of Australia, or riding the bow-waves of passing ships, dolphins exude a real sense of joyfulness.

Bow-riding is not instinctive behaviour: it is something dolphins learn, a knowledge that has been handed down through generations for thousands of years. One wonders when dolphins first discovered that they could get a free ride by slipping into the pressure field created within the waves that unfurl each side of the bow as a ship ploughs through the sea.

Another activity solitary or friendly dolphins seem to enjoy is swimming along in the wake of power-boats. Jojo, a friendly dolphin who lives in the waters of the Turks and Caicos Islands, will perform quite spectacular leaps and corkscrew turns in the foam behind a boat. It is thought that he adopts this position in order to enjoy the 'jacuzzi' effect, for the stream of bubbles created by the outboard motor gives an invigorating body massage.

Dolphins in captivity often invent their own games to alleviate the boredom of their existence. When Brighton dolphinarium in the United Kingdom closed its doors to the public, and the dolphins were left to spend their time as they chose before being flown to the 'Into the Blue' rehabilitation centre in the Turks and Caicos Islands, the animals would play with certain 'toys' for hours on end. A female dolphin called Missie seemed to favour a red hoop, which she pushed along on the tip of her snout and trailed by her tail flukes, occasionally proffering it to onlookers. Without prompting, her companion, Silver, discovered for himself how to play 'catch' with a rubber ball, flicking it over and over again to anyone who cared to join in the game.

In the wild, dolphins will improvise, towing around pieces of seaweed or driftwood. Fungie, the friendly dolphin living in Dingle Bay, Ireland, has been seen entertaining himself by playing with guillemots. He will come up underneath one as it lands on the surface and flip it back into the air with his rostrum (snout). He then rushes over to the spot where the bird is about to drop back into the sea, and tosses the now rather disorientated guillemot up into the air again and again and again.

When playing, dolphins often seem to behave quite mischievously, and it is difficult not to believe that they possess a real sense of humour. There are countless instances of friendly dolphins apparently amusing themselves by tugging at divers' masks so that they fill up with water. One friendly dolphin, Simo, seemed to enjoy taking snorkellers by surprise. He would approach them from behind, rise up vertically into a tailstand, and then gently bop them on the head with his beak, dislodging their mask and snorkel in the process, before sinking back into the sea. Dolphins soon seem to tire of the games they invent, and after pursuing this activity for a while, Simo would look for another source of entertainment. One of Fungie's favourite tricks is to come up on one side of a boat when everyone is looking for him over the other, then drench them with an enormous leap. Yet, even when at their most boisterous, these dolphins have never shown any hint of malice towards their human playmates.

Feeding

When not playing, dolphins are usually busy feeding. Often, the two activities seem to go hand in hand. For while getting their full quota of fish is essential for survival, dolphins also appear to derive pleasure from their foraging.

The dolphin is a large animal with a higher metabolic rate than terrestrial mammals of a similar size, so it needs to consume a good many calories to sustain its energy levels and bodily functions. The dolphin's diet consists of a high-protein fish or squid diet with almost no carbohydrate. Typically, a dolphin in captivity will eat about 20lbs of fish a day, but wild dolphins may eat much more, being far more active. If food supplies are abundant, the creatures will probably spend less time feeding than if food is in short supply. Food consumption also varies from species to species.

To locate their prey, dolphins use their sophisticated sonar system. Dr Kenneth Norris suggests that dolphins are also capable of stunning or even killing fish by emitting a stream of pulses or clicks. There is still some doubt as to whether this is actually the case, but there is good reason to suppose that fish may be disorientated by this sort of acoustic attack. With their conical teeth, dolphins then grasp their prey and swallow it, usually whole.

Dolphins tend to feed on the fish that are indigenous to the waters in which they live. Squid seems to be an important part of their diet. It furnishes them with the arachidonic acid, one of the w6 series of essential fatty acids which is apparently important for the dolphin's brain tissue. In captivity, dolphins often show a preference for mackerel and herring.

While dolphins do feed alone, when in a pod they often hunt together. Whilst observing a group of dusky dolphins, Dr Bernard Wursig noted that each took turns to go through the fish school while the others kept the fish tightly packed together. Wursig realized that such cooperation required highly refined communication, otherwise certain individuals might grab more fish and spend less time herding. He reckoned that the dolphins knew and trusted one another enough to control the situation.

According to Dr Susan Shane, who has been studying bottlenose dolphins for over 15 years, local groups develop feeding traditions that are handed down from generation to generation. In certain areas, groups of wild dolphins have traditionally helped the local fishermen make their catch by driving schools of fish into their nets.

Dolphin trainers use fish rewards to entice dolphins to do 'tricks'. If the dolphin refuses to perform, it often goes without its fish. But sometimes the dolphin has the final say. In a collection of papers entitled *Dolphin Cognition and Behaviour*, the editor, Robert

Schusterman, describes an experiment in which a bottlenose dolphin was being asked to make a series of choices. Each time it got the right answer, it received a fish from an automatic feeding machine. After many correct responses, one day the dolphin made a string of wrong ones. An examination of the machine revealed that the fish inside it had dried out and become unpalatable. Once these were replaced with fresh ones, the dolphin started getting the correct answers once again.

The tale of a trained dolphin called Tuffy also appeals to us, because it suggests that these clever creatures have got their own priorities worked out, and feeding is certainly one of them. Tuffy was put to work as a messenger on a project run back in 1965 called Sealab II. He was kitted out with a harness onto which could be hooked waterproof bags. He then carried post, tools and sometimes medicine to a group of human underwater explorers living in the Sealab capsule on the ocean floor. Tuffy was the only live link these divers had with the outside world. From time to time the divers left the capsule to explore the dark depths. If the divers got lost, they only had Tuffy to turn to. So, time and again, they ran tests, pretending to be lost. A diver would hide behind a rock or clump of seaweed and set off a buzzer which was Tuffy's signal to come to the rescue. Seconds later, the dolphin would dive down, swimming first to the Sealab capsule where he slid his snout through a ring tied to a rope, which was in turn attached to Sealab. He then scanned for the hidden man and, having found him, brought him the lifeline. For these efforts, Tuffy was given a fish reward. But on one occasion something went wrong. The explorer tugged at his bag, but could not get it open, and pushed the dolphin away. But Tuffy did not move. He stared at the man for a moment, then raised one of his flippers and bopped the man over the head.

Being sensitive creatures, it is not suprising that dolphins may go off their food when they are upset. There have been instances when, after a close companion has died, dolphins in captivity have refused food to the point of starving themselves to death.

Making Love

When dolphins are not playing or feeding, they may well be engaged in some kind of sexual activity. Like people, dolphins do not simply mate to reproduce, but seem to indulge in sex for the pleasure of it. For dolphins, sex appears to play a role in establishing and reaffirming bonds of friendship. Amongst the dolphins in Shark Bay, Australia, there is constant sexual interaction, both heterosexual and homosexual, which suggests that much of the activity is purely social. Even at two days old, baby male dolphins have been seen with erections. Their mothers seem perfectly happy to let their offspring explore them sexually, which confirms the notion that sex, for dolphins, is often a social affair.

It may be that the fact of animals like the dolphin indulging in a great amount of sexual activity unconnected with reproduction is correlated with a large brain and expanded neocortex. Certainly, there seems good reason to believe that when dolphins are happy and relaxed they will show it by making love. For there's no doubt that dolphins are highly promiscuous. Males and females do not form long-term pair-bonds or mate for life. Females often make love several times a day and with a number of different males. In his book *Water and Sexuality* Dr Michel Odent points out that in the Sind, a province of Pakistan in the lower Indus Valley, the female dolphin is a sexual symbol. According to a legend, the first *bulhan* (nymphomaniac) was born of a woman who used to make love with dolphins, and the local troubadours still celebrate the Indus, the dolphins and love all together.

Although females can make love all year round, their readiness to mate for the purpose of reproduction is relayed by various cues such as changes in the shape and colour of their genital area, and possibly a surge of hormones detectable by the males. In Shark Bay, pairs and even trios of male dolphins have been seen 'kidnapping' a female, presumably for the purposes of mating. Randall Wells also reports that male bottlenose dolphins have unusually large testes, and that sperm concentrations in their ejaculate are 300 times greater than those of humans.

It appears that there are seasons in the sea, as well as on dry land, and that dolphins' mating behaviour falls under their influence. Since 1985, Bob Morris, a bio- and geo-chemist and cetacean researcher, has been studying a small group of resident dolphins in Newquay Bay, Wales, by observing as well as listening in on them using sophisticated naval sonar buoys. From the unusually excited sounds and splashes he has heard during April and May, Morris reckons that the dolphins were having what amount to sexual orgies at these times. They correlate neatly with the dolphins' birth times, which in this region are in March and August.

The dolphin's courtship is described in explicit detail by Anthony Alpers in his book *Dolphins*. When a male starts to pay attention to a female, he 'postures' in front of her. His body forms an S-shape with his head uplifted and tail bent down. Later, he may swim up under the female and pause with his head just beneath her tail. She responds by patting his head with her tail flukes in a gentle, affectionate way. He may also swim across her back, lightly stroking her with his flippers, or he may turn over and do this from underneath, so that their flippers touch as if the dolphins are holding hands. These actions are a sort of foreplay and take place when the dolphins are resting. More vigorous things occur when the dolphins are feeling energetic. The male may rush at the female as if to collide with her head-on, but at the last moment turn away so that their bodies rub vigorously against one another. This is accompanied by enthusiastic 'pulsed yelps'. Occasionally, the female swims away, perhaps leaping out of the water as if to evade the male. He then darts to the spot where she is likely to re-enter, in order to be vigorously rubbed once more.

Dolphins are one of the few animals that, like us, make love belly to belly, which suggests that both dolphin partners can reach an orgasmic state. Indeed, among dolphins, the whole act is incredibly graceful, like a ballet, with what looks like real love being transmitted between the two participants. There are times when the dolphins softly nuzzle each other with their snouts and gently nibble each other's flippers. Should another male get in the way at such a moment, he will be warned off with a loud jaw-clap.

Reproduction

Just like other mammals, female dolphins carry their young inside their wombs. The gestation period for dolphins is between 10 and 16 months, depending on the species. The pregnancies of bottlenose dolphins last for almost exactly one year.

The way that dolphins give birth is unusual amongst mammals, yet it is remarkably similar to ours. Just before the birth, the other female dolphins seem to sense the climax is nigh, and gather around the mother-to-be. They will help keep curious males, as well as sharks, at bay. The baby emerges tail first, and the birth usually takes about half an hour, although longer deliveries have been recorded. The baby dolphin normally wriggles its way to the surface by itself, but should it need assistance, its mother is on hand. If need be one of the female 'aunts' may also step in to help, taking on the role of midwife. Unlike land mammals, a mother dolphin will not eat her placenta. This is characteristic of marine-dwelling creatures.

The newly born baby dolphin is like a miniature version of its mother. It is normally around three feet long and weighs about 25lbs. It has bristles around its snout, hinting at the dolphin's primordial terrestrial beginnings. Its teeth are below the gums and do not cut through until a few weeks later. Like land mammals, baby dolphins suckle from their mother. Her teats are located in grooves towards her tail, and through muscle action she is able to squirt milk directly into her baby's mouth. The mother dolphin's milk is much fattier than ours and is supposed to have a fishy aroma. A young dolphin will continue to suckle from its mother for up to two years and, as previously mentioned, will stay closely bonded to her for three to six years before joining up with other dolphins of its own age.

After birth, the baby instinctively takes up a protected position beside its mother's dorsal fin. Initially, swimming does not come easily. To keep up, the baby has to beat its tail ten to the dozen as it wobbles about. During the first two months, the young dolphin pops its head out of the water, then falls back with a splash. Graceful movement only comes with practice.

Sleeping

With feeding, playing, making love and reproducing taking up so much of their time, it would seem as if dolphins hardly have a moment in which to sleep. They do, but in a manner quite different to our own. The people of Dingle in Ireland fondly claim that when the sun sets, Fungie the friendly dolphin retires to a nearby cave where he sleeps with a seal. But the truth is that dolphins do not have regular sleeping and waking patterns linked to night and day. If anything, the animals are often at their most active during the dark night hours.

Dolphins take short 'cat-naps' whenever they need to rest. It is not possible for dolphins to lose consciousness in the way that we do when sleeping, because their breathing is under voluntary control, so only one half of their brain switches off at a time. The dolphin then floats just below the surface, periodically fanning its fins so that it rises to take a breath. Dolphins may also sleep with one eye open and the other closed.

Do dolphins dream? It seems unlikely. Brain-wave patterns reveal that dolphins do not exhibit REM (rapid eye movement), which is usually linked to dreaming. But at present scientists do not know what goes on inside the dolphin's mind when it drifts off to sleep — and possibly they never will.

···

Chapter Six

DOLPHIN INTELLIGENCE

INTRODUCTION

The notion that dolphins might be as intelligent as we are has long captured the human imagination. In an attempt to find out just how clever these creatures really are, scientists have probed the animals' brains, taxed their ability to learn and understand various orders, and scrutinized their behaviour. But the quest to determine a dolphin's intelligence is riddled with pitfalls. To begin with, we invariably ignore the fact that dolphins have embarked on a completely different evolutionary path from our own. As Douglas Adams amusingly writes in *The Hitchhiker's Guide to the Galaxy*: 'On planet Earth, man has always assumed that he was more intelligent than dolphins because he had achieved so much – the wheel, New York, wars and so on – whilst all the dolphins had ever done was muck about in the water having a good time. But conversely, the dolphins had always believed that they were far more intelligent than man – for precisely the same reasons.'

Nevertheless, anyone who has ever spent time in the presence of a dolphin cannot come away without thinking that these animals have active and inquiring minds. They also appear to be knowing, highly sensitive and even intuitive. When considered along with the countless tales of their remarkable capacity to learn, discriminate and invent games, these impressions suggest that dolphins are indeed highly intelligent beings.

We may well regard ourselves as intellectually superior to all animals, yet we are wreaking havoc on our precious planet. We have already depleted the Earth's natural resources and polluted the oceans and atmosphere to a degree that is placing our own existence and that of many other creatures in a precarious position. Dolphins, by contrast, live in a state of total harmony with nature. They neither exploit, plunder nor destroy their environment. Perhaps the time has come to climb down off our pedestal and rethink some of our theories on intelligence. Whilst observing dolphins from terra firma, it is perhaps easy to feel superior to them, but once one is plunged into their environment, they are the ones who are in control and command one's deepest respect. If we are – or believe ourselves to be – masters of our universe, then the dolphin is surely the king of his domain.

EARLY SIGNS

The ancient Greeks were the first to note that the dolphin was probably more intelligent than man's closest cousin, the monkey. In Aesop's tale of 'The Monkey and the Dolphin' we have one of the first accounts, albeit a fable, that asserts that the dolphin was more intelligent than the average primate.

Aesop's fable recounts the rescue of a monkey by a dolphin. At that time it was customary for seafarers to take with them an animal companion, usually a lap dog or monkey. On one particular voyage, a passenger brought a monkey on board to keep him company. A violent storm capsized the ship just off the coast of Sunium, a promontory of Attica, and everyone on board was thrown into the water and had to swim for their lives. The monkey also was struggling in the water, but was fortunate enough to be spotted by a passing dolphin, which, mistaking him for a man, went to his aid. The dolphin carried him on its back and headed for Piraeus, the main harbour at Athens. When the dolphin asked the monkey if he was an Athenian, the monkey replied that he was. 'Then of course you know Piraeus,' said the dolphin. The monkey answered that he did, and, thinking that this name referred to a distinguished citizen, added, 'He is one of my most intimate friends.' Whereupon, indignant at this pretence, the dolphin dived at once to the bottom and left the poor monkey to its fate!

It was not until dolphins were brought into captivity, in the early 1960s, and were taught tricks and given tasks to perform, that it became patently obvious that we were dealing with very special creatures. The marine biologist D.O. Hebb, who spent many years studying dolphins both in the wild and in captivity, was one of the first to rate dolphins second to man on the intelligence scale. Hebb noted that certain aspects of their behaviour were concerned with emotions rather than gut reactions. This placed them in a top ranking position among the higher animals on what he refers to as the 'Phylogenetic scale'. The fact that dolphins recognize one another, as well as humans, form individual attachments, and exhibit fear of unfamiliar inanimate objects, suggested to him that dolphins are capable of thinking and have an imagination. Their success in problem-solving is also evidence of insight, a sure sign of intelligence.

One of the first people to attempt to measure the dolphin's intelligence scientifically was the neurophysiologist and father of the 'New Age', Dr John Lilly. Lilly initiated much of the work on dolphin intelligence and communication. Using complex electronic equipment, he drove electrodes into his captive dolphins' brains while they were fully conscious. His aim was to determine the structure and function of the brain by measuring its response to various stimuli. We may shudder at the way he went about his work, but, viewed in a positive light, John Lilly's findings did much to kindle our respect for dolphins. For in his book, *Man and Dolphin*, Lilly remarked that dolphins may be our intellectual superiors. His work attracted the attention of many other scientists, for what he discovered was indeed remarkable – that dolphins have a brain that is as large and apparently complex as our own.

However, Lilly's research has had its shortcomings and some unpleasant repercussions. It was taken up by the US Navy, which perceived that an aquatic creature with an intelligence equal to man's could well be exploited to assist in defence programmes. Lilly himself also now regrets taking dolphins out of their natural environment in order to study them, and he regrets the fact, too, that due to his ground-breaking work, dolphins have been used to satiate man's greed and indulge his warmongering nature.

THE 'BIG BRAIN' CONNECTION

The human brain is the most complex and highly developed structure that exists. Although the dolphin is very different to primates and has spent some 50 million years in the sea, its brain bears remarkable similarities to our own. It is much larger than that of our nearest anthropoid cousin, the gorilla, and certainly far more complex. In size proportion, the dolphin brain runs a close second to man's. The human brain weighs on average 1,400 grams, whereas the dolphin brain weighs from 200 to 6,000 grams, depending on the species. In both man and dolphin, brain size is relative to body size. Weight for weight, man has the largest brain of all terrestrial dwellers, whilst in the sea it is the dolphin who has the most developed brain. In *Communication Between Man and Dolphin* John Lilly pointed out that one of the main reasons that the largest brains on earth – belonging to the whales and dolphins – have evolved in the sea rather than on land is due to basic Newtonian mechanics. On land, large brains and small bodies, he explains, just do not go together: 'Brain size must be relative to body size because of gravity and rotary acceleration through movement.'

Unlike the human brain, however, there is no single dolphin brain model: it varies across the species in size and anatomy. For example, the Ganges river dolphin has a very simple brain, weighing about 200g, whereas the Atlantic bottlenose brain weighs up to 1.5 kg and is highly complex and convoluted. However, like us, dolphins are born with their brains in an advanced state. Full brain development occurs between the ages of nine and 10 years, which is half the total period for humans, but considerably longer than for most other mammals.

The brains of both man and dolphin are made up of many different parts which control a wide variety of functions and activities. Paul D. MacLean, chief of the Laboratory of Brain Evolution and Behaviour at the National Institute of Mental Health, in the United States, has identified three separate physiological levels of the human brain, each corresponding to our evolution. The most ancient part of the brain – the Reptile Brain – comprises the spinal cord, the brain stem and the mid-brain. This brain controls basic survival and reproductive instincts and life-sustaining functions such as respiration, heart regulation and blood circulation. The same primitive brain was present in ancient reptiles. The next layer is the Paleomammalian, also known as the horse brain or limbic system. This part of the brain is the control centre for the emotions and for states of mind such as fear, panic, pleasure and bliss. Messages received from our external environment pass through the limbic system on the way to the neocortex, the newest part of the brain. The limbic system is the area in which responses such as affection, sexual behaviour, altruistic impulses and even love originate. Within this area, the hypothalamus is the predominant controller. It regulates all bodily functions such as thirst, hunger, body temperature and sexual drive, and has ultimate control over the production of neurochemicals such as adrenalin and endorphins. It is also very important in the relationship between mind and body. While the primitive brain evolved first, the cerebrum, also known as the neocortex, is the latest part of the brain to evolve. What has fascinated scientists is the fact that roughly the same proportion of the dolphin brain also comprises cerebrum. The latter consists of densely packed nerve cells which form a region of 'grey matter' referred to as the cerebral cortex. The cerebrum is divided into two hemispheres – the left and right brains – and contains three main areas – sensory, association and motor. Responsible for the burst of evolution that produced the 'thinking' primate, *Homo sapiens*, this 'roof-brain' is the seat of our high-order abstract, cognitive functions – memory, judgement and intellect – and also receives and processes audio-visual perceptions. It is here that we are able to remember the past, to anticipate the future, to create and manipulate language. This is where our conscious thinking is done, and where we control our voluntary movements and actions.

It is the neocortex of the dolphin which is of particular interest to researchers, because it does indeed bear similarity to our own. In 1986, Harry Jerison, a microbiologist at the University of California Medical School, proposed that, given the close positioning of the laminates of the neocortex in the dolphin's brain, motivational functions such as intimacy and feelings might be more active in the dolphin's neocortical processes than in humans', and that dolphins' thoughts might be more emotionally charged. He also suggested that given the large neocortex, the dolphin's echo location processes created a perception of the outer world and of the self that was similar to our own.

Others, however, are not so lured by the idea that the dolphin's big neocortex makes it special. Peter Morgane, a senior scientist at the Worcester Foundation of Experimental Biology, and his colleague Ilya Glezer, an anatomy professor at the City of New York Medical School, along with other researchers, primarily from Russia, have succeeded in mapping portions of the dolphin's brain, especially the cerebral cortex, by using electrodes placed into an anaesthetized dolphin brain. Morgane suggests that the dolphin's neocortex may have got bigger, but it still has an ancient organization, as the dolphin has kept this brain structure since it first went into the sea. This raises the question of how intellectually advanced the dolphin's ancestor was when it took to the water.

The dolphin's brain does have its own extraordinary features. The cerebellum, the part which controls movement, accounts for 20 per cent of the dolphin's brain. It is therefore little wonder that the dolphin is so agile and graceful and possesses great aquatic prowess. Unlike us, it has no olfactory system, in other words, no sense of smell. It therefore relies more heavily on the senses of sight, sound and touch. Scientists have also noted that the dolphin's thalamus – the area of the brain where sensory impulses, particularly pleasure and pain, are analysed and relayed to the cortex, rather like a telephone switchboard – is very well-developed. It has an extensive area of intrinsic nuclei – groups of cells that do not receive any external information. They are called 'silent' or 'associative' zones, and both man and dolphin have roughly the same percentage of 'silent' zones in the cortex. These zones are capable of activities that are not stimulated by external senses, and therefore many people believe that the zones are associated with abstract thinking, and even with spirituality. This idea was originally put forward by John Lilly, who suggested that dolphins could reach meditative states very easily and that they were potentially spiritual creatures. However, such speculation aside, it is important to note that much of the research into the dolphin brain remains inconclusive, and many of the theories put forward are still hypothetical.

The evolutionary aspect of the development of the sea-dwelling cetacean brain in comparison to that of big-brained species on dry land – in other words, man, gorilla, and chimpanzee – is worth looking at for clues as to dolphin intelligence. New research has shown that nutrition has much to do with the development of brain capacity, and scientists have pinpointed the essential fatty acids, arachidonic and docosahexaenoic acid, as being of particular relevance. While protein is important for muscle and mineral development, lipids (fats) appear to be related to the nervous system and to the brain and vascular systems. The lipids used to build the tissue of various species differ, with one exception – the brain. A paper entitled 'Nutritional Influences in the Evolution of the Mammalian Brain' argued that carnivores obtained significantly higher concentrations of fatty acids in their diet, which could explain the difference between the higher degree of brain development in the carnivores when compared to that of the herbivores. However, the most developed carnivores have still lost an enormous amount of brain capacity. But what about the cetaceans and, in particular, dolphins? Biochemically, they had an important advantage. Unlike the land mammals, they had easy access to omega 3 fatty acids, particularly docosahexaenoic acid, which is found in plankton, the microscopic class of ocean plants, and, on land, in grains and nut oils. The other form of fatty acids essential for brain development, omega 6, found in sea plants and in grains and nuts, however, was more difficult to find, but it seems that dolphins were expert in seeking it out.

The obstetrician Michel Odent is carrying out research into the nutritional impact of fatty acids on the human brain by studying a group of pregnant women at Whipp's Cross Hospital, London. Intrigued by the work of nutritionist Michael Crawford, who has initiated much of the research into omega 3 and omega 6, and interested in the human/

dolphin connection, Odent wants to find a link. 'How is it that our brain and that of the dolphin, is bigger than all other creatures'? I am sure that fatty acids are the key,' he muses. Odent is encouraging a number of women to eat a diet rich in fatty acids, particularly omega 3, while they are pregnant. He will then observe if this marine-rich diet makes a significant difference to the brain development and the intelligence of the children born to these women by comparison with those who have not eaten a diet abundant in seafood. He believes that this will throw light on the importance of fatty acids in brain development, man's link with dolphins, and our aquatic past.

THE NATURE OF INTELLIGENCE

Many people, and scientists in particular, find it incredibly difficult to come to terms with the idea that there are some animals who may be as intelligent as us. Perhaps this reaction is not altogether surprising, as it is deeply ingrained in us that we are the most intelligent life-form on the planet. We even called ourselves *Homo sapiens sapiens* – 'Wise, wise man'! The notion that animals were not capable of thought or feelings was put forward by René Descartes in the 16th century. He proposed that animals were automatons not guided by a mind, whereas humans had a mind, free will and the attributes of reasoning. More recently, the animal behaviourist Susanne K. Langer suggested that 'All animal reaction is instinctive and that instinctive behaviour may be quite devoid of intelligence.' So, although attitudes are changing, our underlying mental block about animal intelligence still holds true.

What is intelligence? It is difficult to quantify at the best of times. Having largely done away with the basic function of survival, man has been able to indulge his brain. We have time to sit around and think, to learn new skills, to invent things; something which we loosely define as 'cognition' – the ability to perceive, to know and to learn, which goes beyond purely instinctive responses. In the quest to become increasingly 'civilized', humans have placed much importance and emphasis on the left-brain functions such as logic, rationality and analytical thinking. In recent years, we have begun to realize and respect the importance of the right brain, which is the seat of creative thinking, inspiration and intuition. 'Whole-brain thinking', as it is termed, is more effective, makes our life richer and more fulfilling, and makes us less tunnel-visioned. As we come to realize the importance of such a balance, of combining both left- and right-brain thought, perhaps we also have to rethink our ways of perceiving dolphin intelligence. As John Lilly pointed out, we cannot judge dolphins on our terms. 'It [the dolphin] doesn't build anything. It doesn't write anything. It doesn't record anything, outside of its self. So, you start completely out of the ball park of human definitions of intelligence.' Lilly also remarked that this was similar to dealing with an extra-terrestrial being, because the dolphin comes from an alien environment, has its own method of communication and has a different physical body to our own. 'If you were dropped naked in the middle of the Gulf Stream, in the middle of the night, could you survive? How is your intelligence used in these circumstances, without your usual artefacts? Now, if you could put on a dolphin suit and swim at six or 10 knots, then you would be sufficiently interesting to them. But, with our present swimming equipment, all they can do is push us ashore, and say, "Get the hell out of here, this is not your league." So, it's very hard to identify with this, to analyse what this intelligence is doing.'

Signs of Intelligence

The organic chemist and dolphin expert Bob Morris believes that the volume, proportion, weight, cell-count and sheer complexity of the dolphin brain favour the development of intelligence. In other words, the dolphin is equipped to analyse situations, not just to react to them, and to make decisions on the basis of its findings much in the same way as we do.

But defining intelligence is not easy, although there are certain characteristics which apply whether we are referring to man or to monkey. Flexible behaviour, inventiveness, forward planning, and learning ability are all qualities which signify the potential existence of intelligence. The ability to do the right thing on the right occasion, that is, flexible behaviour, reveals a consciousness of what is going on. Dolphins exhibit such behaviour, appearing to be aware of their situation and acting in an appropriate manner. One of the world's leading researchers who has been studying both dolphin communication and intelligence is Dr Louis Herman. Based at the University of Hawaii's Kewalo Basin Marine Mammal Laboratory, Herman has been exploring both these aspects since 1966. His aim is to look at ways to communicate with dolphins more effectively and to understand their intellectual skills. Herman defines intelligence as flexibility. 'Intelligent animals are able to construct a detailed image of the world based on experience and accumulated knowledge in order to behave, react, and respond appropriately when different aspects of reality emerge. Intelligence therefore relies on the ability to store and utilize new knowledge, along with strategies and rules that have been learned or that may be devised.'

In one of his studies, Herman showed that dolphins can remember new sounds heard after delays of several minutes and that they could also remember things briefly shown to them after delays of several minutes. He also proved that dolphins could report the absence of objects as well as their presence, and that they were therefore capable of understanding things that have nothing to do with the dolphin's natural environment, survival, or reproduction.

While the dolphin's flexibility reveals one aspect of its intelligence, the creature also exhibits the ability to invent and to plan ahead. Many dolphin trainers have recounted stories which are perfect examples of the dolphin's capacity for creative forethought. Gordon Panitzke, a dolphin trainer who has tremendous respect for dolphins, told us this story of ingenuity. His dolphins realized that they could get a reward for retrieving stones that had accidentally fallen into their pool. At first, they brought the occasional one or two; then they came up with an endless supply. Panitzke eventually discovered a store of stones stashed away in an underwater pipe. The dolphins had managed to get pebbles to collect in the pipe by swishing water over the gravel around the edge of the pool with their tail flukes, and proceeded to bring out the stones whenever they felt in need of extra fish.

Furthermore, in answer to the question that many scientists have posed, as to whether dolphins are really capable of thinking things out, J.F. Eisenberg of the University of Florida, Gainesville, says that dolphins have neural mechanisms that operate in a similar way to the processes observed in humans when engaged in higher mental activities. Eisenberg also suggests that despite their lack of hands, dolphins can learn to carry out a variety of manipulative tasks. To many people, the versatility and complexity of the dolphin's behaviour makes it obvious that it must often be acting intentionally, with some understanding of the likely results of its behaviour. For instance, when one dolphin is trained to perform complex manoeuvres, the next dolphin, even though it may have been isolated, often performs the complex actions without prior experience or practice. Obviously, the second dolphin realizes that by copying the other dolphin's performance, it, too, will be rewarded.

Dolphins and Learning

Like children, dolphins invent their own games, both in the wild and in captivity. Many trainers have commented that the dolphins actually teach *them* to play games. One example of this took place at a research laboratory in California. A dolphin which was being taught to imitate human speech managed to emit a squeak which sounded like the word 'ball', but always followed it with a very different sound. After a few repetitions, he refused to repeat 'ball', but kept up his own sound. After initial disappointment, the trainer finally realized what was going on, and imitated the second sound. The dolphin then leapt out of the pool, circled the tank several times, and returned to the lesson: he would only play the game if the trainer was participating too.

It is clear also that captive dolphins appear to comprehend messages from their trainers. The kind of learning of which they are capable is far more significant than merely being able or willing, and in their play, dolphins show signs of solving problems by grasping a principle, rather than fumbling by trial and error to get it right.

Although we encountered a number of dolphin trainers who insisted that dolphins were 'no more intelligent than the average dog', none the less, one of the most respected and controversial dolphin conservationists, Ric O'Barry, the ex-trainer of Flipper, has no doubt that dolphins are intelligent, no matter what definition is applied. When working at Miami Seaquarium's Top Deck Show, he began to realize that there was more to the dolphin than met the eye and 'that it was not I who was training dolphins, but they [who] were training me. When they leaped, I tossed a fish. When they tail-walked, I tossed a fish. Whatever they did, I tossed them a fish. Who taught them to leap and turn flips originally? I have no idea. But, knowing what I know now, I suspect that nobody taught them — they taught themselves, in order to be fed. Yes, the trainer "shapes" behaviour, as animal psychologists say, but no more than the dolphin "shapes" the trainer's behaviour.'

Many scientists and trainers have compared the dolphin's intelligence to that of a human toddler. O'Barry comments: 'Dolphins are not little wind-up toys; they're complex individuals with likes and dislikes, fears, moods and dispositions, good days and bad. In general dolphins are a fun-loving bunch; cautious, impressionable, sensitive and intuitive, loyal to one another, highly adaptable, curious, willing and yet malleable, easily spoiled and then quite demanding, possessive and apt to throw tantrums, lovable, sensuous, mischievous and highly intelligent. They are almost anything you might say of a human child.' Yet he is anxious that we should not seek to draw too many comparisons between dolphins and ourselves. 'I am guilty of making comparisons myself, but it isn't really fair play. The criteria that work for determining our intelligence, do not work with regard to dolphins. What is clear to me is that they are far more intelligent in their world than we are in ours.'

Another example of insightful behaviour is the ability of some experienced animals to 'check out' training criteria by running through a series of variations on a learned behaviour. Trainers have also reported many incidents which show clearly that dolphins are not only capable of learning, but also of remembering what they have learned. One example of this is an event which took place at the Brighton Dolphinarium in the United Kingdom before it was closed down in 1991. Staff watched uneasily as Missie, the resident female dolphin, tried to remove Minnie, her three-month-old calf that had just died, from the main pool, by pushing her through the wooden bars into the rear holding pen. In the past, all the dolphins that had died in the aquarium had been put in this pen. An ex-dolphin trainer, Doug Cartlidge, suggests that Missie knew that this was where her calf belonged. She herself exhibited real terror of the holding pen, and could not be enticed to enter it under any circumstances. When she was being transferred from Brighton to a rehabilitation centre in the Turks and Caicos Islands, she actually broke a diver's nose whilst attempting to evade being forced into the holding pen preparatory to making the journey.

In about 1965, at Sea Life Park in Hawaii, Karen Pryor, now Commissioner of the Marine Mammal Commission, Washington DC, was working with a newly captured rough-toothed dolphin. Pryor taught the dolphin to associate the sound of a whistle with the arrival of fish — the primary reinforcer. As she watched at the tank-side, the animal happened to lift its tail from the water. She blew the whistle and threw it a fish. Within minutes, the dolphin was lifting its tail repeatedly, earning one fish after another. Then it happened to make a noise, a little squeak — rough-toothed dolphins, like many other species, rarely make audible sounds. Pryor reinforced the noise-making behaviour several times. Then the animal lifted its tail again, and Pryor made a training mistake: more interested in the noise, she failed to respond. The animal became visibly upset. It had no previous experience of failure to earn reinforcement in a training situation, and rushed around the tank breaching before going over to the far side of the tank and turning its back on her. It took a few 'free' fish to get the dolphin to participate again (a common trainer's device to stimulate the offering of behaviour in an animal that is not responding, by making it clear that reinforcement continues to be available).

Pryor then clarified the 'rules' with signals for tail-lifting and the noise. After doing these several times, the dolphin swam to the other side of the tank as Pryor was busy rinsing her hands, and then came over to her and with one flipper stroked her arm up and down very vigorously, an affiliative signal frequently seen between dolphins, but never in Pryor's experience performed by a dolphin towards a human. Loosely interpreted, the dolphin appeared to be saying that it understood what she meant and 'forgave' her for her error.

By contrast, there are some trainers who have said that dolphins are stupid because they won't perform the tricks that the trainers want them to. But judging by the kind of tasks that are requested of dolphins, it comes as no surprise to us that the animals should be reluctant. The captive environment gives dolphins little, if any, chance to show their intelligence, which was not developed to entertain us with back flips and somersaults. It is rather an intelligence that is geared to living in harmony with the natural environment, to locating and catching food, and to survival. Many dolphin experts have even claimed that to keep dolphins in captivity is of great detriment to their own intelligence. One such expert, the Swiss scientist Professor Giorgio Pilleri, director of the Brain Anatomy Institute of the University of Berne, has studied dolphin behaviour and intelligence for 20 years. From his experience of observing dolphins in captive environments – something which he now deeply regrets – he feels that it is impossible to gain any real knowledge about their intelligence, because captivity distorts the very nature of the dolphin. He states: 'Even when the purpose is scientific study, the animals are so physically and psychologically deformed in the process that any discoveries made are distorted and give a thoroughly inadequate picture of true behaviour in the wild.'

So perhaps it is time to abandon comparisons between dolphins and ourselves, and to turn our attention instead to appreciating the ways in which dolphins communicate.

Chapter Seven

....

DOLPHIN COMMUNICATION

INTRODUCTION

The idea of talking to animals has always enchanted and intrigued us. But, apparently isolated as we are in our ability to speak, this notion has always seemed to belong to the realm of fantasy. Yet is it really so far-fetched? When scientists started 'eavesdropping' on dolphins, what they overheard sounded remarkably like a kind of conversation. Could such a cacophony of whistles, squeaks and squawks be a form of dolphin language, and, if so, could we learn and understand it? Back in the 1960s, Dr John Lilly seemed to be breaking new ground when he taught his dolphins to repeat certain words in English. (His work inspired the film *The Day of the Dolphin*.) Lilly predicted that within the next decade or two, we could be conversing with the bottlenose dolphin. His dream has yet to come true, but scientists working in the field of animal communication do believe that the sounds and body postures of the dolphin convey a wealth of information about its emotions and state of mind. By deciphering and interpreting such signals, researchers are coming even closer to understanding the 'language' of the dolphin.

SOUND SENSE

Of all the dolphin's senses, hearing is by far the most sensitive and sophisticated. Dolphins read or assess their oceanic environment by interpreting its sounds, and glean far more information from the noises made by the inhabitants and elements of the sea than we can begin to imagine. As the classical Greek poet Oppian so aptly wrote, 'They rejoice in the echoing shores.'

Because sound travels faster and for longer distances in water than it does in air, it is not surprising that the dolphin's acoustic sense is so highly developed. It is said that dolphins can hear the sound of a whistle from about 12 miles away, and bottlenose dolphins can pick up each other's signals over a distance of some six miles. Whereas the hearing system of most land-dwelling mammals, ourselves included, comprises an ear or pinna, eardrum and cochlea, dolphins have barely visible pinhole tubes located behind and slightly below their eyes. External sounds pass through these tubes directly to the eardrum.

To navigate and obtain precise information about their environment, dolphins have developed a highly sophisticated sonar system. With this, they are able to locate the shoreline, sea-bed and objects of all shapes and sizes, including those that are almost invisible to the (human) naked eye. The sonar system works in the following manner: dolphins send out a stream of loud, low frequency 'clicks' which one can hear underwater. It sounds rather like a door slowly creaking open. This stream of sounds is generated within the dolphin's nasal sacs, which are situated just behind and slightly above the 'melon', which itself lies just above the eyes. This organ acts like a lens, focusing the sound into a narrow beam which is projected from the dolphin's forehead. As this blast of sonic vibrations hits an object, it is deflected back almost immediately. The dolphin receives a sort of three-dimensional picture of the object, composed of information which is picked up by the structures located in the creature's mouth. Scientists believe that the vibrations are then transmitted to the brain via the mandibular nerve, just below the lower jaw. Upon the dolphin's receiving the initial echo, another 'click' is generated. The time lapse between the 'click' and the returning echo enables the dolphin to determine how far away the object is. A string of continuous 'clicks' allows the dolphin to track a fish, and signals picked up on either side of its head provide information about the direction in which it is travelling. To scrutinize an object in more detail, dolphins will switch to 'clicks' of a higher frequency. Researchers have noted that some dolphins 'play' with sound, shifting back and forth from a high to a low frequency. So sophisticated is their sonar that they can echo locate on two different targets simultaneously and, at the same time, communicate with each other by whistling.

Two experts on marine mammals, Dr Kenneth Norris and Bertel Mohl, suggest that, as mentioned in Chapter Five, dolphins may even be able to stun and kill their prey by blasting them with high energy 'clicks'. A source of controversy, this 'Big Bang' theory postulates that dolphins use loud impulse sounds to upset the sensory systems of fish, so disorientating them and making them easy to catch.

Yet despite being so highly developed, the dolphin's sonar is by no means infallible. Many dolphins have lost their lives because they have been unable to detect the fine nylon mesh of modern drift nets.

Ultrasonic Imagery

What the dolphin receives when using its sonar may take the form of a three-dimensional image, rather like the kind produced by equipment used in hospitals to scan internal organs, and, in submarines, to navigate the ocean depths. Some people suggest that in this way, dolphins may be able to 'see' right inside us, and even to discern such details as the contents of our stomachs. Certainly, dolphins seem to pay special attention both to pregnant women — which indicates that the animals may be able to detect the presence of a fetus — and to those who have metal plates or pins in their body.

This has led some researchers to speculate that dolphins may pass on information to one another in the form of 'pictograms'. Sonic imagery, such people claim, negates the need for a language: for, if dolphins can see inside one another, and build up holographic images, why should they need to ask questions or make statements regarding the wellbeing of their companions? A dolphin detecting the presence of a shark, for example, does not to need to sound a verbal alarm — it simply sends out a series of 'clicks' that correspond to the sonic picture created when its echo-location beam rebounded off the approaching shark. The echo that rebounds may also be picked up, not just by the dolphin that emitted the 'clicks', but by others in the vicinity, so that they can share the information.

The 'visual' translation of sound is illustrated by the classic experiment carried out by Dr Jarvis Bastian from the University of California. Bastian's experiment involved two dolphins, Buzz and Doris. Bastian set up four underwater levers in a tank, two for Doris and two for Buzz, and two lights — one that flashed intermittently and one that shone continually. Both of the dolphins had to press their right-hand lever when they saw the continuous light and their left-hand lever when they saw the intermittently flashing light. If they did this correctly, they both got a fish. Bastian then took the experiment a step further. Buzz had to press his lever before Doris could press hers. If she pressed the lever before Buzz, neither dolphin was rewarded. But if Buzz pressed the correct lever, they both got a fish.

The final and most difficult stage of the experiment seemed to prove without a doubt that the dolphins could not only understand the principle behind the experiment but could communicate information to each other using sound. Bastian divided the tank in two, separating the dolphins with a wooden screen. This time, only Doris could see the lights, but to get the fish she had to get Buzz to press the correct lever (either the left-hand one or the right-hand one, depending on which light was flashing) before she could press hers. Doris went over to the screen and whistled to Buzz, who returned her call. He responded by pressing his lever, and she in turn pressed hers. They both got their fish. Obviously Doris must have been telling Buzz that the light was either flashing or continuous for him to know which was the correct lever to press.

The cetacean expert and acoustics researcher Bob Morris is not convinced that dolphins communicate by means of such 'pictograms'. 'The 3-D image picked up by a dolphin through the reflection of sound gives it a "mental image" of an object. However, this is not what it sends directly to other dolphins,' he asserts. Instead, Morris suggests that the dolphin translates this information into a two-dimensional sound like a whistle. Whether or not that whistle then paints a mental picture in the dolphin's mind remains, however, a mystery.

DO DOLPHINS HAVE A LANGUAGE?

Many evolutionists postulate that when dolphins took to the water after living on land, they brought with them a basic collection of mammalian sounds, such as pulsed barks, squeaks and squawks. These noises are used to convey the same kind of messages as they do in land mammals, and appear to have evolved into a complex variety of sounds, which may carry all kinds of information from one dolphin to another. The tone of these sounds seems to convey information about the dolphin's emotional state. Sounds used for socializing are of a lower frequency than the sonic 'clicks', which means that they fall within our hearing range. Squeaks, squawks, barks and grunts are thought to be used in self-expression, while pure-tone whistles, taking the form of 'trills', 'arpeggios' and 'glissandos', are used to keep in touch. These whistle sounds are more akin to those used by birds than to the noises of any land-dwelling mammal. Researchers have identified over 30 whistle-type sounds, each of which has a specific meaning, and Denise Herzing is amongst those people who are convinced that every dolphin has its own 'signature' whistle, very much like a name, which it uses to attract the attention of other dolphins. In this way, dolphins can identify one another in less than half a second. When a baby dolphin is born, its mother whistles almost continuously to 'imprint' her sound on the baby. It then takes between one and two years for the baby dolphin to develop its own signature whistle, which is probably derived from its mother, and is therefore in a sense inherited – much as we inherit a surname. Mothers also signal to their offspring to return to them using one distinct whistle.

Squeaks and barks are often used to convey danger, protest, anger and irritation. 'As the level of emotion rises, the number and loudness of the sounds also rise,' state the communication experts Melba and David Caldwell. They have noted that the sounds shift in very subtle ways – the frequency or number of pulses per second can increase or decrease depending on the situation. The Caldwells compare these 'graded signals' to our own use of sound. 'A mother calling her child in for dinner uses a considerably less intense vocalization than she does if the child is engaged in a dangerous pursuit.' Similarly, when dolphins are in danger, they emit a sharp 'crack' sound which acts like an alarm.

But do the various sounds that dolphins make actually constitute a language? This is a very controversial area, and, while some researchers think it possible, others are not so sure. Dr Richard Ferraro, a senior scientist at the Institute of Applied Physiology and Medicine in the United States, and an expert in the field of dolphin communication, believes that only some groups of dolphins have developed a vocalized language, and that this can vary in degree and complexity. He thinks that this may have come about by chance. Because dolphins live in tightly woven family groups, it is possible that one member of the group develops a vocalized language and passes it on to the family, which then passes it on from generation to generation, so evolving a language and dialect unique to that group. Ferraro has yet to prove his theory, which will take many years of research, but he is convinced that all dolphins have the potential to develop language.

Bob Morris feels that the complexity of the structure and pattern of dolphins' whistles certainly suggests that they have a language: we should interpret their whistles like a package of information which has a beginning, a middle and an end. As linguists have pointed out, whistle languages are also used by humans. The natives of the Azore Islands, and some tribes in Mexico, communicate over distances of three miles using quite a complex series of whistles.

Body Language

Like us, dolphins do not simply communicate through sounds. Their body posture also gives away a lot about their emotional state and can actually alter the meaning of their whistles. Although it was once thought that dolphins had fairly underdeveloped eyesight, experts now believe that the animals have good vision both above and below the surface of the water, and that they use visual signals in the form of body posture and speed of movement to convey certain messages. When threatening another dolphin, for example, a dolphin takes up a frontal position, arches its own back and opens its mouth. Conversely, submission is signified by a closed mouth and by turning the body sideways. (However, it should be noted with regard to visual signals that there are some species, such as river dolphins, which have very poor vision – the muddy, murky waters in which they live render their sight pretty useless.)

Like humans, dolphins are also tactile by nature, both enjoying and using touch to communicate with one another. In sexual relationships, and those between mothers and babies, touch is particularly developed and important. Used most prominently by the Atlantic bottlenose dolphin, tactile communication consists of touching flippers, stroking, nuzzling and nudging, which can convey a wide range of signals, ranging from affection to comfort. A mother will punish a disobedient infant by gently holding it down or by pushing it up out of the water. This signifies that the baby dolphin should 'behave' and take up its proper position – swimming parallel alongside its mother. As young dolphins grow, punishment may also take the form of blows and bites if their behaviour is intolerable.

Dr Richard Ferraro initially worked with John Lilly on the JANUS (Joint-Analog-Numerical-Understanding-System) project and, more recently, with Louis Herman in Hawaii. Ferraro's goal is to combine the study of dolphin communication both in the wild and in captivity, and he himself has designed equipment which he hopes will aid this research. His particular interest is body language, and he believes that by studying this aspect of dolphin communication we are more likely to be able to understand dolphin behaviour and intelligence. He and other scientists believe that the vocal aspect of dolphin communication is very small by comparison with those of motion and body language. But body language is much more difficult to study, because researchers have to get into the water themselves and watch the dolphins carefully for long periods of time without disturbing the animals' natural behaviour.

The scientist Denise Herzing, Research Director of the Wild Dolphin Project and an affiliate of the University of Ohio, has been studying dolphin communication for 20 years. Unlike much of the previous research, her recent studies, as mentioned in Chapter Five, have been carried out by observing wild dolphins off the coast of the Bahamas since 1985. There, a pod of 50 spotted dolphins has become used to Herzing and her fellow researchers, who have consciously tried not to disturb the dolphins' natural behaviour. Herzing's project works by interacting with dolphins on their terms. Her research priorities include establishing a respectful and trusting relationship with the dolphins, identifying individuals and family groups, and documenting social behaviour and acoustic communication. By means of video recordings of the dolphins and computer analysis of dolphin sounds, Herzing has been able to build up a gradual picture of how the spotted dolphins use particular sounds and body language to communicate. She has been able to isolate their signature whistles, certain vocalized feeding sounds, and the meaning of many body postures in conjunction with certain whistles and squeaks. Although this does not quite constitute a vocabulary, it is a positive approach to communication, because it involves learning the dolphins' language, rather than teaching them ours. Other dolphin sounds that Herzing has identified include a baby dolphin's call on separation from its mother; an 'SOS' emitted by an injured or sick dolphin; an 'I'm bored' signal whistled by dolphins separated from human or dolphin contact; the 'Keep together' signals of the pod; and the mating call and 'Hands off' warning from one dolphin to another.

THE LANGUAGE BARRIER

While, as mentioned at the start of this chapter, the question of communication with another species is something which has captured the human imagination throughout history, it is important for us to realize that such communication could exist on many levels, and not depend solely on language. Although it is clear that dolphins who actively seek human companionship are eager to break down the barriers of communication between our two species, as humans we have been unable to decipher the complexities of dolphin language. The communication frequency which dolphins use is about 10 times higher than the highest frequency of human hearing and this has been one of the major stumbling-blocks in communication between humans and dolphins. But with the advent of modern computers has come the possibility of creating a common language – a sort of 'hi-tech' human/dolphin patois. However, this approach has its drawbacks. A team of researchers who were studying wild dolphins reported an incident which illustrates human naivety. Armed with a battery of sophisticated computer equipment which synthesized dolphin vocalizations, the team played a number of carefully chosen sounds within the dolphin's hearing frequency underwater to the dolphins. The latter repeated the vocalizations once or twice and then began to add complex variations. Naturally, the scientists were unprepared for this improvisation, and were then unable to decipher what the dolphins were 'saying', since, by comparison to the dolphins' abilities, their equipment was so primitive.

Talking with Dolphins

In the 1960s, the neurologist Dr John Lilly pioneered research into dolphin communication and commented that 'Within the next decade or two, the human species will establish communication with another species. Non-human, alien, possibly extra-terrestrial, more probably marine; but definitely highly intelligent, perhaps even intellectual.' He suggested that this would be *Tursiops truncatus*, the Atlantic bottlenose dolphin.

Lilly was much inspired by the work of the Greek natural historian, Aristotle, who stated: 'The voice of the dolphin in air is like that of the human in that they can pronounce vowels and combinations of vowels, but have difficulties with consonants.' It was obvious to Lilly that the Greeks had attempted to communicate with dolphins. Up until the mid-20th century, scientists had vehemently scorned the idea that dolphins 'spoke' to one another, as they believed that the creatures had no vocal chords; they were also unaware that whales and dolphins had such complex ultrasonic apparatus. But in 1960, Lilly set up a laboratory in St Thomas, and founded the Communication Research Institute. He and his fellow researchers were aware of the dolphin's eagerness to mimic the human voice, and in Miami, Florida, studies were already under way involving researchers Dr Morgane, Dr Eugene Nagle, Dr Will McFarland and Dr Paul Yakovlev of Harvard University Medical School, who were concentrating on the neurophysiological and neuroanatomical aspects of communication. Lilly was particularly interested in sound, which he felt held greater potential than sign language. Like humans, dolphins can vary their vocal communication by adjusting the loudness, frequency and pitch of their sounds very rapidly. Inspired by these similarities, Lilly and his fellow scientists developed JANUS – the Joint-Analog-Numerical-Understanding-System. The 'brain' of the computer that they used had one set of inputs for man and one set for dolphins. The sonic inputs were sensitive to the frequencies most easily detected by dolphins – 3,000Hz–80,000Hz – and humans – 300Hz–3,000Hz.

Convinced that the arrangement of the dolphin's brain signified that it possessed the ability to communicate in a similar way to man, and that dolphins did in fact have a language, Lilly focused his attention on one particular dolphin named Elvar, which was isolated from its fellow dolphins and spent its time with Lilly and his researchers. Elvar was encouraged to repeat words and phrases, and proved to be an excellent mimic. An astronomer and cosmologist, Carl Sagan, who visited Lilly at his laboratory in 1963, recounted an incident which he believed showed that the dolphin was not just repeating the words and phrases parrot-fashion. Elvar swam up to Sagan, rolled on to his back and demanded to have his stomach rubbed. Sagan obliged and Elvar then swam away, before returning with his belly just under the water. Sagan rolled up his sleeves and rubbed Elvar's stomach. Showing signs of great excitement, Elvar swam away and returned again, this time submerged by about a foot under the water. Sagan stroked him again, and yet again the dolphin swam away, returning the next time about three feet underwater. At this point, Sagan ignored Elvar because he (Sagan) did not want to get completely soaked. Elvar reacted by standing up on his tail and saying 'More', thereby showing that he understood exactly what the word meant. He had not just picked at random any word that he had learned.

From this and similar incidents, Lilly reported that dolphins had a language, which he dubbed 'delphinese'. However, his contemporaries argued that all Lilly had shown was that dolphins could repeat a few words and phrases in English, similar to the mimicry of mynah birds and parrots. Others posed the significant question: why should we expect dolphins to speak to us in our language?

Lilly may have been a pioneer of communication research, but the man who has given most credibility to this field is the psychologist Dr Louis Herman, director of the University of Hawaii's Kewalo Basin Marine Mammal Laboratory. For the past 10 years, Herman has been working with two Atlantic bottlenose dolphins, Phoenix and Akeakamai (nicknamed 'Ake'), methodically testing their ability to understand and execute commands in two kinds of artificial language. The language used for working with Phoenix consists of electronically generated computer whistles, while that used with Ake is based on hand and arm gestures. Each language has a 'vocabulary' and a set of rules governing how the sounds or gestures are arranged in sequences that form thousands of sentences. Using these languages, Herman has shown that dolphins understand the meanings of the words in their languages and, even more importantly, how word-order affects meaning. This ability is considered to be the core of most human languages, and a trait that many linguists and philosophers would argue is a sign of intelligence. Herman has found that dolphins can differentiate between phrases such as 'pipe fetch surfboard' – which translates as 'Get the pipe and take it to the surfboard' – and 'surfboard fetch pipe' – 'Get the surfboard and take it to the pipe'. The commands are issued in two different ways – through a set of computer whistles broadcast through an underwater speaker, and also by means of a series of hand and arm gestures. For the latter, a trainer stands at the tankside, wearing dark goggles to prevent giving unintentional visual cues. The trainer then makes a series of gestures that construct a 'sentence'. David Premack, a former ape-language researcher at the University of Pennsylvania, who has retired from his animal-language work, claims that Herman's 'free use of a sentence' is a problem. Human language, Premack argues, consists of abstract concepts, not just objects and actions. Other ape-language researchers also imply that the animals learned this behaviour to earn rewards, and that this is therefore not a demonstration of 'language'. Herman, however, contends that the fact that the dolphins get rewards does not invalidate the involvement of language, and that they 'develop an understanding of the words for their language at the level of a concept'. For example, 'under' means 'passing beneath', and the dolphins will raise an object from the bottom of the tank in order to swim below it in response to the 'under' command. He has also demonstrated that dolphins understand references to absent objects. When asked 'Ball question', which means 'Is there a ball in the tank?', Ake searches the pool and responds by touching a 'Yes' or 'No' paddle. When she presses the 'No' paddle, it implies that she has understood the sign, formed a mental image of the object referred to, and deduced that the ball is not there. Called referential reporting, this ability has previously been documented in apes and man.

In another project involving analysing the 'language' of dolphins, in order to identify their different whistles, Peter Tyack, an assistant scientist at Woods Hole Oceanographic Institute in the United States, attaches a primitive contraption called a vocalite to the head of a dolphin, using suction cups. The gadget lights up whenever the dolphin makes a sound. With the aid of Dr Richard Ferraro, Tyack is also developing and testing more sophisticated technology, in which a microcomputer records each sound and then transfers the time of every vocalization into a second computer. These recordings are analysed to determine which dolphin was communicating, what the sounds were and what behaviour was occurring at the time. With support from the Office of Naval Research in Arlington, Virginia, Tyack is also studying the social function of the whistles, by recording the sounds of captive dolphins at the New England Aquarium and at Chicago's Brookfield Zoo, and analysing the signature whistles of a wild dolphin population in Sarasota Bay, in the hope of discovering a common pattern.

Telepathic Communication

Mythology and a plethora of mariners' tales have given us many examples of dolphins which have come to the rescue of swimmers in distress and shipwrecked souls. These stories imply that dolphins are not only compassionate and caring, but that they are capable of picking up distress signals. While some people say that the creatures pick up sound signals (for example, shouts and cries for help), or react to body language, others have put forward the idea that dolphins possess a sixth sense – in other words, that they are telepathic. An erstwhile dolphin trainer, Ric O'Barry, is among those who are convinced that this is true: 'Sometimes they'll perform a trick before you even ask or signal – it's just as if they are reading your mind.' According to O'Barry, if dolphins can transmit sounds and read the echo, they may also be able to transmit sonic images, from one dolphin to another. This, he suggests, could be a type of mental telepathy. Christine Bowker, who worked in Britain's first Sea World, is one of the many trainers who have also reported what may be telepathic experiences with dolphins: 'They were always trying to get one-up on me . . . For example, I was trying to get two dolphins to jump on either side of me and was actually thinking, "How am I going to tell them, or indicate to them, something as complicated as that?" when they both did exactly what I wanted, and then went whizzing around the pool making those funny chuckling noises they make when they are pleased with themselves.'

Frank Robson, author of *Pictures in a Dolphin's Mind*, claims to have trained dolphins simply by using mental telepathy. 'I visualize what I want the dolphins to do, and they do it. I don't have to use a reward system like other trainers. The dolphins perform because they want to. They enjoy pleasing me and communicating in this way,' he writes. Some people have also claimed that dolphins can actually pick up and tune in to our brain waves and are therefore able to gauge our emotional state. This kind of 'entrainment' could explain why they react differently to different people during an encounter. It has also led to the suggestion that they have the power to affect our emotional state and so alleviate conditions such as depression and fear.

Alien Beings?

On a more esoteric level, researchers from SETI (the Search for Extra-Terrestrial Intelligence) have taken a keen interest in the research of Dianna Reiss, an animal-and-human communications professor at San Francisco State University, and director and founder of Project Circe at Marineworld in Vallejo, California, USA. Far-fetched as it may sound, Reiss's work on decoding dolphins' communication systems is similar to the quest to find extra-terrestrial intelligence.

As guest speaker at a NASA conference, and recipient of a grant from the Pasadena, California-based Planetary Society, she spelled out the problems these two endeavours share. 'How do we detect signals and recognize patterns when we are unsure of the nature of the signal?' she asked. 'How does an observer of one species penetrate the communication system of another when we are really blind and deaf to that system?'

During an eight-year study, Reiss has concentrated on analysing both vocal and non-vocal signals. Working along similar lines to Louis Herman, Reiss constructs 'ethograms' — behavioural codes — by watching and videotaping the dolphins, tape recording her observations, then sorting the various kinds of behaviour into categories. She then looks for a relationship between the dolphins' sounds and their other behaviour. Reiss has also designed an underwater keyboard with nine keys for the dolphins to use. Each of the keys has a symbol, such as a fish, ball or hoop. When a dolphin pushes a key with its beak, a computer records which key has been pressed and then produces a sound specific to that key. The dolphin then has to repeat the sound to get its reward, which will be, as appropriate, a fish, ball, or hoop. In other words, the dolphin learns to associate a certain sound with an object. Reiss believes that this is a form of 'common language' which both dolphin and human could develop, share and understand.

....

Part Three

ENCOUNTERS WITH DOLPHINS

Chapter Eight
....
FRIENDLY DOLPHINS

INTRODUCTION

In ancient times, as we have already mentioned and will discuss in more detail in this chapter, extraordinary encounters between humans and dolphins were recorded by classical scholars. Once regarded as myths and fables, such interactions have none the less long been a source of fantasy and fascination. However, it is only recently that people have begun to realize that these stories are not figments of the imagination, but, in all probability, essentially true accounts. Friendly dolphins are now emerging throughout the world, often becoming a focus of attention for locals and attracting people from miles away who make pilgrimages to see and swim with the animals.

For meeting dolphins in their natural environment can be a magical experience. Few people fail to feel overcome with joy and wonder at the sight of these graceful creatures leaping and gambolling in the waves. For example, imagine for a moment that you are on a yacht cruising through glistening turquoise waters. Out of the blue, a pod of dolphins appears. Like shimmering grey shadows, they glide beneath the surface of the sea. Only an occasional glimpse of dorsal fins reveals their presence as they breach to take air. Then, although most seem content to keep their distance, two of the dolphins move cautiously towards the yacht. Soon they are swimming in synchrony right beside you, keeping perfect pace with the boat. Heads raised slightly, these two smiling creatures are looking right at you. Their eyes look so human that you cannot help feeling that they are gazing deep into your soul.

Their curiosity quenched, the two dolphins turn away, and, diving deep, disappear from sight. The magic melts. But looking back out to sea, you notice the others drawing closer. Suddenly there is a tremendous splash. The inquisitive duo are back. Did they go off to fetch the rest of their pod? This time, they weave back and forth across the bows. Cadging free rides on the waves that form as the yacht moves forward, the dolphins skim through the water, spinning and turning as they go. Every so often, they leap exuberantly into the air. Now the boat is surrounded by dolphins. Some are mothers accompanied by their calves; others give the impression of being young lovers and sedate elders. Yet all exude the same aura of vitality and contentment.

The dolphins hold you spellbound in a world far removed from reality. Their *joie de vivre* is catching. Overwhelmed by a sense of intense excitement and happiness, you hope that they will stay, but after a while the dolphins slowly begin to swim off to the open seas. The two 'friends' are the last to leave. Just before they disappear from sight, they perform a series of aerial jumps, as if to say farewell.

How long were they there? It is impossible to tell, for it was as if time stood quite still. And, even though they have gone, the impression of their presence lingers on. The memory of this event is so potent that it returns over and over again, even in your dreams, each time rekindling that same inner glow.

Both of us were lucky enough to experience separate encounters of this kind personally. Not only did this stimulate our fascination for dolphins, but it also made us realize that meeting them in the wild was a special and moving event. We soon discovered that we were not unique. Many people who have come into close contact with these magnificent creatures in their natural environment appear to be touched in the same way; and all report feeling honoured that the dolphins had chosen to grace them with their presence.

THE BONDS OF FRIENDSHIP

Traditionally, seafaring folk have always regarded dolphins as a good omen, and most fishermen felt fortunate to be accompanied by these creatures as they went about their work. The ancient Greeks also thought that dolphins were maritime guides that would navigate vessels out of troubled waters and steer those which had strayed off-course back to safety. A story relating to the retrieval of Serapis, a god-like creature that features in Greco-Egyptian religion, illustrates this idea.

According to legend, the Serapis appears to have strengthened the position of the Ptolemaic dynasty which ruled Egypt after 323 BC. It is said that the unknown god itself, which was a strange synthesis of Osiris, king of the underworld and Apis, the sacred bull of Memphis, came to Ptolomy Soter in a dream and told him where to find it. The king then sent two men, Soteles and Dionysius, to Sinope, on the north coast of Turkey, in order to find the Serapis and bring it back to him.

On their journey, the two men were driven off-course beyond Malea by a violent wind and lost their way completely. As if sensing their dismay, a dolphin appeared at the prow of the ship, seeming to invite them to follow. It then escorted the vessel through calm, safe waters to the port of Cirrha, where the men offered thanks for a safe landing. From there they must have recovered their bearings, for the Serapis was duly installed in the Serapeum in Alexandria. The cult of Serapis was famous in Egypt and Greece, and in later times spread throughout the Roman world, too, so it is possible that in those days dolphins were widely viewed as divine messengers and guides.

An instance of a dolphin forging an actual friendship with a young boy is reputed to have taken place near the city of Iasus, not far from Miletus in Karia (present-day Turkey), and is recorded by Pliny and Plutarch, both of whom lived in the 1st century AD. According to this tale, the dolphin and the boy, who was called Hermias, swam and played together during the day. When Hermias mounted the dolphin's back, it happily carried him wherever he chose to go. All the inhabitants of Iasus flocked to the shore to watch each time this happened. One day, a violent storm blew up unexpectedly. The boy slipped off the dolphin's back and was drowned. Then, according to Plutarch, 'The dolphin took the body and threw both it and itself together on the land and would not leave until it too had died, thinking it right to share a death for which it imagined that it shared responsibility.' In memory of this calamity, inhabitants of Iasus have minted their coins with the figure of a boy riding a dolphin.

Theophrastus, a zoologist and pupil of Aristotle, reported that friendships between boys and dolphins similar to the one at Iasus took place at Navpactos (in the Gulf of Corinth), Amphilochus and Taranto. And some 200 years later, the Roman scholar Pliny the Elder recounted two further such instances in his *Natural History*. The first took place in the reign of Augustus, and concerns a dolphin brought into the Lucrine Lake, not far from Naples. Although it is not clear, it would seem that this dolphin was actually caught and kept captive. With their penchant for circuses, it would come as no surprise to learn that the Romans had dolphinariums.

According to the story, on his way to school at Pouzzouli, a poor man's son used to stop at the salt-water lake and, by calling 'Simo, Simo' he was able to attract the dolphin. (Pliny explains that the Romans' pet-name for the dolphin was Simo, which is actually a Greek word meaning 'snub-nose', referring to the shape of the dolphin's snout. Pliny says that dolphins would answer to this name and 'liked it better than any other'.) After a while, the boy lost all fear of the dolphin and would leap into the lake and clamber on its back. The dolphin would take him right across the bay to school, and come to collect him again at the end of the day. This went on for several years, until the boy died from an illness. But the dolphin continued to come to the customary place until it also died, as Pliny claims, 'quite undoubtedly from longing'.

Some years later, another dolphin appeared at Hippo Diarrhytus, a Roman colony in Tunis, on the north coast of Africa. This dolphin would feed from people's hands, allowed itself to be stroked, played with swimmers and carried them on its back. The tale of the Hippo dolphin is told in meticulous detail by Pliny the Younger in a letter to his poet friend, Caninius, in which he writes, 'I have a story for you which is true though it has all the qualities of a fable, and is worthy of your lively, elevated and wholly poetical genius. I heard it the other day at table when conversation turned on various miraculous events. The man who told it is completely reliable, though what is that to a poet? However, you could depend on his word even if you were writing history.'

From this introduction, we can be fairly sure that Pliny has not unduly 'embroidered' the story. He continues: 'There is in Africa a Roman settlement, near the sea called Hippo. The inhabitants of all ages are very fond of fishing and boating, and of swimming too; especially the boys . . . Their idea of glory is to be carried out to sea, the winner being whoever leaves the shore and his rivals the furthest behind. In a contest of this sort one lad, who was bolder than the rest, was getting far out, when suddenly a dolphin came up to him. First it swam in front of him, then it followed him and then it went round him. Then it dived under him again, and to his horror, started carrying him out to sea. But then it turned back and restored him to his companions and dry land. The news of this got round and everyone rushed to see the boy, as if there were something supernatural about him. They eyed him and questioned him, listened to him and passed his story around. The next day, they lined the shore, gazing out to sea and watching the lagoon. The boys went swimming and among them our hero, but with more care this time. The dolphin duly appeared and made for the boy, who fled with the rest. At that the dolphin, as if inviting him back, started leaping out of the water and diving and twisting and twirling about. This happened again the next day, and on the third day, and for several days, until the men of Hippo, born and brought up by the sea, began to be ashamed of their fears. They went up to the dolphin and played with it and called to it. They even touched it and it encouraged them to stroke it . . . they grew venturesome. In particular, the boy who had had the first encounter with it swam beside it in the water and got on its back and was carried to and fro. Feeling that the dolphin knew him and was fond of him, he became fond of the dolphin. There was now no fear on either side and the boy's confidence and the dolphin's tameness increased together . . . What is also remarkable, another dolphin accompanied this one but only as an onlooker and escort. It did none of the same things and submitted to none of the same familiarities; it merely conducted the other one to and fro, as the other boys did with their companion.'

According to Pliny, the dolphin would beach itself on the sand and, on one occasion, the governor's legate, Octavius Avitus, was reported to have rubbed ointment into its skin. Pliny suggests that this 'superstitious' act made the dolphin 'languid and sickly', but on reflection, it seems possible that Avitus was trying to save the dolphin from sunburn and dehydration. However, sadly, unlike the friendly dolphin of Iasus, this one did not die because it was stranded, but was purposely killed by some of the Hippo people because, it was said, they could no longer meet the expense of entertaining all the officials who came to their town to see the spectacle. For although the Romans found the dolphin entertaining, they did not hold it in as high regard as the Greeks, who would have considered it a sacrilege to kill such a creature.

This difference in attitude is highlighted by a tale told by Oppian, a Greek poet and philosopher, who obviously held dolphins in great esteem. This friendship between a single boy and a dolphin took place approximately 100 years after the incident at Hippo, in a harbour near Poroselene, a town on one of the Hectasonnesi islands that lie off Lesbos. It is likely to be a true account, for the Greek traveller Pausinias, who is not known for his flamboyant and imaginative prose, wrote: 'I saw the dolphin obeying his call and carrying him whenever he wanted to ride.' Oppian, who spins a rather more romantic yarn, suggests that an intensity of love that surpassed all others existed between the boy and the dolphin.

The dolphin in this story came into the harbour as a baby, having lost its mother and the rest of the pod. It was befriended by an elderly couple and their young boy, who fed it fish and gave it a name. As the boy and dolphin grew up together, a strong bond of affection formed between them. When the boy rowed his boat out to sea and called to the dolphin, it would come speeding up to him. When the boy dived into the water, the two would swim together side by side. Oppian writes: 'Thou would'st have said that in its love the dolphin was fain to kiss and embrace the youth: in such close companionship it swam.'

The dolphin carried the boy on its back and reputedly took him wherever he wished to go. Although especially fond of its particular companion, it also acted warmly to others. When fully grown, the dolphin not only caught fish for itself, but would also repay acts of kindness by bringing fish back to its relations. News of the friendly dolphin travelled and many strangers, as well as the townspeople themselves, would turn out to watch the boy and dolphin playing together.

Like a great many of the old stories about friendly dolphins, this one also has a tragic ending if we are to believe Oppian, who tells us that the boy died and that 'like one sorrowing, the Dolphin visited the shores in quest of the companion of its youth; you would have said you heard the veritable voice of a mourner – such helpless grief was upon it. And no more, though they called it often, would it hearken to the island townsmen or would it accept food when offered it, and very soon it vanished from the sea and none marked it any more, and it no more visited the place. Doubtless sorrow for the youth that was gone killed it, and with its dead comrade it had been fain to die.'

On the other side of the world, the Maoris of New Zealand believed that dolphins or *taniwhas* escorted canoes across the sea, guiding them to islands that they wished to reach. They also thought that dolphins would come to the rescue of those whose canoes capsized or were wrecked. Maori folklore accounts for such friendliness in the story of Ruru, who was turned into a dolphin as a punishment. According to the legend, two Maori men fell in love with the same girl. One of the men, named Ruru, was rejected by her and, in a fit of jealousy, he threw her from the top of a cliff. His rival took revenge and attacked Ruru, who fell off the edge, but was not killed. As he plunged towards the sea below, he uttered a powerful curse, normally reserved for Maori chiefs. The curse saved Ruru's life, but unfortunately killed a dolphin which happened to be swimming in the sea below. When Ruru saw the dead dolphin washed up on the shore, he sought help from the *tohunga*, or tribal priest, and offered to do penance for his behaviour. The *tohunga* was none too sympathetic to Ruru's plea, and ordered that Ruru enter into the dolphin's body and spend the rest of eternity at the coast, greeting each canoe that passed.

This tale was recalled centuries later, when a famous dolphin named Pelorus Jack took to accompanying steamships across the Cook Strait which separates the North and South Islands of New Zealand. When he first appeared, in 1888, Pelorus Jack was known as 'the big white fish'. He was later identified as a Risso's dolphin, a species which has a squarish profile with no beak and a soft smile. For more than 20 years, this friendly dolphin regularly met and escorted ships journeying back and forth between Wellington and Nelson in a certain stretch of water off Pelorus Sound, which is how he got his name. It is said that whenever he heard the engine of any boat or ship, at any hour of the day or night, he would abandon what he was doing to join the vessel. He tended to prefer steamers, perhaps because of the distinctive sound they made. He would swim alongside them for about 20 minutes, covering distances of up to six miles, before frisking off again. The faster they could go, the better he seemed to like it, for he could leap and play in the bow-wave. Sometimes he came so close to the boats that people thought he was actually rubbing up against the vessels.

During a long lifetime, Pelorus Jack was seen by hundreds of tourists from overseas who made the Nelson crossing especially to make his acquaintance. This exceptional dolphin was featured in articles and described on post cards somewhat inaccurately and naively as 'the only fish [sic] in the world protected by an Act of Parliament'. For at one point during that time someone on board one of the steamers had fired at him with a rifle. The motive is unclear, but financial incentive may have been a factor, for at that time any museum in Europe would have paid dearly for the animal's body. Fortunately, Pelorus Jack was not hit, but as a result of the attack, there was public demand that he should be protected by law. When the Order of Council was first made, Pelorus Jack had been greeting each passing vessel day in, day out for 15 years. Towards the latter years, he occasionally failed to put in an appearance, and in 1912 he went missing for the last time. It was rumoured that he had fallen victim to the harpoons of a small fleet of Norwegian whalers known to have anchored off Pelorus Sound in April of that year; others more optimistically suggested that he could have died of old age.

In any event, Gabriel, the first recorded friendly dolphin since ancient times, certainly suffered as a result of putting his trust in humans. In 1814, this 13-foot male bottlenose dolphin made his home in the River Dart at Stoke in England. There he befriended both children and adults. But some entrepreneurial showmen got wind of Gabriel's presence and thought it would be lucrative to put him on display at the Haymarket in London. They caught him in a net, put him on a bed of straw in a farm wagon, then set off for the city, exhibiting him along the way. Before they had gone far, Gabriel died, slowly and painfully, from internal injuries.

Over a century elapsed before any further encounters with friendly dolphins were reported. Then, in 1945, came news of a 13-year-old American girl called Sally Stone who played with six wild dolphins in Long Island Sound near New York. Eight years later, at

Fish Hoek, near Capetown, South Africa, a pair of female Indian Ocean bottlenose dolphins mingled with bathers, giving them rides on their backs and towing them along with their dorsal fins. Apparently they favoured one young girl above all the others and would single her out from the crowd.

In 1960, a large female dolphin named Charlie (christened before her sex was known) began playing boisterously with boats off the east coast of Scotland and formed a close relationship with a man called Hans Cranston. She then migrated south to the fishing port of Eyemouth and in 1976 she was reported to be fraternizing with scuba divers, readily joining in any games they invented.

In recent years, the person most responsible for kindling an awareness of these remarkable human/dolphin relationships is Horace Dobbs. In his first book, *Follow a Wild Dolphin*, Dobbs gives an enchanting account of his own experience of meeting and getting to know a wild dolphin called Donald (see 'Famous Dolphins', below). The ancient tales of the classical scholars came to life when Donald lifted Dobbs' young son, Ashley, onto his back and carried the boy around the bay. When first published in 1977, Dobbs' book sparked an unprecedented interest in friendly dolphins, and during the 1970s, many other examples of such animals were reported all over the world: for example, there was Nina in Spain, Dobbie in Eilat, and Horace in New Zealand. All were of the bottlenose variety, except for Sandy, a spotted dolphin who interacted with holiday-makers on the island of San Salvador, south-east of Miami.

The interest in friendly dolphins continued into the 1980s with the appearance of Percy and Freddie in England, Simo in Wales, Jean-Louis in France, Jojo in the Turks and Caicos Islands and Fungie in Ireland, to name only those dolphins which have been in the public eye. Many of these dolphins became celebrities in their own right, and have starred in films, television documentaries, magazine and newspaper features. Those who have swum with these particular animals regard them as special 'friends', for although there are similarities in their behaviour towards people, each has a distinctive personality. In an attempt to illustrate this, we will now profile a handful of the most famous friendly dolphins, relying on both our own experiences and first-hand accounts of the dolphins wherever possible.

FAMOUS DOLPHINS

Opo

The story of Opo has all the qualities of the classical dolphin tales. Early in 1955, the boat-owners of Opononi, a parochial township nestling on the western coast of New Zealand's North island, noticed a lone dolphin lingering in Hokianga Harbour. Not long before, a youth with a rifle had boasted about having fired at a family of dolphins and shot one. As Opo was thought to have been about a year old at the time when she first appeared, it is possible that the dolphin that died was her mother. As word spread of Opo's presence, people out fishing in boats began to look for her. Seemingly curious, Opo, in turn, came closer to them. After someone discovered that the dolphin liked being scratched with an oar or mop, Opo began following the boats to the wharf and beach. Writing about her in an article for *Te Ao Hou* ('The New World'), a Maori farmer called Mr Toi reported: 'I was returning from Rangi Point School at about 6.30 p.m. . . . suddenly there was a big splash and a boiling swirl. A large fish [sic] was streaking for my boat . . . when about 10 yards away it dived and surfaced on the other side. It played round and round the boat. I was afraid she would hit my outboard, so I went inshore as close as I could. When I was in about four foot of water I looked back. She was about three feet out of the water, standing literally on her tail and looking at me from a distance . . .'

By the New Year, Opo would make an appearance almost every day, and always responded to the sound of an outboard motor. As her fame spread, thousands of people started flooding into Opononi. Signs were quickly erected which read 'Welcome to Opononi, but don't try to shoot our Gay Golphin', referring to the nickname the local children had given her. A song was even written about Opo which became a hit single at the time.

In his book *Dolphins*, New Zealander Antony Alpers writes: 'On this mass of sunburned, jostling humanity the gentle dolphin had the effect of a benediction — there were no cases of drunkenness, fights or arguments — everyone was in the gayest of holiday moods.'

It was some time before anyone got very close to Opo, but once her trust had been gained, she became incredibly friendly. She seemed particularly fond of children and would swim up to them, almost begging to be petted. Amongst her young admirers she would seek out those who were gentle and avoid those who were rough and loud. Her favourite was a 13-year-old girl called Jill Baker, who lived in Opononi and swam almost every day. As soon as Jill entered the water, Opo would leave all the other children and swim off by her side. 'I think the reason why the dolphin became so friendly with me was because I was always gentle with her and never rushed at her as so many bathers did,' Jill wrote. 'At first, she did not like the feel of my hands and would dart away, but after a while when she realized I would not harm her she would come up to me to be rubbed and patted. On several occasions when I was standing in the water with my legs apart, she would go between them and pick me up and carry me a short distance before dropping me again. She would quite often let me put little children on her back for a moment or two.'

It was reported that Opo seemed to hear and enjoy the laughter of a crowd. However, if she felt swamped by people trying to touch her and clutch at her tail, she would move out of reach, smacking the water every few yards as she went. Her annoyance was never any more intense than this.

Total strangers would talk freely to one another about their experiences with Opo. Like many friendly dolphins, she seemed to break down the social barriers to friendship and bring out the better qualities in people. So beloved was she that throughout the country it was felt that she should be given protection. An Order of Council was issued saying that it was unlawful for anyone to take or molest any dolphin in the Hokianga Harbour.

However, on the day that the regulation became law, Opo did not arrive in the harbour as she usually did. She had been playing with bathers the day before, and some fishermen had seen her in the morning, but that afternoon she could not be found. An elderly Maori collecting mussels at low tide eventually found the dolphin's dead body jammed in a crevice between some rocks at Koutu Point. Some felt that Opo had become stranded whilst seaching for fish, whilst others suspected foul play. When word reached the village, everyone was overcome with gloom. Opo was buried with reverence beside the Memorial Hall and her grave was covered in flowers. Letters and telegrams expressing sympathy, especially to the children, flooded in from all over the country, showing how much happiness this gentle dolphin had brought to so many people.

Nina

In 1972, a solitary female bottlenose dolphin began following fishing boats in and out of the small seaport of La Corogna on the north-west coast of Spain. One day a local diver called Luis Salleres looked over his shoulder to find the dolphin watching him intently as he went about his business of collecting clams from the seabed. From then on, she became his close underwater companion, and as their friendship grew, Nina seemed to delight in being touched and stroked.

On one occasion, Salleres invited his friend José Vasquez, who was interested in marine biology and animal behaviour, to meet Nina. While Salleres went to fetch his camera, Vasquez got severe cramps in both legs, and not being a competent swimmer, he panicked and waved for help. Within seconds, Nina appeared and, as if understanding his distress, hung motionless in the water beside him so that he could place his arms around her.

This friendly dolphin became truly famous when she was filmed by Jacques Cousteau, who also recorded her story in his book *Dolphins*. Nina extended her friendship to all, allowing bathers to pet her and hold her tail. At weekends the streets of La Corogna were packed with visitors who had come especially to see her, and at times some 2,000 people flocked into the water all at once.

So precious was Nina that the local council banned the use of fishing nets and grenades to stun and catch fish in the area. Her welfare was even made the concern of the Spanish Navy. Despite such precautions, one day she appeared to be distressed, and five weeks later, she was found dead, washed up on some rocks. It is thought that some fishermen had begun to use grenades again, and that one of these had killed her. The whole community mourned her loss and the council ordered a monument to be built in fond memory of this friend and national heroine.

DONALD/BEAKY

This charismatic male bottlenose dolphin first made himself known to divers off the coast of Port St Mary on the Isle of Man. They became aware of a dolphin eyeing them from a distance as they sat in their boat and watching them underwater as they went about their tasks.

Thought to be about 16 years old, Donald was, by all accounts, a rather spirited and mischievous dolphin with a real sense of fun. His adventurous life is described in graphic detail by Horace Dobbs in the book *Follow a Wild Dolphin*. Although Dobbs swam with Donald on numerous occasions, the first to befriend this dolphin was a woman called Maura Mitchell. Donald took an instant liking to this gentle woman who had a way with animals, and he allowed her to stroke him and stayed close by her as she swam. A special bond formed between them. Maura could tell by his expression what kind of mood Donald was in. If he came up to her slowly with eyes closed, he was feeling affectionate and needed a cuddle. If his eyes were bright and alert, she knew he wanted to play, and they would romp around in the water together.

Although he had a particularly soft spot for Maura, Donald enjoyed the company of other people, especially Dobbs and his son Ashley. On one special occasion, when Ashley was snorkelling underwater with a camera, Donald started boisterously jumping about. He then made a headlong run at Ashley and to Dobbs' amazement lifted the boy out of the water so that Ashley was riding on the dolphin's back with his legs astride, just as depicted on ancient Greek coins.

Donald delighted in playing games, and often invented his own with human participants. He enjoyed interrupting divers as they tried to carry out underwater tasks. If he wanted the game to continue, he would pull at their flippers as they clambered back into the boat. If no one was in the water, Donald looked elsewhere for some fun. In his spare time, lifeboatman Norman Crelin would catch lobsters. As he reached out to grab hold of the buoy on the end of the string of pots, Donald would grasp the rope between his teeth and deliberately tow it away. Teasing a Jack Russell terrier called Spratt, which used to travel with its owner in a small rowing-boat, was another source of amusement. By jumping first at one side of the boat, then at the other, Donald found that he could stir the little dog into a frenzy of barking. He took even greater delight in drenching the poor creature completely.

Donald did not like missing out on any fun, as Horace Dobbs discovered. On one occasion, Dobbs was riding on an aquaplane with Donald beside him, when the dolphin started prodding his arm with its nose, then grabbed his elbow between its teeth. Dobbs determinedly held on until Donald came up under him and pushed him off the aquaplane. The dolphin then grabbed the board between its teeth and got a free ride. As if to make amends, it then swam under Dobbs and presented its dorsal fin. Dobbs placed his arms around it and held on as Donald took off at speed.

Donald's fun-loving life was also fraught with hazards. In 1972 a gunman pumped bullets at him. Two struck his head, narrowly missing his eye, while another three wounded his body. The next spring, John Moore and Willie Kneale found him stranded in the mud. Fortunately, they got hold of a mechanical excavator, and managed to lift him in a steel bucket and dump him back in shallow water, where he seemed none the worse for the experience. On another occasion, when underwater explosives were used to deepen the harbour at Port St Mary, Donald nearly got entangled in the wires connecting the explosive charges, and had to be enticed out of the area. In March 1974 he disappeared, and was presumed dead.

Some months later, a friendly dolphin, which locals named Dai, turned up at Martin's Haven on the coast of Pembrokeshire in Wales. Dobbs accompanied Maura Mitchell on a visit there. He recalls how Donald (for it was he) hovered vertically in the water for a full 30 seconds, looking at them. He then dived and appeared on the other side of the boat to get another glimpse. When Maura entered the water, he greeted her like a long-lost friend. There was little doubt that he recognized them both.

Ever accident-prone, Donald managed get a mooring-rope caught around his tail flukes, and was stuck for two days. He was eventually found by Peter Pearson and his son Simon. As they rowed past, Donald lifted his tail as if to explain his predicament. After this incident he moved on again.

His next port of call was Penzance, in Cornwall (in the United Kingdom). He was first spotted by Geoff Bold, a mechanic at the Penlee Lifeboat Station, in January 1976. As mentioned in Chapter One, the dolphin's arrival transformed the quality of Bold's life, for at the time, he was suffering from bouts of deep depression. One day this suddenly lifted for no apparent reason. Bold looked around and saw Donald watching him as he worked. Although Donald moved on again, whenever Bold felt low, he simply thought about the dolphin and his spirits lifted.

Some time later, a wild dolphin appeared in Falmouth. One dinghy took the creature's fancy, and he would spend hours around it, just as Donald had done at Port St Mary, Martin's Haven and Penzance. By the spring of 1977 he was winning the hearts of the local people, but whatever happened to him after then seems to be a mystery.

Jean-Louis

In 1976, a Breton fisherman spotted a fin in the water which he thought was a 'Jean-Louis' — a local nickname for the blue shark. While the man was hauling in his lobster pot, he realized that the fin belonged not to a shark, but to a dolphin, which was playfully pulling at the end of the fisherman's rope. He named the animal Jean-Louis, which was guaranteed to cause much confusion, as it turned out that the dolphin was in fact a female. She soon became a friend of the fishermen in and around the Baie des Trepasses in Brittany. Her favourite place was Dolphin Rock, a rough cove where she played in the frothy waves and surfed, often with human companions.

Solitary female dolphins like Jean-Louis, Nina and Opo exhibit different behavioural patterns to those of the more aggressive and boisterous males, such as Percy and Freddie (see below). Jean-Louis generally preferred gentler, more sensual games, although she also enjoyed frolicking and gambolling with canoeists. One of her favourite games was that of hide-and-seek, and she was also reported to enjoy mimicking her swimming companions' body postures, twisting and turning in a sensual synchronization that resembled a lyrical water-ballet. She also loved to swim at top speed in the wake of an inflatable boat whilst positioned just beneath the propeller, and then to overtake the boat and jump in front of it.

Jean-Louis often exhibited a keen sexual interest in many of the male divers whom she encountered, by rubbing herself between their legs. The film-maker and marine photographer, François Pelletier, struck up a special friendship with her. She would swim closely by his side, make apparently sexual advances towards him, and, when encouraging him to play, put her beak up to his mask, withdraw, and shake her head. Horace Dobbs commented that Jean-Louis was like a flirtatious woman. 'Not only did she get her own way, in his opinion, but she was much more subtle than Donald in achieving it. I tried hard to get close to Jean-Louis, but she would not allow more than fleeting contact, even when we were playing a complex game.'

Jean-Louis showed great interest in sound and music. Dobbs rigged up an underwater xylophone which amused her briefly, but she was more enchanted by the high-frequency clinking sounds made by anchors and chains. The film director Peter Gillbe, who with Dobbs made a film for British Channel 4 about Jean-Louis, was deeply moved by his encounter with this dolphin. The film, called *A Closer Encounter*, was seen by 900,000 people and aroused a lot of interest in swimming with friendly wild dolphins. It is uncertain what has now become of Jean-Louis. Some say that she is still in the area, while others believe that she has moved on to a new location.

Jojo

First sighted in early 1980 by fishermen and divers off the coast of Providentiales (Provo), in the British West Indies, Jojo has become a celebrity in his own right. For some reason, this dolphin chose to stay in the protected waters of Provo, where his regular encounters with humans began in 1982. Ric O'Barry has speculated that Jojo might actually be

Liberty, a captive dolphin that O'Barry released in the Bahamas in 1972, but there is little evidence to prove his assumption.

An amazing friendship has been forged by a Californian man, Dean Bernal, and Jojo. The latter has become Bernal's near-constant companion. They swim along together at the same pace, and when Dean free-dives, the dolphin dives with him. Together they explore the seabed, with Dean picking up shells and other items from the bottom while Jojo watches intently. Often, Jojo brings Dean 'gifts' in the form of sunglasses, money, seashells and broken necklaces that the dolphin has retrieved from underwater.

But Jojo is not just interested in quiet pastimes. He possesses a sense of bravado and seems to thrive on excitement. He harasses sharks, which often bite him back, and on one occasion the dolphin chased away a nine-foot hammerhead when it came too close to the diver Jacques Mayol and his team. By using his rostrum (nose), Jojo pushed the shark at least one 120 feet down to the floor of the reef, and proceeded to fend it off as it made attempts to return to threaten the divers.

Jojo will often involve Bernal in these dangerous games. In sport, Jojo rams sharks, pins them to the seabed, then herds them towards Bernal, often into his arms, as if offering him a toy. Other such 'gifts' include manta rays. Unlikely as it may sound to human ears, these tokens appear to represent Jojo's affection and friendship.

Jojo interacts with other humans, but is devoted to Bernal and will abandon other swimmers in preference to him. Bernal has noticed that the dolphin has a particular fondness for children. He has been known to place his jaws around a child and rub their stomach with his tongue. One of his more unusual companions is a golden labrador called Toffee belonging to Tim Ainsley, a catamaran owner. When the dog sees the dolphin, he leaps into the water and swims after him, barking with delight. The dolphin teases Toffee by swimming underneath him and nibbling his paws. Both seem to enjoy one another's company.

Although as a rule gentle and sensitive, Jojo is by no means passive and will retaliate if provoked. If people chase him, he will respond with a sharp flick of the tail, which is capable of knocking someone out; or, if crowded, he will butt someone out of the way. On one occasion, he got into a 'fight' with an aggressive New Yorker who tried to grab him. Jojo responded by knocking the man on the head, whereupon the man tried to punch the dolphin on the snout. Jojo, however, simply opened his mouth and let the fist settle between his teeth. For his efforts, the man lost a solid gold ring encrusted with diamonds, which Jojo later found and brought back to Bernal.

An explorer at heart, Jojo likes to roam around the islands, and Bernal has a calling device which Jojo can detect from a great distance. This helps to lure him away from any potentially dangerous situations, for Jojo, like Donald, is accident-prone. Having settled in a tourist resort, most of the dangers to which he is subject are normally brought about by humans. For example, Jojo enjoys jumping and spinning along in the wake of powerboats

– but this has encouraged people to 'herd' him with their craft. In July 1989, he was run over by a ski-boat when he surfaced to breathe, and received serious injuries. He had deep cuts caused by the propeller, which just missed his eye. A few months later, a sharp object also damaged his right eye.

In June 1990, Jojo went missing. He had become entangled in a turtle seine net, set in the Pine Cay channel, and was trapped for about two days, struggling to survive exposure to the sun and drowning. By the time he was found, his skin was severely chafed and sunburnt and he had deep lacerations in his tail flukes and fins from the ropes.

Bernal's main concern is that with every new encounter, Jojo's risk of survival decreases. He has been poked, prodded, hit by both water skis and jet skis, and caught in nets. How long can he go on without getting into really serious danger? To protect him, the Jojo Dolphin Project has been set up to find out more about dolphin ways and interspecies communication. On the recommendation of the Public Service Commission, Bernal has been appointed as National Parks Warden with a special responsibility for Jojo's welfare. Jojo has recently been joined by the 'Into the Blue' dolphins, Missie, Silver and Rocky, and appears to be happy with his new companions.

Percy

A male bottlenose dolphin, Percy first appeared in 1982 in Portreath, Cornwall (in the United Kingdom), close to Godrevy Island. One of his favourite haunts was a place called Gull Rock, where he was often to be found fishing and cavorting. It was first thought that he might in fact be Donald, but Horace Dobbs realized that this creature was instead a 'new' friendly dolphin. A mature male of between nine and 12 feet long, Percy was smaller than Donald and had different scars and markings. Dobbs named him Portreath Percy, or Percy for short, and this name stuck.

Percy was first discovered by Bob Holborn, a local guest-house proprietor, who gradually built up a close friendship with him. Percy used to trail about a foot behind Holborn's inflatable boat, slowly and steadily becoming more inquisitive as time went by. Eventually, Holborn joined him in the water, floating quietly on his back and waiting for Percy to approach, slowly building up a sense of trust.

'He came right up to me, opened his beak and mouthed me from the tips of my flippers to the top of my head. When he seemed satisfied, he laid his head across my chest and I stroked him,' Holborn says. Percy attracted the attention of many divers who came from near and far to swim with him. The dolphin was as intrigued by them as they were by him. For three summers, Percy enjoyed leaping and playing outside the harbour entrance, and delighted in following the fishing boats back and forth. Those who observed his behaviour commented on his sense of humour, love of fun and the enjoyment that he derived from playing games with the fishermen. One story that illustrates Percy's comic nature describes an occasion when a couple of fishermen were anchored in the bay to pick up some lobster creels. Before hauling up the last pot, they decided to take a lunch-break. They got their sandwiches out and began to eat, while Percy apparently watched with growing impatience. After a while, he disappeared below the surface, went down and picked up the pot himself. He then resurfaced, knocked on the boat hull to attract their attention, and presented them with the creel! He also revelled in playing 'tag' and frantically chasing swimmers and divers to and fro. One of his favourite games involved anchors. Mischievously, he would lift them up from the seabed and so move the boats along.

Like all wild dolphins, Percy was constantly under threat from fishing boats, nets and pollution. In August 1983, locals spotted him doing a series of peculiar backward flips into a strong current, and apparently hitting his head on the water. On closer inspection, they discovered that he had a fish-hook with a line attached to it embedded in his left eye. Unfortunately, no one could help him, and it took some time for the hook to work itself free.

In common with the majority of solitary male dolphins, Percy was also very sexually active, frequently exposing his penis and rubbing it against swimmers. In dolphins, however, this is not just sexual behaviour. It is also a sign of friendship and shows trust and acceptance, although it understandably caused some alarm amongst those swimming with Percy, who misunderstood his body language.

In the summer of 1984, a scientist and cetacean researcher, Christina Lockyer, made a study of Percy which included his swimming patterns, interaction with people and home range. In her paper, she noted several traits that bore comparison to those of Donald and other solitary dolphins, such as towing boats, nuzzling propellers and showing a keen interest in fishermens' activities. On one occasion Lockyer noted that Percy deliberately entangled Bob Holborn's lobster pots. When Holborn dived to sort them out, Percy untangled them for him so that they did not have to be cut, thereby showing that the dolphin had a capacity for both problem-solving and memory.

He often exhibited peculiar behaviour. Once, he apparently swam belly up to urinate over the stern of a boat, startling its occupants. Instances of this kind of 'sense of humour' were often noted by Lockyer. She ascribed his altered moods, sexual activity and behavioural patterns to spring and autumn peaks. She also noted that the rake-marks caused by another dolphin's teeth indicated that Percy was probably still in contact with other dolphins, and so was not a truly solitary dolphin.

At the end of 1984, he made his last appearance and had his final encounter with Tricia Kirkman, a woman who had also been very close to another dolphin, Simo (see below). Percy's encounter was observed by Horace Dobbs, who noted that in Kirkman's presence the creature was very gentle and sensitive. According to Dobbs, Percy allowed her to rest her hands on his head so that she could float safely. He then towed her gently and smoothly along in a circle around an inflatable boat. Sadly, since this meeting, he has not been seen again, and it is not certain where he disappeared to.

Fungie

Fungie, also known as Dorad or Tarquin, has become a superstar in his own right and is the subject of several books and films – the best-known book being Heathcote Williams' *Falling for A Dolphin*, and the most recent film Kim Kindersley's *The Dolphin's Gift*.

In the winter of 1983, fishermen noticed an unusual presence in Dingle Harbour, Co. Kerry, on the south-west coast of Ireland. Some had spotted a fin in the water around their boats, while others remarked that they had seen a shark following them – although it would have been almost unheard-of for sharks to come in so close to the boats. However, it soon transpired that the 'shark' was in fact a dolphin.

One year, on a day when the German market for herring collapsed and the fishermen dumped their catch back in the water, the dolphin raced around among the shoals of fish and flung them in the air, with some landing back on the decks of the ships. Over the next few days, crews on board each boat reported having a dolphin for company as they set out fishing. Fungie, as he became known, would escort them as far as the Crow Rock, then break off and head back. He was inquisitive as well as playful, often leaping in the air right beside the boat, looking in to see what was going on. Often the fishermen would hear a tapping noise from the stern, and find Fungie hitting each blade of the propeller with his beak. Sometimes he jumped clean out of the water over the boats, giving the occupants the fright of their lives.

In April, he was spotted by swimmers at Beebawn (Binn Bann) Strand near Dingle and Slaidin. His first two years at Dingle harbour passed quietly. John O'Connor was one of the first to attempt to get close to Fungie. The dolphin would swim to within 10 feet of O'Connor, then stop and stare. O'Connor says: 'If we made any sudden movement, he [Fungie] would respond by a startled reflex – at other times he seemed to shiver with nervous excitement.' Their first meetings were thus charged with tension on both sides. 'Just as we were about to give up on him, his attitude changed,' O'Connor adds. 'From then on, when we went diving, he was always there, peering over your shoulder, at times being a perfect nuisance.' Even when trust was established, Fungie would first swim up cautiously, and only on recognizing them would he allow them to touch his skin.

The dolphin has shown that he can differentiate between new divers and people he already knows. O'Connor points out: 'He is more inquisitive of unknown divers but also more cautious, returning to the diver he has known for the longest for reassurance as he allows a newcomer the briefest of touches.' Fungie clearly gets pleasure from playing tricks on new visitors. Approaching them from behind, he gently nudges their shoulder or armpit and appears to enjoy his subjects' looks of surprise when they find themselves face to face with him. And, if he is deliberately ignored, he will often go to great extremes to get attention. Often he will swim very fast from behind you, then do a flip-turn, landing right up against your face-mask, and will then gently peck the mask with his nose. If he is pushed aside, he becomes furious, and will for example grab at divers' flippers, tugging on them until he gets attention.

One of the best-known friendships that the dolphin has established is that with 19-year-old Siobhan Daly. She has reported that Fungie is able to read her thoughts and emotions, sensing when she is frightened, happy and even angry. 'Not long after I met him, we were playing one day and he leapt over my head and landed very close. I screamed in fright and he came right up to me and scanned me with his sonar. He became very gentle and after that refused to jump if I was in the water. He sensed that I was frightened and he wouldn't jump for months after that.'

The poet Heathcote Williams comments on Fungie's aquatic grace and awe-inspiring presence in the book *Falling For A Dolphin*:

The dolphin descends,
Swimming around you, mercurially,
And you pursue it again below.
It whirls and coils,
Describing three-dimensional hieroglyphs in its
Watery space,
Then glances at you.
A pencil-thin stream of bubbles pours from its blow-hole
As it speaks.
Again, you are lost for a reply,
Immersed in this element,
Knowing less than nothing.

Fungie has apparently changed a lot over the past few years. Those who first swam with him have commented that he has become less interested in human company, and it is now quite difficult to gain his attention because he has such a wide choice of companions. People make pilgrimages from all over both Ireland and the world to see him. Locals have commented that it is rather like visiting Lourdes, and that such people are often seeking a 'divine' experience. The number of tourists and boats has increased dramatically, and Fungie is constantly bombarded with visitors, distractions, and playthings. Plans to build a new marina and holiday homes also threaten his environment, so it may not be long before he disappears from Dingle, perhaps opting for a quieter, more remote habitat, where he can be more selective about exactly which people he chooses to interact with.

Simo

In the spring of 1984, a young male dolphin appeared in the Welsh fishing port of Solva, on the Pembrokeshire coast. The locals named him Simo, a name which, as we have mentioned, derives from the Greek word meaning 'snub-nose', a common nickname for dolphins in ancient times. Simo attracted the attention of local fishermen, who were captivated by his curiosity, especially regarding underwater activity. He showed great interest in divers, following them around underwater, as if looking over their shoulder at what they were doing. Some of his favourite pastimes included such raucous games as pushing canoes and tipping people off their airbeds, both of which seemed to delight him. He also enjoyed swimming around the fishing boats, leaping and frolicking in their wake. Indeed, one of Simo's main characteristics was this gregarious, almost rumbustious nature, and his overpowering and enthusiastic antics, especially his annoying habit of nipping people with his sharp, conical teeth, frightened many of his swimming companions. Often, he would approach swimmers from behind, rise up vertically in a headstand posture, and hit them on the head with his beak, dislodging their masks and snorkels, before sinking back into the water.

The fact that he was also very active sexually and would rub his erect penis against people disturbed and upset quite a few of those who sought his company. But Simo openly loved attention to be lavished on him, and adored being scratched at the base of his pectoral fins. Often, as a sign of affection, he would put his head gently on people's shoulders to greet them, and offer them dorsal and belly-up pectoral fin tows.

Simo seemed to prefer female company when given the choice, and struck up several close relationships with women. One such devotee who befriended him, Anne Marks, was so enchanted by him that she kept a diary of his activities. He allowed her to stroke his head, beak and eyes and would present his abdomen to be stroked — a sure sign of trust. He also engaged in a friendship with Clare Sendall. She reported that one of his quirks involved snuggling up to her shoulder and offering her a pectoral fin tow. He would then dive deep and leap out unexpectedly, almost landing on top of her. Sometimes, he blew bubbles at her underwater, a signal that she believed was a form of communication. Another woman who became very close to Simo was Tricia Kirkman. Although she could not swim, she always felt at ease in his presence. Kirkman had a problem with her circulation, and had had electric-shock therapy to dilate the blood vessels in her feet. Once when she was floating alongside Simo, she remarked on a tingling sensation in her right hand. When she came out of the water, she noticed that her hands felt warmer, and she began to wonder if Simo had some kind of healing power.

During the summer of 1985, encouraged by Dr Horace Dobbs, Kirkman spent a lot of time with Simo and became very close to him. In response to her love, the dolphin became visibly protective and possessive of her. While she was in the water, he never left her side, devoting all his attention to her, and on one occasion he actually drove about 10 swimmers out of the water, biting two and buffeting another around the head in the process, apparently so that he could have Tricia to himself. Perhaps this was a sign of dolphin jealousy, or perhaps Simo preferred 'one-to-one' relationships.

Towards the end of that summer, Anne Marks noticed that Simo was behaving strangely. He appeared to be sluggish and listless, and instead of his usually energetic activities, he would loll around apathetically. Rather than chasing after the fishing boats, for example, he appeared to be struggling for sufficient energy to surface for a breath. One day, he was seen to surface slowly beside a boat, open his mouth and sink back into the water. Marks never saw Simo again after this incident. Locals hoped that he had rejoined a local pod of dolphins further up the coast, but no one can be sure of his fate.

Freddie

Freddie, a mature male dolphin, first appeared just outside Amble harbour off the rather bleak coast of Northumberland, in the United Kingdom, about five years ago. At first, he was very wary of both boats and people, but as time passed, he became bolder and more interested. One incident which occurred in 1989 marked a turning-point for Freddie. A dolphin-lover, Virginia Farrow, untangled some fishing line that was caught around the animal's fins. This act of kindness and concern seemed to establish his trust in humans, and now, playful, gregarious and charismatic, Freddie loves their attention and company. When anyone gets in the water, he appears beside them almost immediately, eager to examine them and to establish contact. Freddie has been known to offer his dorsal fin to those he likes, and tows these people gently for a brief ride. He also exhibits the dog-like behaviour of dragging people along by their arm, which he takes gently in his mouth.

Gordon Easton, a lifeboat master, takes people out to see Freddie almost every day. Easton has become very attached to the dolphin, and looks after his welfare. Since Easton spends much of his time trying to protect the dolphin from over-enthusiastic visitors, he advises that it is best if no more than two people get in the water at a time.

Liz Sandeman, who has swum with Freddie on several occasions, describes her experiences of him: 'He really enjoys being stroked and rubbed and is very tactile. He can also be quite boisterous, but he has definite times when he is quiet and pensive. I suppose you could say that dolphins are susceptible to mood swings just like humans.' Margaux Dodds, who has also swum with Freddie, recounts one telling incident that reveals the dolphin's ability to anticipate how different people will react to his behaviour. 'He swam up behind me, put his head on top of my head and took me under with him. It was quite overpowering, but I think he did it because we had spent a long time together in the water building up a relationship – he obviously knew that I trusted him and that although it was a bit frightening, I would not be disturbed by it.' Many other people who have swum with this dolphin have made a similar observation that he seems to be able to 'read' people very easily.

A tactile dolphin, Freddie has been known on many occasions to hook his penis around a swimmer's knee. Some have suggested that these displays signify 'sexual frustration', and consequently there have been many scaremongering stories that suggest Freddie may be 'dangerous' and should be avoided. However, it seems unlikely that a dolphin which has shown such interest in and enjoyment of human company would seek to harm anybody unless deliberately provoked.

Unfortunately, Freddie has become too much of a celebrity for his own safety. The growing number of visitors, and the noise and danger of jet skis and motor-boats, threaten both him and his immediate environment. In the autumn of 1991, he was badly injured by a police launch that could easily have killed him. He had 12 cuts on one side of his body and it was touch and go whether he would survive. (The water in Amble is so polluted that the wounds could easily have become infected.) Freddie is often also seen lingering by the sewage outlet close to the harbour mouth, which presents another serious hazard to his health. And, although he undoubtedly enjoys human companionship, there are now fears that he may literally be killed by kindness and effectively suffocated by too many people over-eager to experience his vivacious company – that is, if he survives the environmental perils that surround him.

TERMS OF ENDEARMENT

Just why, when most dolphins usually flee the scene as soon as people enter the water, do these particular ones act in such a friendly manner towards us? Can we really flatter ourselves to think that they prefer our company to that of their own kind?

Cetacean experts have their own theories. In *Follow a Wild Dolphin*, Horace Dobbs ventures his fanciful view that such dolphins are on a mission to learn more about us in order to survive. Imagining himself inside Donald's mind, Dobbs writes, 'We need to know something about what motivates their [humans'] trend towards apparent self-destruction. In other words we need to know about the vibrations of their minds. When he (my mentor) sent me on my mission, he knew I would be gone for a long time, for in order to accomplish it I would have to isolate myself completely from close contact with dolphin vibrations.'

Viewing the scenario from a more scientific standpoint, Dr Peter Evans posits that 'friendly' dolphins tend, for some reason or other, to have become excluded from their social set. 'It may be an old dolphin who cannot keep up with the group or perform its role within the unit, or a younger dolphin that is too aggressive. When this happens it may start a new group or try to join another pod. If it fails, the dolphin will remain on its own. Solitary individuals are usually males and this occurs most commonly amongst the bottlenose variety. Being a coastal-dwelling species, these dolphins are likely to come into contact with humans, especially if they take up permanent residence in a particular area. Inquisitive by nature, they show interest in swimmers and often behave towards then in a friendly and playful way.'

Meeting dolphins in their natural environment can be a moving and magical experience.

*Spinner dolphins (*Stenella longirostris*) off the Leeward Islands, Hawaii.*

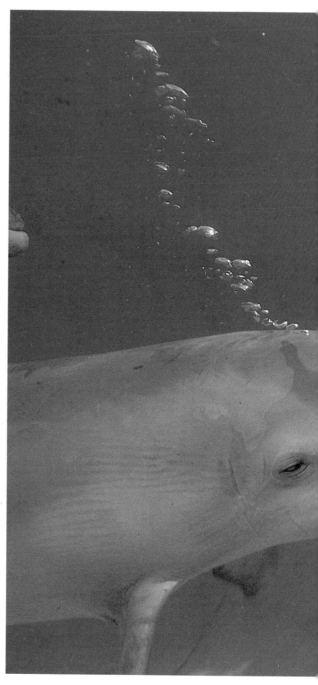

Encounters with solitary wild dolphins have captured man's imagination for centuries. Here, a bottlenose dolphin gently caresses a diver's hand.

The sour side of captivity: dolphins held in a small 'petting pool' at Seaworld in San Diego, California, USA.

Traditionally, dolphins have always cooperated with fishermen and have been regarded as a symbol of good fortune.

At Monkey Mia, in Western Australia, families of wild dolphins have been interacting with humans since the 1960s.

Kept in captivity in Brighton Dolphinarium for most of their lives, Missie and Silver now roam free, after being rehabilitated and released through the 'Into the Blue' project.

Fungie, the resident bottlenose dolphin at Dingle, County Kerry, Ireland, frolics with a human companion.

Man and dolphin show a natural curiosity towards each other. Since ancient times, stories of friendships between dolphins and young boys have been widely documented, yet only now are we beginning to realize their relevance and authenticity.

A diver and a dolphin swimming together in synchronicity.

Captive dolphins at the Theater of the Sea, Florida Keys, USA.

Jojo (a wild bottlenose dolphin) and Dean Bernal at play in the warm waters of the Turks and Caicos Islands.

Jojo and Dean Bernal wrestle with a nurse shark.

A wild bottlenose dolphin.

Thousands of dolphins die each year as a result of modern fishing techniques. Here, a striped dolphin is caught in a drift net off the Azores.

Drift netters in the north-east Atlantic haul aboard a trapped dolphin.

Other people propose that friendly dolphins may be alone because their relations or companions have perished after being caught in fishing nets or stranded on the rocks. Being social creatures which need to form close associations with one another, it is perhaps not surprising that such dolphins then regard friendly humans as surrogate mates or companions. The local people of Amble, for example, found a female dolphin washed up on the shore at around the same time that Freddie appeared in the harbour. Some speculate that the dead dolphin may have been his mate, and that the reason why he tends to act so amorously towards many swimmers, especially women, is that he misses her company.

In *Encounters with Whales and Dolphins*, Wade Doak recounts a similar incident that took place in 1983. According to the people of Chira Island off the Pacific coast of Costa Rica, a lone dolphin followed a boat back to their village after its companion had been shot by a fisherman. Developing a friendship with young and old alike, it usually appeared as soon as people began swimming out from the beach. The dolphin seemed to be particularly fond of small children and would push them around in tiny dug-out canoes. It also followed them right up onto the shore and often had to be pushed back into the sea. So trusting was this dolphin that it would allow people to pick it up and hold it for short periods of time. When it wished to return to the water, the dolphin would simply roll out of their arms. Sadly, its faith in human kindness was hideously betrayed. In November of that year a fisherman called Raphael Conteras found the dolphin entangled in his net, calmly waiting to be released. Instead, he hacked it to death with a machete and took the carcass back to the horrified villagers. The story goes that a week later, while sheltering from an electrical storm in the bottom of his boat, Conteras was struck dead by lightning.

With regard to the theory that friendly dolphins may have become separated from their natural companions, it is worth noting also that, in the tale already cited earlier in this chapter, the dolphin that came into the harbour of Poroselene all those years ago was thought to have been a calf that had lost its mother.

Whatever the true case may be, today's friendly dolphins, like those in ancient times, often seem particularly attracted to children, perhaps because dolphins can relate better to children's high-pitched voices and playful nature. Children are also generally more intuitive and sensitive, and less manipulative, than most adults, which may explain why dolphins enjoy their company.

People who spend a lot of time with friendly dolphins invariably say that the creatures are prone to favouritism: while attracted to some individuals, they take an instant dislike to others. Graham Timmins, who moved to Dingle to be near Fungie and set up his own research and conservation centre, Seventh Wave, says: 'One of the dolphin's most impressive skills is his ability to differentiate between different people. Two interesting instances of recognition come to mind. On one occasion I was swimming with the dolphin and three friends. Carina is such a favourite of his that the rest of us decided to banish her to the boat for a while so we could get some attention too. This worked until Carina started resting the tips of her [diving] fins in the water. In an instant the dolphin was back by the boat waiting for her to get back in. He even took her fins in his teeth and pulled them, so we gave up trying to manipulate the situation and let Fungie have his way.

'Another time I was swimming with one of his old favourites, a mural artist called Lief Bruylant. She assumed her characteristic posture, swimming in a circle on her side with arms and legs curled back, which often entranced him. But strangely, he seemed to ignore her, playing quietly with me and a couple of other people until, after 10 minutes, he suddenly seemed to recognize her. He made a beeline for Lief, charging excitedly round her a few times and mimicking her, exactly as he had done on previous occasions. Maybe dolphins can characterize subtle differences in the way we swim and move our limbs in the water, and this is how the Dingle dolphin recognizes his favourite companions.'

Dolphins may go further than mere preferences, too, and may form a particularly strong attachment to certain individuals. At the Cabana del Sol resort in Cuba, a captive male dolphin called Juan shows all the signs of being 'in love' with an 18-year-old girl named Leah Lemieux. Juan lives with three other dolphins – two females and another male – in a spacious seawater pen fenced off from the ocean. Leah's relationship with Juan began three years ago when she begged permission to swim with these dolphins. Right from the beginning, the dolphin was attracted to her, and ever since, a special bond has grown between them. When Leah is with him he ignores the female dolphins completely. If she does not visit he becomes listless and refuses to perform, and on these occasions he will not even accept fish from his trainer: only Leah can entice him to eat. Once, Leah was given a red rose while Juan was watching. When she entered the water, he immediately came to her side. Then he swam away and returned with a leaf which he gently placed on her shoulder. This case is of particular interest because, while it is true that friendly dolphins are often loners, Juan's attachment to Leah challenges the theory that dolphins only make do with human companionship because they lack that of their own kind.

Groups of Friendly Dolphins

Considered by some to be one of the 'wonders of the world', Monkey Mia is perhaps the only place on earth that one can encounter families of wild, friendly dolphins in safe, shallow water. Five hundred miles north of Perth in Western Australia, in a region called Shark Bay, Monkey Mia – *mia* is an aboriginal word meaning 'home' – is a remote area where the only sign of civilization is a caravan park frequented by keen fishermen and dolphin-watchers.

No one really knows what initially attracted the dolphins to the warm shallows of Monkey Mia. One theory is that in the 1960s, a young girl who was holidaying in the bay lured a dolphin that the fishermen had nicknamed 'Old Charlie' into the shallow waters. Apparently, she built up a friendship with the dolphin, which came in to see her every day.

Perhaps other dolphins were then attracted by fishermen throwing them the odd cast-off fish from the wooden jetty. Other people suggest that the connection may even go back to a time when coastal-dwelling Aborigines fished in harmony with the dolphins, a phenomenon that still occurs in some parts of Australia.

One of the first people to report on the events at Monkey Mia was an underwater explorer, Ben Cropp. In 1978, while he was out sailing, he took shelter from a storm in the Monkey Mia bay. There were several dolphins on his bow as he cruised in towards the shore, something with which he was familiar, but he was taken by surprise by the sight of a group of dolphins surrounding fishermen who were sharing their cast-off fish with them. An ex-dolphinarium owner, Cropp was completely amazed by the interactions that were taking place. He and his companion leapt into the water and began playing with the dolphins, who responded quickly to their advances. In captivity it would have taken up to six months to train dolphins to interact in this way, and yet the Monkey Mia dolphins chose to meet and trust people of their own free will.

In 1976, Hazel and Wilf Mason became the proprietors of the caravan park, and they both started to document the comings and goings of the dolphins. The Masons have noted that the Monkey Mia dolphins are particularly fond of children and pay the latter special attention. Normally, the dolphins greet people who wade into the water by raising their own heads above the surface. If a fish is presented, they open their mouths to receive it. Often, they will return the favour by tossing the onlookers a fresh herring or a piece of seaweed. Sometimes they will allow strangers to stroke and touch them, while at other times they will swim away if people reach out over-enthusiastically. There was originally a group of only eight friendly dolphins, but there are now reported to be as many as 200 of the animals residing in the area. Some of the best-known dolphins include Holey Fin, easily identifiable by her somewhat battered and pierced fin; her daughter, Holly; Crooked Fin; Puck; Nicky; Goldie; BB; Joy; and Beautiful. A full-time warden looks after the welfare of the dolphins, ensuring that they are not maltreated. Critics, however, are opposed to the dolphins being fed by the public. An American cetacean researcher, Ann Spurgeon, who spent a lot of time with the Monkey Mia dolphins, reported in *Whale Watcher Journal* in 1981: 'We looked often into the dolphins' eyes and the quality of the look they returned was unlike that of any animal we have known . . . It is possible that, if the human species can become more gentle, open and compassionate towards other life forms, Monkey Mia could be a prototype for the future – a voluntary exchange, mutually rewarded and inspirational.'

Apart from the Monkey Mia phenomenon, throughout the summer of 1991 a group of three wild dolphins interacted with swimmers off the coast of north-west Ireland. Although they are by no means as trusting as Fungie, they are nevertheless remarkably curious and friendly for wild dolphins.

EAVESDROPPING ON WILD DOLPHINS

While friendly dolphins act towards people in a particularly trusting and open fashion, whole pods of wild dolphins will also allow us to mingle with them if the conditions are sufficiently conducive.

The person largely responsible for pioneering such encounters is a New Zealander, Wade Doak. A former language and graduate student with a long-standing passion for deep-sea diving and underwater exploration, Doak traces the beginnings of his fascination for dolphins to an event that took place in 1971. He was at a depth of some 20 metres during a diving expedition off Poor Knights Islands, when the sea suddenly turned black. Doak looked up to see a school of dolphins watching him intently. Four years later, whilst sailing with his wife Janet, the contact was reinforced when the couple came across another group of dolphins that were performing barrel-rolls and spins. This time, the Doaks dived overboard into the sea. Whereas wild dolphins, as mentioned earlier, usually swim away when people enter the water, these stayed close by the excited couple. From that moment on, Wade turned his mind to unravelling the mystery of how dolphins behave in the wild.

In the 1970s, his interest in dolphin and human interaction was fuelled by two particular incidents that occurred right on his doorstep, as it were, in New Zealand.

First came reports of a common dolphin cruising in the estuary of the Ngunguru River. It was a young female, who became known as Elsa. Children standing on the banks would call to her, and she responded by swimming through the shallows towards them. The total trust and passive surrender that she exhibited were quite extraordinary, as Doak reports in his book *Encounters with Whales and Dolphins*.

Later, another lone dolphin turned up, this time in Hawke Bay, and set up station around a marker buoy, attracting attention to himself with some spectacular leaps. Christened Horace (after Horace Dobbs), the dolphin soon established quite a rapport with the locals as he frolicked with any boats leaving or entering Napier Harbour. Horace seemed to have a particularly mischievous streak, for as yachts crossed the channel, he delighted in nudging their rudders to throw them off-course. Yachtsmen often found their centreboards and rudders strangely immobilized after Horace had been around. The first person Horace befriended was a diver, Quentin Bennet, but as the dolphin's trust grew he began playing with other swimmers too. Frank Robson, who gave Horace his name, recalls that on several occasions the dolphin actually came to the rescue of people who, having ventured too far out of their depth, were struggling in the water, and deposited them close to the shore.

Wade and Jan Doak established Project Interlock to coordinate and assemble accounts of dolphin/human encounters in an attempt to identify any special patterns of communication and interaction. Unperturbed by Jacques Cousteau's experiences of free-swimming dolphins fleeing as soon as divers entered the water, the Doaks set out to re-establish contact with the common dolphins off Poor Knights Islands, close to their home at Whangarei. In an attempt to be as inconspicuous as possible, Jan Doak dressed up in a wetsuit that was especially modelled to make her look like a dolphin. Wade recounts how a group of about two dozen inquisitive dolphins circled her when she entered the water. After lingering for about 15 minutes, all but three swam away. The Doaks named these lingerers Average White, Small Scar and Sideband, with reference to their colouring and markings. Finally only Sideband, who had a white vertical band on his left side, behind his dorsal fin, remained. This dolphin was so curious that he came within four feet of Jan, following her as she dived and then rose to the surface. When she attempted to copy Sideband by swimming 'dolphin-style', he responded by throwing his tail up and head down as if mimicking her in return.

Following this successful encounter, the Doaks went on to explore various ways of establishing mutual trust and communication. When sailing out to meet dolphins, they began playing certain types of music. They found that the sound of flutes and tinkling bells seemed to attract the dolphins' attention. It also enabled the animals to identify the catamaran acoustically.

To acclimatize the dolphins to their presence in the water, the Doaks first lay either on the bows of the catamaran, or in hammocks suspended beneath them. When the dolphins came close, the Doaks were particularly careful not to make any sudden movements or lunge towards them. The couple also did not reach out to touch the animals before confidence and trust had been established. Soon, the strange-looking wetsuits became redundant as the dolphins began feeling comfortable in Jan's and Wade's presence. Before long the Doaks were enjoying amazingly close encounters with these free-spirited creatures.

From their own experiences, the Doaks believe that dolphins make meaningful gestures to us during such interactions, including leaping as the boat is leaving, deliberately splashing people on boats after making eye-contact, and whistling or vocalizing in response to being called. If a dolphin swims in short spurts in a certain direction, it may be trying to guide a diver to a lost partner or object or lead a yacht past an underwater obstacle. Defecation may signal excitement and can even be a show of acceptance. Touching, however, is the dolphin's ultimate gesture of trust and friendship.

As dolphins are notorious hybridizers, they may extend their courtship behaviour towards humans. There is no doubt that dolphins can tell the difference between male and female people even when these are dressed in wetsuits. Because the male dolphin uses its penis as a tactile organ, what is merely playful behaviour may be mistaken for a sexual advance. However, it not unknown for solitary male dolphins to attempt intimacy. During sexual foreplay, a dolphin may take your arm or flipper in his mouth. If in a more boisterous mood, he may rush at you head-on, which could easily be mistaken for aggression. There have also been occasions when dolphins have enticed or towed female swimmers right out to sea as if attempting a 'kidnap', which can be unnerving.

One thing is certain. Dolphins are far more intrigued by active people engaged in some kind of underwater pursuit, be it simply diving for shells on the seabed, than they are by passive floaters. Strong swimmers who can plunge to the depths and rise to the surface, dolphin-style, seem able to sustain the animals' interest longest. Inquisitive dolphins often glide alongside such people, mimicking their body postures and movements as if accepting them as members of their own species.

The Doaks' pioneering work has set a precedent for those wishing to 'eavesdrop' on dolphins. The couple's approach to achieving a special rapport with these curious yet shy, sensitive beings is one from which we can all learn. The Doaks insist that mutual respect and openness are an essential part of the 'etiquette' involved in making contact with wild and friendly dolphins alike. Wade Doaks feels that the real barrier is man's manipulative, domineering attitude towards nature. 'I would have thought it self-evident not to throw yourself onto other creatures,' he emphasizes. 'You must allow them to get to know you before you can expect any meaningful interaction to take place.'

GUIDELINES FOR SWIMMING WITH DOLPHINS

We should remember that even friendly dolphins are not tame pets. They are wild creatures that can at times act rather boisterously and unpredictably. To establish a good relationship with dolphins, it is important to be sensitive to their moods and actions. Anyone who is fortunate enough to have the opportunity to swim with wild dolphins would be wise to follow the guidelines listed here, both for her or his own safety and that of the animals.

1. When in the water, move as gracefully and rhythmically as possible, with your hands crossed behind your back. Reaching out may be regarded as threatening if a dolphin does not know you. Only when a bond of trust has built up can you try this without unnerving your aquatic companion.
2. Take off any rings and other pieces of jewellery before entering the water. Sharp-edged items can cut a dolphin's skin, leaving it open to infection.
3. Do not touch a dolphin near the blow-hole: it is akin to somebody placing their hand over your nose, and, quite justifiably, a dolphin may react aggressively. On one occasion, Jojo smacked a woman very firmly with his tail flukes after she had attempted to poke her finger down his blow-hole.
4. Menstruating women are advised not to swim with dolphins, as this state can sexually arouse the males. Even competent swimmers may find it alarming to be pursued by an over-amorous dolphin, no matter how gentle and good-natured he usually is. Dean Bernal also warns that anyone wishing to swim with Jojo should not float on their back, because this sexually excites the dolphin and may lead to him becoming angry and frustrated. This

may or may not apply to other dolphins. Jaw-clapping and violent tail-slapping are sure signs of irritation or agitation. If a dolphin seems to be getting over-excited, it is probably wise to leave the water.

5. Do not crowd or swim after a dolphin. This may be perceived as threatening behaviour, and could provoke a defensive reaction. Be patient and wait for the dolphin to come to you. It is also advisable for no more than two people to swim close to a dolphin at once. If one person is enjoying all the attention, do not try to distract the dolphin away: the chances are that it will simply leave the scene altogether.

6. Do not swim when you are ill. Apart from the obvious danger to yourself, dolphins may be susceptible to human diseases, particularly those affecting the upper respiratory tract.

7. If taking an underwater photograph, do not use a flashlight bulb. Dolphins have sensitive eyes.

8. Friendly dolphins are often known to have particular likes and dislikes as well as different moods. Get to know something about their personalities from people who spend a good deal of time with these dolphins. This will help you to establish a better rapport with the animals.

9. Try not to be manipulative in any way. Dolphins are not there to perform for you. Establish trust and be open to whatever may happen.

WILD DOLPHIN PROGRAMMES

Wild Dolphin Project
Grand Bahama Island, The Bahamas.
This is run by the behavioural psychologist, Denise Herzing, who is at the forefront of research into wild dolphin behaviour and communication. Each week, six people are allowed to accompany researchers on-board the 60-foot catamaran which serves as a floating field station. Encounters are principally with a pod of some 50 wild spotted dolphins that have become acclimatized to the presence of humans. The project runs from May to September.
Contact address: Wild Dolphin Project, 21 Hepburn Avenue, Suite 20 Jupiter, Florida, USA.

Project Dolphin
Grand Bahama Island, The Bahamas.
This is operated by Claude Charest and Terry Berryn, who belong to a group called Oceanic Society Expeditions, based in San Francisco. (See p. 131 for the address.) When they sail out to study dolphins on their 70-foot schooner, the *Jennifer Marie*, they have places for eight paying volunteers on each eight-day trip to help with their research. Wild spotted and bottlenose dolphins are the focus of their study. The researchers take care that

volunteers do not disturb the dolphins' natural behaviour in any way. The project begins in November and December, and then runs from May until September.

Dolphin Watch
Key West, Florida.
'Captain' Ron Canning takes people out for one day trips on his catamaran to see a pod of around 26 wild bottlenose dolphins, just off the coast of Key West. Canning is wary of exploiting the wild dolphins and is cautious about letting people leap off the boat to swim with them. Although not involved in any established research projects, he is very knowledgeable about dolphins and has their best interests at heart. The safest time to visit here is from May to July, when the seas are calmest.
Contact address: Dolphin Watch, P.O. Box 4821, Key West, Florida 33041, USA.

COMMERCIAL SWIM PROGRAMMES

In response to a growing interest in swimming with dolphins, a number of centres have sprung up that attempt to recreate such encounters, but in a controlled environment. Having experienced all but one of the swim programmes currently in existence, we feel that these interactions lack the magic of meeting dolphins in their natural habitat.

The underlying reason for this can be summed up very simply. Wild dolphins are free to interact with us as they wish, whereas those involved in these swim programmes are not. Although the dolphins that we saw were kept in seawater in spacious pens that sometimes bordered on the open ocean, the animals were nevertheless constrained. At regular intervals throughout the day they had little choice but to interact with a number of different people for a limited period of time. And, to ensure that everyone has an enjoyable experience, the dolphins are invariably 'trained' to jump over your head, peck you on the cheek, lie on their side so that you can stroke their soft skin, and give you a dorsal fin tow for which they will get a reward. This means that the dolphins are not really interested in you, but are simply responding to a command, and throughout the encounters their attention is focused on the trainer with his or her bucket of fish.

In these convenience-orientated times, swim programmes have an obvious appeal. For those who have neither the patience nor the inclination to spend hours bobbing around in boats waiting for dolphins to appear out of the blue, such programmes are the perfect solution. And there is no denying that it is a real pleasure to have such close contact with these amazing creatures. The cetacean expert Dr Kenneth Norris claims, 'There is no experience as powerful as the direct contact provided by the swim programmes.' He also posits that by making us more aware of the nature of dolphins, such encounters inspire a desire to save wild dolphins. 'These remarkable animals become beneficiaries of wonder and care,' he adds.

Benjamin White Jr, founder of the Dolphin Rescue Brigade branch of the Sea Shepherd

Conservation Society, agrees that swimming with dolphins can be a 'transcendental experience', but disapproves of the whole notion of packaging it for the sake of convenience. He maintains that dolphins participating in swim programmes are behaving 'unnaturally', because they are under an obligation to let you touch them. In the wild, it is rare for dolphins to come that close. As White stresses, 'If we really love and respect these animals, we should meet them on their own terms.'

Apart from being restrained in pens, one of the main criticisms of swim programmes from the dolphins' perspective is the stress of meeting so many different people day in, day out. After all, wild dolphins only allow such an invasion of their personal space once a strong bond of trust has been established. The conservationist and ex-dolphin-trainer, Ric O'Barry, speculates that from the dolphins' viewpoint it must be like being trapped in a small room with a number of people who desperately want something from you. He recounts a rather hideous incident observed by a colleague of his who monitors swim programmes, wherein a drunken man, weighing some 300lbs, having paid his $50 for a 15-minute encounter, was allowed to clamber into a small pen with a dolphin.

O'Barry's greatest concern, however, is that a frazzled dolphin may lose its temper and injure someone. 'Despite their permanent smiles, and contrary to stories about their wild counterparts' unflagging love of humanity, captive dolphins do have a breaking-point, after which they will lash out,' explains O'Barry, who once worked with Flipper.

There is also concern over the possibility that we may transmit illnesses to confined dolphins. Thomas Dohl, a research biologist working at the Long Marine Laboratory, at the University of California in Santa Cruz, points out that dolphins are particularly susceptible to upper respiratory infections caused by cold and 'flu viruses. This may give them pneumonia, which can be fatal. Although his fears are shared by many, including marine mammalogist Dr Hal Markowitz, at present, conclusive evidence is lacking.

The National Marine Fisheries Service (NMFS), which is responsible for issuing and renewing permits for swim programmes in the United States, has taken these objections into consideration. At present, all swim programmes in America operate on a purely experimental basis and are being closely monitored. The NMFS has drawn up a summary of regulations that sets certain limitations on the interactions:

(a) Swims should be restricted to two hours per dolphin, followed by two hours of rest.

(b) No more than two people at a time should swim with any one dolphin.

(c) An escape route ought to be available so that a dolphin can leave if it chooses to end the interaction.

(d) Swim participants should complete a brief health profile; anyone with a respiratory disease or who is taking medication that suppresses immune function should be excluded from swimming.

(e) Infants should not participate in programmes.

(f) Swimmers should shower with soap and water both before and after the swim.

The swim programmes that we visited seemed to follow most of these guidelines. However, in our opinion, these encounters lacked the spontaneity and excitement of those we had enjoyed with free-swimming wild and friendly dolphins. The question of whether or not such interactions generate an appreciation of dolphins that justifies keeping the animals in this way hangs precariously in the balance. There is no doubt that such swim programmes are a money-spinning venture. Most centres will charge up to $60 for a swim that lasts around 20 to 30 minutes. And the prospect of entrepreneurs bringing 'swim with the dolphins' ventures to hotels and holiday resorts, in an attempt to stir up extra business, is too grim to contemplate.

Our worry is that, even in the right hands, such programmes serve to perpetuate a domineering and manipulative attitude towards nature that lies at the root of our current environmental problems. But, as everyone is entitled to their own opinions, we are nevertheless providing a brief description together with our own impressions of each.

Theater of the Sea

Islamorado, Florida.

A Dolphin Adventure Programme is the star attraction of this marine park where dolphins, sealions, sharks, turtles, sting rays and a wealth of other marine life are on display. The seven dolphins live in a man-made lagoon reputed to cover some four acres, which is apparently fed by seawater from the ocean. However, during our visit, all but two of the dolphins were confined to small, fenced-off pens. The swim takes place in a slightly larger area. The programme begins with a half-hour seminar on dolphins, then swimmers spend the rest of the hour in the water. Six people swam with two dolphins only. The sessions are conducted by a trainer, who, by using hand signals and fish rewards, entices the dolphins to interact in various ways. Regulations prevent incompetent swimmers, pregnant women and children under 13 years of age from participating in the programme.

Dolphins Plus

Key Largo, Florida.

This centre is run by the Borguss family, who have extensive experience in training dolphins for shows. Some years ago, they decided to try a different approach and put their dolphins in a deep, man-made canal which connects to the ocean. This canal, in turn, is divided up into a number of high-fenced pens. This is one of the first facilities to introduce dolphin therapy under the supervision of Dr Betsy Smith. The swim programmes are run quite separately, and include a one-and-a-half-hour briefing, given by a marine biologist, which covers various aspects of dolphin behaviour, intelligence, communication and anatomy. This is followed by a video to show people how to act towards the dolphins in the water and what to expect from their experience. We felt that this was both valuable and highly informative.

The actual swim lasts 30 minutes. Two sessions were conducted simultaneously, and only four people at a time were allowed in the water with the same number of dolphins. Theoretically, it was therefore possible to have a one-to-one interaction, but two of the dolphins were too absorbed in their own exuberant game to take much notice of their human visitors. The other two were more interested in interacting with us, and we both experienced some touching moments. Interestingly, these animals paid particular attention to one woman, who we later discovered visits the centre on a regular basis. They obviously knew her and preferred her company to that of total strangers. Two men complained that the dolphins they swam with ignored them completely. We liked the fact that staff on duty kept a strict eye on the swimmers and that interactions were unprovoked, or, in other words, the dolphins were not cajoled with fishy rewards into paying us attention. The facility is clean and well-organized, but we felt that the pens were cramped. Although Dolphins Plus claims that its dolphins are semi-captive and free to leave if they choose, we saw no evidence of their being able to swim out to the open sea.

Dolphin Research Center
Marathon Shores, Florida.
This facility is set in a natural lagoon that faces out to sea. Again, the lagoon is fenced off into pens, some being much more spacious than others. There are around 17 resident dolphins here, but the number varies as the centre loans out its dolphins for TV and film performances (its dolphins starred in *The Big Blue*), and takes in others that are in need of a vacation from dolphinariums. As guests of Dr David Nathanson, we were able to watch a therapy session here, but were unable to participate in the normal swim programme.

The Dolphin Encounter, which lasts one-and-a-half hours, includes an orientation session, a swim lasting up to 30 minutes, and a final workshop and discussion period.

The Dolphin Research Center also runs Dolphinlab, a special seven-day programme which covers instruction on dolphin behaviour, language research, biology and training.

The atmosphere was pleasant enough, but the dolphins' facilities gave the appearance of being rather dilapidated and shabby.

Dolphin Quest
The Hyatt Regency Hotel, Waikoloa, Hawaii.
This programme is run by two veterinarians, Rae Stone and Jay Sweeney. Six dolphins live in a 35,000 ft sq. lagoon fed by the ocean. The 30-minute swims with the dolphins are only available to 30 guests each day. As there are apparently up to 2,500 hopefuls, participants are chosen by means of a lottery system. An introductory educational talk which covers

the basics of dolphin behaviour, social life and physiology is followed by a briefing on etiquette to follow while in the water with the dolphins. Interactions are not forced by feeding the dolphins fish, and dorsal tows are forbidden. There is a 'free zone' in the lagoon where the dolphins can seek refuge from people. However, staff do use a net to force the dolphins back out of this pen and into the main lagoon again if they stay there 'too long'. According to an independent vet, two dolphins have died here as a result of poisoning by reef fish.

The Dolphin Experience

Port Lucaya, Grand Bahamas.

Part of the Underwater Explorers Society (UNEXSO), The Dolphin Experience was in the process of being moved to a new facility when we visited. This is just as well, for the original comprised a small pen in the middle of a busy, visibly polluted marina. But, as proprietor and head trainer Mike Schultz points out, the new nine-acre lagoon which branches off the man-made canal connecting the marina to the sea is now the largest of its kind. To make full use of this space, the organization had just brought in three new dolphins – Scarab, Cocoon and Echo – who had starred in the film *Cocoon*.

The Dolphin Experience claims to run a semi-captive programme, for their dolphins are taken out to the open ean, weather permitting, every day. Mike Schultz also claims that the dolphins can escape if they want to because the fences are low enough to jump. According to locals, the animals sometimes do get out, but every effort is made to recapture them.

Various options are open to those wishing to interact with dolphins. The ordinary swim programmes are conducted by the trainers, who give a brief introductory talk on dolphins before letting participants enter the water. The sessions are well organized. Responding to the trainers' commands, the dolphins give dorsal-fin pulls, twist beside you and leap out of the water above your head before they finally 'wave goodbye'. Young children were allowed in the water, including toddlers. One screaming baby appeared to be utterly terrified by its dolphin experience, which its parents were intent on capturing on video. Regulations seemed somewhat lax, but then, the Bahamas are outside US jurisdiction.

Another tantalizing encounter on offer involves going out to the reef in the open seas with two of the dolphins. Those who are qualified divers kneel on the seabed while the dolphins circle around them: snorkellers can view the encounter from the surface. Again, the interactions are fuelled by fish rewards. On rare occasions these semi-captive dolphins are joined by wild spotted dolphins which seem intrigued by the proceedings. Rumour has it that these dolphins have tried to 'kidnap' those from The Dolphin Experience, but whether there is any truth in this remains to be seen.

DOLPHIN HOLIDAYS

Bernadette and Barry Norris, M.V. Francis, Sheppards Marina, Gibraltar. Daily trips to see the dolphins.

Dolphin Swim, P.O. Box 8653, Santa Fe, New Mexico 87504. Rebecca Fitzgeralds runs one- to two-week boat trips to see and swim with wild dolphins in the Bahamas.

Friends of the Sea, P.O. Box 2190, Enfield, Connecticut, USA. Trips to see the spotted dolphins in the Bahamas.

Jacques Plettener, Los Arcos, 1 No − 13. 38640, Los Christianos, Tenerife. Organizes dolphin-watching trips in the Mediterranean.

Kaikoura Tours Ltd, P.O. Box 89, Kaikoura, New Zealand. Three-hour tours to look at the Hector dolphins as well as at whales, seals and the bird life of the area. Trips run twice daily.

Oceanic Society Expeditions, Fort Mason Center, Building E, San Francisco, California 94123, USA. Holidays in North and South America, the Pacific and Caribbean for dolphin-watching.

Richard Fairbairns, Sea Life Cruises, Quinism, Dervaig, Isle of Mull, Argyll PA75 6QL, UK.

Tim Ainsley, Beluga, Box 385, Providentiales, Turks and Caicos Islands, British West Indies. Arranges trips to see Jojo and look for wild dolphins off these islands.

Western Isles Sailing Exploration Company, Prospect House, Hollands Road, Haverhill, Suffolk CB9 8PJ, UK. Sailing holidays to look for dolphins, including holidays in Tenerife.

Part Four

....

DOLPHINS IN PERIL

Chapter Nine

CAPTIVITY

INTRODUCTION

Keeping wild animals in captivity has always raised some important ethical questions. The most fundamental of these can be summed up very simply. What right have we to pluck free-living creatures from their natural habitat to display for our interest and entertainment? It is small wonder that dolphins, which have often been seen as symbols of freedom itself, have recently been at the forefront of the captivity debate.

With their endearing smiles and playful, friendly nature, dolphins are the star attraction at many aquariums, marinelands and oceanariums. Those trying to justify confining dolphins claim that these creatures bring inordinate pleasure to millions. Indeed, they act as ambassadors for their species. Only by seeing dolphins in the flesh can we appreciate them fully and feel inspired to protect them in the wild.

However, in our own minds, we have no doubt that holding creatures born to roam the open seas in small pens or concrete pools is inherently wrong. It goes against the law of nature.

EARLY DAYS

While the Romans may have caught dolphins and kept them in lakes (see the story of the Pouzzouli dolphin in Chapter Eight), it is only in the last half-century that dolphinariums have become a worldwide phenomenon. The first person to hit upon the notion of exhibiting dolphins as a novel way to attract crowds was a Mr C. H. Townsend, curator of the New York Aquarium. After travelling for three days from North Carolina, where they were caught, five bottlenose dolphin 'pioneers' arrived at this establishment on 12 November 1913. Never in the aquarium's 12-year history had there been a more successful exhibition, Mr Townsend reputedly enthused. But the excitement was short-lived, for 21 months later, all the dolphins had died, most succumbing to pneumonia.

At the end of the 1930s, there was a surge of interest in taking dolphins from the wild, for both public display and scientific research. When the Marine Studios in Florida opened in 1938, crowds gathered to see the spectacle of these magnificent creatures at such close quarters. At first, the dolphins simply circled the pool and occasionally jumped for fish. Only by accident was it found that they could perform amusing tricks.

One evening, Cecil M. Walker, who was responsible for maintaining the water-purification pumps, saw a dolphin push a pelican feather across the water. He took the feather and threw it back, whereupon the dolphin retrieved it again. He then tried the same game with a ball, the inner tube of a bicycle, small stones and a variety of other objects. Other dolphins started joining in the act, which was to evolve into the kind of repertoire seen at shows today.

None the less, it was not until the early 1950s, when the sealion trainer Adolph Frohn was appointed by Marine Studios to 'teach the dolphins dressage stunts', that professional displays began in earnest. So extraordinary were Frohn's performing dolphins that, along with ordinary members of the public, world-renowned scientists flocked to watch them in action. The internationally famous zoologist Heini Hediger was so impressed by one especially gifted dolphin that, in a scientific paper on animal psychology, he wrote: 'But Flippy wasn't a fish, and one almost had to suppress the question as to whether it was an animal at all, when it was looking at you sideways with a twinkling eye from less than half a metre away.' This highlights how little even the experts knew of dolphins in those days.

At this time, Marine Studios boasted 11 dolphins, which were kept in a pool measuring a mere 22.5 metres across and 3.6 metres deep. Marine Studios set an early precedent for dolphinariums, which popped up like mushrooms throughout the 1960s and 1970s. The cult children's TV show *Flipper* was largely responsible for this growth of interest in dolphins. It portrayed the dolphin as man's, or more accurately boy's, best friend, an ever-faithful companion who came to his friend's aid in times of trouble. So popular was this delightful dolphin that every entrepreneur in the land must at one time or another have pondered 'If only we had our own Flipper . . .'

In reality, six dolphins took it in turns to play the part. The original Flipper was actually a female dolphin called Mitzi, who came from the Santini Porpoise School (now the Dolphin Research Center) in the Florida Keys. Her successors were Susie, Kathy, Patty, Squirt and Scottie, who belonged to the Miami Seaquarium. Amongst those who looked after and helped to train these dolphins was Richard O'Barry. In his book *Behind the Dolphin Smile*, O'Barry claims that the only way that the dolphins were cajoled into performing their amazing stunts was by rewarding them with food. 'The main pressure in training is hunger,' he writes, 'If they [dolphins] are not hungry, there's no way to teach them anything.' Sometimes even a food reward was not enough to entice a dolphin to carry out certain acts. O'Barry recounts how the programme's director, Ricou Browning, wanted Flipper to swim through an underwater cave for one scene. Dolphins, O'Barry explains, have an instinctive fear of swimming under anything, perhaps realizing that if they get trapped and cannot reach the surface, they will die. O'Barry waited until Kathy was hungry and ready to do as he asked before swimming to the cave. She followed. He then thrust his arm into the opening, a signal for her to follow, but she did not move. O'Barry swam inside and tried to lure her from within with the prospect of a fish reward, but she refused to budge. Eventually he had to put his arm around her back and literally thrust her into the cave. She was trembling with terror, almost scared to death, he recalls. Kathy never conquered her fear, but the director eventually got the shot he wanted.

Hollywood's portrait of the dolphin was to take root and flourish. The fact that Flipper was a mythical character that did tricks no ordinary dolphin would normally dream of was neither here nor there. Today, shows still portray these creatures as performing stars eager to entertain us.

It was some years before O'Barry came to the conclusion that perpetuating this myth was wrong. The turning-point came when he returned to Miami Seaquarium to find Kathy languishing in her lagoon, her whole body covered in blisters. He leapt into the pool to be close to her, and she died in his arms. The cause of death, he believes, was acute captivity. Susie also perished when she caught pneumonia after being sold to a travelling circus in Europe as 'the original Flipper'.

Risking excommunication from the dolphinarium industry, many trainers, as well as those people generally concerned with animal welfare, have recently led a campaign to highlight the plight of dolphins in captivity. The notion of these creatures being happy in their confinement, these people claim, is a cleverly crafted illusion. If one compares the lifestyles of both wild and captive dolphins, the campaigners certainly have a good case.

LIFE IN CAPTIVITY

Some dolphins are born in captivity, but most are taken from the wild. Teams of professional captors embark on special expeditions to 'acquire' dolphins either for displaying in aquariums or for scientific research purposes.

Ric O'Barry went on countless catching expeditions in Biscayne Bay when working for Miami Seaquarium in the 1960s. He describes how dolphins innocently came up alongside the collecting boat and rode the bow-wave. They had no idea that they were in any danger until the net was set. Once encircled, the dolphins raced around in a state of confusion and panic. 'Those we didn't want — the males and older females, and those with any scars or shark-bites — we turned loose. It got to the point where we caught some of them rather regularly,' he writes.

Some of the dolphins, including pregnant mothers and nursing calves, were fatally maimed during such capture attempts. Others even died of shock. In an investigative report published in 1975, W.A. Walker estimated that as many as two out of five *Tursiops* died during captures in southern Californian waters between 1966 and 1973.

Doug Cartlidge had been an international dolphin trainer for over 10 years before he went on one of these outings off the Great Barrier Reef for Sea World in Australia. 'We were looking for a young, spotless male dolphin to do shows. We spotted a group of three and followed them into an estuary. Having cornered them, we put down the nets and waded in. The first dolphin we picked up was an old male that was too large for the show, so we let him go. The next was a large female who was covered in scratch-marks. She was no good so we hauled her over the net too. The third was a young male with flawless skin, just what we were looking for. So we netted him. For some reason I glanced over my shoulder. The other two dolphins had not swum away; they were lying on their sides watching us. I felt uneasy, but we had a job to do. We lifted him onto a stretcher and went back to the boat. Once on board we had to work fast, covering his skin with lanolin to prevent dehydration and spraying him with water. We were about to leave when I noticed the two dolphins were right beside the boat. They must have followed us back.

'Then it dawned on me — we'd taken away their calf.' From that moment on, Doug realized that he could no longer do this work with a clear conscience.

Wrenching a dolphin from family members and close companions not only disrupts the social structure of a pod. Because dolphins form strong attachments to one another, it must also be very distressing for both the individual and those it leaves behind.

Recent studies by the Center for Post Traumatic Stress Disorder in the United States indicate that human and animal victims of severe trauma sustain permanent changes in brain chemistry which trigger adrenalin surges, panic attacks, depression and physical and emotional numbing. Literature on dolphin captures indicates that wrenching wild dolphins from their social groups and habitat is a traumatic event of comparable magnitude and intensity to those which produced the brain changes in animals within the afore-cited studies. The stress of capture may have a lasting effect on such sensitive animals.

In an investigative report into the causes of death of captive dolphins, Karen L. Steurer suggests that the high number of deaths that occur during the animals' first two years in captivity may well be linked to capture shock. 'If stress in the captive environment is indeed a factor in mortality, it would follow that some forms of stress develop only after a considerable period of time,' she postulates.

Limitations on taking dolphins from the wild are lax. In the early days, it was a free-for-all situation: anyone could go out and catch as many dolphins as they wished. Even rare animals were not protected, and dolphinariums had no qualms about putting them on display. O'Barry tells of how he was involved in capturing the only known albino dolphin in the world in South Carolina. She was nearly eight foot long with pure white skin, pink eyes and mouth, and black teeth. They pursued her for 10 months before eventually netting 'Carolina Snowball' along with her calf, who was named Sonny Boy. Although her trainer was the infamous Adolph Frohn, she proved to be an intractable sort, learning only one simple trick. But she was the Seaquarium's star attraction, drawing millions of people from around the world to see her. Three years later she developed an infection at the base of her tail. She began swimming erratically one day and, to the horror of watching tourists, veered into the picture window with a sickening thud. She died shortly afterwards.

Between 1938 and 1980 the United States took a minimum of 1,500 live dolphins from the sea. When demand from dolphinariums rocketed during the 1960s there was barely any proper monitoring or record-keeping of the number of dolphins being caught.

Now, however, America is one of the few countries that has legislation regarding the harassment and capture of dolphins. The Marine Mammal Protection Act, passed in 1972, rules that any prospective catcher must apply for a permit. Requests are considered and permission is granted by the National Marine Fisheries Service. Unfortunately, many other countries throughout the world have no restrictions on catching dolphins in their territorial waters. In the last 10 years, Japan alone has captured 500 dolphins for amusement parks, and many dolphins are still being sacrificed for the sake of our entertainment. In 1980, for example, a capture attempt made by the International Dolphin Show, a dolphin trading outfit run by the Swiss entrepreneur Bruno Liendhart off Taiwan's Penghu Islands, resulted in the horrific deaths of 60 dolphins.

Although this scandal was hushed up, others have caused a public outcry. The plight of Lemo and Nemo, two of Leindhardt's dolphins, attracted attention from the British press after the animals were abandoned in the Meridien Hotel's swimming-pool in Cairo. The dolphins were close to starvation and obviously traumatized by the time aid arrived. Doug Cartlidge, sponsored by the animal charity Zoocheck, flew into Cairo to care for them. He was later joined by Mr David Taylor, an international 'dolphin' veterinary surgeon. After a court order was granted, Lemo and Nemo were flown to Marineland in Antibes to recuperate. And yet, because they are still the property of Leindhart, their story remains unresolved.

A New Life Begins

Dolphins beginning a life in captivity must wonder what on earth is happening to them. Having been lifted from a naturally buoyant environment and put on a stretcher, they experience the pull of gravity for the first time. Heavily sedated to prevent panic, for some, the whole event must seem like a dream or, more accurately, a nightmare. After a journey which may even involve a plane flight, the dolphin eventually arrives at its new home. If lucky, it may be taken to a seawater lagoon. More likely, the dolphin's new home will be a large concrete tank resembling an outsized swimming-pool. In *The Rose-Tinted Menagerie*, William Johnson, animal welfare consultant to Prince Sadruddin Aga Khan's Bellerive Foundation, writes: 'From the moment of capture every single individual must be kept afloat by injections of synthetic vitamins, broadspectrum antibiotics, fungicides and hormones. Without them they would live no longer than a few days, succumbing to infections and malignant parasites as stress ravages their natural immunity.'

Missing their family and friends, these dolphins may find solace in being among their own kind as they take in their bleak surroundings. Where now are the familiar sounds of the ocean, the gentle rhythms of the tides and passing shoals of fish?

While there are various reports of dolphins comforting and physically supporting others that are in distress (see the story of Pauline in Chapter Five), many ex-trainers say that in their experience, dolphins living under the stress of captivity can be uncharacteristically unkind. Older dolphins, particularly males, may bully youngsters. As Doug Cartlidge explains: 'In the wild, a young dolphin may pacify another by getting out of its way. In a confined pool, where there is nowhere to hide, it gets chased round and round in circles. The aggressive dolphin thinks the youngster is choosing to taunt him and will go on the attack.' Although confrontations doubtless occur in the wild, in captivity the submissive dolphin is definitely at a disadvantage. Such animals are often bitten or bashed by their elders and 'betters'. Dolphins under stress can also become angry with their trainers and keepers. They may snap their jaws loudly, or speed towards a swimming trainer as if to ram him, only veering away at the last minute. Even friendly wild dolphins that are annoyed by attention-seekers are known to act in this way.

Eventually, the captive newcomer finds its place amongst the other dolphins. As new friendships are forged, life must seem less lonely. Whether dolphins kept in bland concrete tanks ever really acclimatize to their new environment is highly questionable. With its wealth of marine life, the ocean is an unending source of stimulation for these inquisitive and intelligent creatures. In the wild, dolphins spend much of their time hunting for fish, an activity from which they seem to derive great pleasure. In captivity, meals, consisting of dead, defrosted fish, are regimented; gone are the days when the dolphin could eat to its heart's content.

In fact, every aspect of its existence is now controlled. Unless pumped directly from the ocean, the water these dolphins live in will be an artificially salted equivalent with disinfectant chemicals added. Chlorine used to kill bacteria may 'bleach' the animals' skin a shade lighter and sting their eyes, which could explain why captive dolphins often seem to be 'squinting'. Concern has also arisen over the potential toxicity of substances formed when chlorine reacts with organic material in the dolphin's faeces and urine.

Showtime

Within the dolphinarium industry, it is generally felt that training and performing is beneficial to the dolphin's wellbeing. On the surface, these creatures seem eager to participate in shows. While carrying out spectacular aerial leaps and flips, they give every impression of having fun. However, the notion that they are performing purely out of love for their trainer or for our entertainment is a clever illusion.

For dolphins deprived of any other stimulation, it is true that learning and carrying out tricks may help to ease the boredom of their existence. Trainers use a technique known as 'positive reinforcement'. This basically means that when a dolphin performs a certain stunt, be it waving a flipper or jumping, it receives a fish as a reward. Dolphins then learn to associate hand signals with certain tricks. (But because dolphins often experiment with different actions that may earn them a fish, trainers often say it is hard to determine who is teaching whom.)

To make sure that dolphins are ready and eager to perform during shows, the animals are kept hungry. Then, after each trick, they receive a fish. Dolphins that let their trainers down by refusing to oblige are 'punished' by having their reward withheld. In their defence, trainers say you cannot force a dolphin to do tricks, but hunger is doubtless a strong incentive.

A diary kept at Brighton Dolphinarium during 1984 and documenting the performances of Missie (then known as 'Baby'), Silver and Poppy, provides a revealing insight into ways of encouraging a reluctant dolphin to toe the line.

11 February. Baby not interested in shows and her food was cut to $3\frac{1}{4}$ lbs.

12 February. Total shutdown on first two shows, showing a little interest on 14.15 show, performed skittles, retrieved a ring and no more, ate fish given. Doesn't seem to be sick. Either Silver is stopping her from working or she's having us on. We'll see what happens tomorrow when she's hungry. Had no fish, only vitamins.

13 February. Baby refused to work on all shows. 3lbs.

14 February. Still not working. 4lbs.

15 February. Eating OK. Looks a little thin. 3lbs.

16 February. Finally starting to work – did bow, as well as hoop jump, somersaults, skittles, teeth-cleaning, kiss, backstroke. $4\frac{3}{4}$ lbs.

17 February. Still very wary of Poppy and Silver but she is also playing up a bit, hoping to get free fish because of what happened to her. $2\frac{1}{2}$ lbs.

18 February. Finally showing signs of improvement – she is looking a little thin but this is to be expected, as I have cut her food consumption down. 4lbs.

19 February. Did every trick asked of her. I think we've broken her!

Bearing in mind that dolphins kept in captivity should receive between 20lbs and 25lbs of fish per day, it is not surprising that Missie eventually gave in to her trainer.

Sadly, this does not appear to be an isolated case. Many ex-trainers admit to having withheld food from disobedient dolphins. Amy Brady, who worked at Ocean World in Fort Lauderdale in the United States for eight months in 1987, claimed that a dolphin named Shadow died during what staff referred to as 'Black July' in that year, after instructions were given by the head trainer not to feed the dolphin because he would not leave his pen.

Being intelligent creatures, most captive dolphins take the line of least resistance, performing on request. Only the most spirited, it seems, refuse to cooperate. To be fair, most trainers whom we met seemed genuinely fond of their wards and had no wish to starve them. But both trainers and dolphins alike are under pressure to put on a good show. For dolphinariums are commercial ventures, and the dolphins are there for our entertainment.

Every day, crowds flock to see 'Flipper's Beach Party' at the Miami Seaquarium. Still portrayed as the hero of the day, Flipper comes to the rescue of a girl trapped in a smoking house by putting out the fake fire with a hose. To get the party rolling, he switches on the radio with his snout, then dances with his glamorous bikini-clad girlfriend. It all seems harmless enough. Yet such tricks give an entirely distorted view of the dolphins' natural behaviour and lifestyle, and in so doing, completely discredit the argument that dolphin shows fuel our appreciation of dolphins in the wild. Instead, we leave with the impression that these creatures are Disney-like characters that wear sunglasses, sing 'Happy Birthday', tow their 'friends' around in dinghies, and wave goodbye to us.

In their defence, trainers say such stunts are only an extension of 'natural behaviour'. Dolphins do flap their flippers and perform aerial leaps in the wild. In shows, however, such behaviour is given new and false meanings. If a wild dolphin began nodding its head rapidly with its mouth open, and uttered a string of squeaky noises, it would probably be extremely angry, for these are blatant signs of aggression. Yet, in a show, we are seduced into thinking the dolphins are 'nodding in agreement' and 'saying yes'. In any case, some tricks are distinctly unnatural. No untrained dolphin would walk backwards on its tail or beach itself on a stage. In our view, the ungainly, jerky movement of tail-walking, which we saw portrayed as 'breakdancing' (!) hardly highlights the grace, fluidity and beauty of dolphins in motion. And yet such shows are invariably greeted with enthusiastic applause. Why?

William Johnson suggests that the demand for such entertainment is a reflection of a sick society. Keeping animals in captivity and getting them to perform for us is, in his view, nothing less than a gross form of exploitation. The belief that other creatures exist solely for our convenience is a legacy we have inherited from the Romans. In those times, anthropocentrism, a view of man as the central figure in the universe, took root and flourished. From this superior position, man felt justified in treating all animals as mere objects of amusement. The Romans adored circuses at which dignified creatures such as elephants, tigers and bears were cajoled into standing upright and dancing in order to portray them as 'human'. While we may pride ourselves on being more 'civilized' these days, in the 1970s dolphins were participating in strip-shows at the Moulin Rouge nightclub in Paris, France.

Anthropocentrism, Johnson continues, may be described as a latent human condition thriving only in environments of greed, materialism, narrow-mindedness and deep-seated insecurity. Just as it contributed to the downfall of the Roman civilization, the belief that we have the right to exploit, dominate and control nature is largely responsible for our current ecological crisis.

Lying at the very heart of the problem is humanity's aversion to what we perceive as chaos and anarchy, something Erich Fromm described as 'fear of freedom'. Yet if we continue to rebel against the supposed capriciousness of Creation, we will never feel truly at peace, and nor will the dolphins that we subject to imprisonment.

Signs of Sadness

Dolphinariums portray their inhabitants as happy, well-balanced creatures, but are they really? Many people concerned with animal welfare are not so convinced.

'The dolphin's endearing smile is its greatest downfall,' says Ric O'Barry: 'It could be going through hell, but because it keeps on smiling, you'd never know.' However, there is good reason to suppose that dolphins held in captivity may suffer from acute stress. For although dolphins do enjoy the company of people, *en masse*, we may appear threatening. In May 1989, three dolphins became ill after being stared and shouted at by more than 1000 people per hour at the newly opened National Aquarium in Baltimore, 50 days after their arrival. 'We looked at everything that we thought could be stressful to them, such as the configuration of the tank, the temperature, being watched by the public, light levels and noise from the pumps,' said Professor Michael Stoskopf of Johns Hopkins University School of Medicine in the United States. 'We found the real problem was the people. They [the dolphins] didn't have enough room to get away from the crowds. Fleeing from the people, they congregated in a spot where noise from the tank's pumps was loudest, and they were more unhappy than ever.' The dolphins were flown to the Dolphin Research Center in Grassy Key, Florida, and within six months they seemed to have recovered.

To our mind, the worst fate for a dolphin is to be held in a 'petting' pool. The pools are small and shallow, so that people can get close enough to touch and stroke the dolphins, which are often completely surrounded by people demanding their attention. Sometimes it is also possible to feed the animals fish. One of the saddest sights we have ever seen was at Ocean World in Fort Lauderdale, Florida. Here a dolphin called Polly, who had one deformed fin, was floating listlessly in a pool no bigger than an average sized swimming-pool, where she had been for the last 24 years. The next day we found out that Polly had died.

Recent studies carried out in the United States suggest that an inordinate number of captive dolphins are indeed falling victim to typical stress-related illnesses such as heart attacks and gastric ulcers. Even back in 1963, at the first International Symposium on Cetacean Research, Dr Kenneth Norris said he believed that 'stress is the most severe health problem we face in keeping cetaceans, particularly those under severe training.'

After studying dolphin behaviour and intelligence both in captivity and in the wild,

Professor Giorgio Pilleri, director of the Brain Anatomy Institute of the University of Berne in Switzerland, believes that dolphins held in confinement are likely to become psychologically deformed. Freedom deprivation, coupled with the destruction of the dolphins' sophisticated social structure, leads to despair, suicidal behaviour, unnatural aggression and feelings of intense claustrophobia — symptoms similar to people kept in prison and solitary confinement. Jacques Cousteau came to a similar conclusion when his own dolphins, confined for study purposes, attempted suicide. His captives hit their heads against the hard edge of their pool until they died. Deeply saddened by this experience, Cousteau made this strong statement: 'No aquarium, no tank in a marineland, however spacious it may be, can begin to duplicate the conditions of the sea. And no dolphin who inhabits one of those aquariums can be considered normal.'

Even dolphins kept in seawater pens that border on the sea can show signs of sadness. 'Poor Juan,' writes Leah Lemieux, a frequent visitor to performing dolphins which live in a lagoon at the tourist resort of Cabana del Sol in Cuba. 'He always stays by the net-fence, sometimes raising his body out of the water as if trying to go over it and making loud noises of frustration. He also pulls on the net over and over again.'

Dolphins may also reveal a lack of happiness by failing to reproduce successfully. During 20 years at Brighton Dolphinarium in the United Kingdom, a dolphin called Missie became pregnant six times. Two of her calves were stillborn, another two lived no longer than a month, one named Souki died aged three years, and Missie's latest baby, Minnie, survived just five months. In a review of American dolphinariums, Karen Steurer found that over half the dolphins born in captivity were dead at birth. Of course, not all baby dolphins survive in the wild either. However, research suggests that their chances are much higher when the natural social structure of the pod is intact.

Perhaps the greatest pity of captivity is that dolphins held in such conditions invariably die prematurely. In the wild, males may live well into their 30s, while females often reach more than 40 years of age. From a census conducted in 1976, two researchers, L.H. Cornell and E.D. Asper, calculated that the average age of bottlenose dolphins in captivity was just 5.4 years. Of the 199 dolphins that died in American dolphinariums between 1975 and 1987, only four died of old age. The most common cause of death tends to be pneumonia, caused by an infection affecting the creatures' respiratory system. Stress and other factors may also weaken their immune systems, making them more susceptible to disease. Some marine scientists also think it possible that dolphins may be at risk from cold and 'flu viruses caught from people.

In spite of such pressures, captive dolphins in their 20s bear witness to the remarkable adaptability and psychological resilience of these creatures, for life in confinement is very different from that in the wild. And yet, as we shall now see, even after years of living such an artificial existence, it seems that some dolphins never lose touch with their natural instincts, and can re-adapt to life in the wild.

INTO THE BLUE: REHABILITATING CAPTIVE DOLPHINS

After the death of Kathy (see p. 137), Ric O'Barry set his heart on releasing dolphins from captivity and preventing any further capture of those living in the wild. His first attempt at freeing a dolphin involved in a scientific research project at the Lerner Marine Laboratory on Bimini was a dismal failure. In true cavalier style, O'Barry stole into the pen in the middle of the night and opened it, hoping that the delighted dolphin would simply swim out to the open sea. But 'Charlie Brown' would not budge despite O'Barry's words of encouragement. Caught red-handed, O'Barry was charged with attempted theft and ended up in gaol.

It became clear to him that dolphins held in captivity are – not surprisingly – nervous of returning to their natural environment. Even though unhappy, they have grown accustomed to confinement, and are dependent on humans for food. Simply setting them free and expecting them to fend for themselves is naïve. Such dolphins have first to undergo a rehabilitation process which involves, amongst other things, teaching them to catch live fish.

In 1970, O'Barry established the Dolphin Project, and with money donated by Stephen Stills (of the band Crosby, Stills and Nash), he bought two dolphins from Milton Santini, a female called Florida and a male called Liberty. After successfully teaching the dolphins to feed themselves, O'Barry flew them to Eleuthera, an island in the Bahamas, where they were released and swam off into the blue. At the time, the project was criticized because the dolphins were not tracked and their fate is still unknown.

The next rehabilitation opportunity arose when Dr John Lilly decided to return his captive dolphins to the wild. Joe and Rosie were taken from the Gulf of Mexico in 1980 for an ambitious project on communication which was set up by Toni, John Lilly's wife. The experiments lasted seven years, and the results were only partially successful. When the research folded, the fate of the dolphins hung in the balance. While decisions were being made, Joe and Rosie stayed at the Dolphin Research Center in the Florida Keys. Meanwhile, Alan Slifka, chairman of the Board of the Big Apple Circus, and three other people, including Virginia Coyle, formed the Oceanic Research Communication Alliance (ORCA). They were granted a permit by the National Marine Fisheries Service to pilot a programme designed to find out how captive dolphins in general should be rehabilitated and returned to the wild.

Joe and Rosie – the latter by now pregnant – were the perfect candidates. Ric O'Barry and a whale biologist, Abigail Ailing, were given the task of 'untraining' these dolphins. O'Barry recalls that the first time Joe caught a live fish he looked very pleased with himself. Because sonar sounds for locating food bounce off the concrete walls of a pool, no doubt creating for a dolphin an impression similar to that of being in a hall of mirrors, captive dolphins tend to stop using this sophisticated system, and it takes a while for it to work efficiently again.

After a while, Joe and Rosie became less interested in their human companions, and began to spend more time by the fence separating their pen from the sea. For some reason, dolphins will not jump over fences even if they want to escape, so, when the dolphins seemed ready to take to the open water they were freeze-banded for easy identification on either side of their dorsal fins – Joe with an arrow and Rosie with a circle – and were then transported to a sheltered tidal creek in the Wassaw Island National Wildlife Refuge on Georgina Island, where they were set free. In the summer of 1989, the shrimpers and other seamen in the ORCA sighting and tracking network spotted Joe and Rosie swimming with wild dolphins at least nine times. They reported that Rosie looked to be accompanied by her calf. In 1990, under the guidance of cetacean expert Dr Randall Wells, two more captive dolphins called Echo and Misha also gained their freedom.

The most remarkable release to date took place in the clear blue waters of the Turks and Caicos Islands in autumn 1991. The candidates of the 'Into the Blue' project were three dolphins from Britain called Rocky, Missie and Silver. This rehabilitation programme was set up by the animal welfare charity, Zoocheck, with active support from Prince Sadruddin Aga Khan's Geneva-based Bellerive Foundation, and sponsorship from the British *Mail on Sunday* newspaper. In many ways, this project was unique, for each of the dolphins concerned had spent most of its life in captivity, and doubts were raised as to whether they could ever be returned to the wild. The 23-year-old male dolphin, Rocky, was the first to arrive at the protected 80-acre lagoon belonging to P.R.I.D.E., a local conservation group founded to protect reefs and islands from degradation and exploitation.

Rocky's chance for freedom had come when the owners of Morecambe Marineland decided to close down the dolphinarium rather than update the facilities as required by impending new legislation. For a while, Rocky's fate seemed uncertain while his owner decided whether to risk releasing a dolphin that had spent 19 years – nearly his entire life – in captivity or to sell him to another dolphinarium. The 'Into the Blue' team, led by ex-trainer Doug Cartlidge and Lucy Maiden of Zoocheck were persuasive, and Rocky was to become a pioneer amongst dolphins. But events did not run smoothly. The day before Rocky was due to depart, he was taken from his home in Morecambe to the Dolphin Centre at Flamingoland in Yorkshire. Eventually a court injunction had to be obtained before he could embark on his journey to the Caribbean. Rocky took the transatlantic flight in his stride and within minutes of being transferred to a special holding pen in the lagoon, he was swimming around and asking to be fed.

Meanwhile, Brighton Dolphinarium's new owners, Sea Life Centres, also came to the decision that the best future for Missie and Silver lay with 'Into the Blue'. Within two months these dolphins, too, were winging their way to a new life. Arriving at the lagoon must have felt like a dream. It was 22 years since Missie had swum in seawater, felt the waves, heard the ocean sounds and seen sunlight and the stars.

Within a few days, all three dolphins were swimming together in unison. They leapt and gambolled in the crystal-clear, shimmering waters, obviously relishing the sheer extent of their temporary home. For the next five months they underwent a programme of rehabilitation. This involved 'deprogramming', to stop them doing tricks for food, as well as teaching them to catch their own fish again.

Once approval had been given by consultant veterinarians, the three dolphins were taken to a release site off the remote island of West Caicos. William Travers, director of Zoocheck, happily reports that these dolphins have been sighted on numerous occasions by local fishermen since that eventful day. 'Silver has now travelled many hundreds of miles and spends time with Jojo, the friendly local dolphin. Rocky and Missie are together and have been spotted swimming with other wild dolphins. All sightings so far are within the reef which forms a natural reserve and makes this an ideal site to release rehabilitated dolphins. As there is no net tuna fishing and the sea here is unpolluted, the dolphins are as safe as they could possibly be.'

At one time, dolphins held captive for so long had no option but to end their days in small pools. Now there *is* another option. Rehabilitation may not be a viable proposition for all dolphins, especially those born into captivity. But ultimately it is up to us to decide whether or not dolphins are given the chance for renewed freedom. For, as William Travers points out, 'Everyone who visits a dolphinarium is, in effect, committing the dolphins to a life in captivity.'

THE FUTURE

Even those who feel that there is nothing wrong in holding dolphins captive, admit that the conditions of their confinement are often less than acceptable. Dolphinariums vary the world over, so it is impossible to generalize about this. While some keep their dolphins in quite spacious seawater lagoons, others hold them in cramped concrete tanks.

In 1985, in a report into British dolphinariums commissioned by the Department of the Environment, Dr Margaret Klinowska of the Marine Mammal Unit at Cambridge University in the United Kingdom commented that the construction of dolphin pools has nothing in common with the dolphin's natural environment, and everything to do with the requirement that the animals must perform. This, in turn, makes it difficult to imagine the animals in their natural environment. Amongst a wide range of recommendations to improve the conditions of captivity, Dr Klinowska outlined mimimum dimensions for pool sizes, based on standards adopted in America. These are due to become law in 1993, and at present none of the British dolphinariums meets such standards. Criteria for keeping dolphins in captivity vary from country to country. In Alberta, Canada, three dolphins are on display in a small tank in the middle of the West Edmonton Mall, merely to entertain shoppers.

Those who oppose keeping dolphins in captivity feel that simply building slightly bigger pools will not make much difference to a dolphin's quality of life. 'In the wild, dolphins may swim distances of up to 50 miles and dive to depths of 100 feet. No pool can ever meet the conditions wild dolphins are used to,' says Ric O'Barry implacably. 'It is the dolphin's birthright to swim in a straight line in the ocean as far as its heart desires.'

One possible solution to the dilemma was raised at the International Whaling Commission (IWC) 'Whales Alive' Conference, held in Boston in 1983. Cetacean scientists recommended that dolphinariums should in due course be replaced with coastal marine reserves. Although perhaps fenced off from the surrounding ocean, in such reserves the dolphins would nevertheless be free to come and go as they pleased. Indeed, they could even choose whether or not they wished to make contact with human beings. The only performance provided for the public would be the experience of observing the dolphins' natural and spontaneous interaction with each other. Under such circumstances, by relinquishing our need to control and dominate these creatures, a bond of true friendship might have a chance to flourish.

Chapter 10

THE DOLPHINS OF WAR

INTRODUCTION

Picture, if you will, the murky waters of Cam Ranh Bay, Vietnam. A dolphin speeds towards a Vietnamese frogman and skewers him with a lance strapped to its beak. Now travel to the Persian Gulf. A team of dolphins dive deep into the ocean and use their complex echo location to hunt down stray torpedoes and detect enemy mines. These are not episodes from Robert Merle's film *The Day of the Dolphin*, nor are they part of any science-fiction series. This is the reality of the dolphins of war, trained by the US Navy to seek and destroy.

Since time immemorial, man has exploited animals and used them to wage war against his fellow men. Horses, elephants and even dogs have been drafted into army service when the need has arisen. Yet dolphins are being abused in a particularly invidious way. Armed with explosives, trained to seek out enemy mines and vessels and to destroy them, dolphin 'kamikazes' are being trained by both the American and Russian navies. But to what purpose? This is surely one of the most sadistic displays of man's inhumanity to man – and to the dolphin.

IN THE NAVY

Such work began with innocent intentions in the late 1950s, when research was initially geared towards analysing the dolphin's hydrodynamics and sonar. The animals were poked, prodded and put through rigorous testing to discover how they could swim at high speeds for such long periods of time, in the hope that the Navy could learn from their aquatic prowess and improve its own vessels. Intrigued by the dolphin's ultrasonic and echo-locative abilities, the Navy also carried out a wide variety of experiments to determine whether dolphins could be trained to locate and retrieve 'lost' objects from the seabed, with a view to using the creatures to replace expensive electronic equipment and human divers. A respected dolphin expert, Ken Norris, was involved in some of the Navy's early research, before this was directed at more sinister aims. Norris reports that the Navy originally intended to use dolphins both as a model for a hydrodynamic torpedo that could move as easily through the water as these creatures, and to develop sophisticated dolphin-like sonar equipment. However, Norris is now opposed to the use of dolphins for war purposes.

In the early 1960s, the work of John Lilly and other scientists investigating dolphin communication and intelligence alerted the Navy to the fact that dolphins possessed an intelligence second only to man's, and that they had the ability to learn tasks quickly and efficiently. The Navy's curiosity was sufficiently aroused to start 'secret' dolphin research, but early reports of these plans quickly leaked out. At the 1963 International Convention for the Study of Cetaceans, Dr L. Harrison from the Zoological Society of London in the United Kingdom was appalled by the suggestion that cetaceans could be exploited in such a way: 'It seems that some people are proposing to prostitute their biological work on the Cetacea and involve the animals in human international strife by training them as underwater watchdogs to guard naval installations from frogmen, or to act as unmanned submarines.'

The ex-dolphin-trainer Ric O'Barry was approached by the CIA at this time and was asked to set up a programme of dolphin research aimed at turning dolphins into 'weapons of war'. At the time, O'Barry was the trainer on the *Flipper* TV series, which had actually used the idea of dolphins progressing from leaping through hoops and performing harmless tricks to attaching magnetic mines to enemy vessels. But to O'Barry, this had only been a fantasy, and he wanted no part in what he considered to be a diabolical affront to both man and dolphin.

However, the Navy remained undeterred, and continued the programme without O'Barry's cooperation. It went ahead with dolphin training, and, as previously mentioned, used dolphins in both the Vietnam and Persian Gulf wars. In fact, from 1960 to 1989, the US Navy is known to have employed 240 dolphins. One of the first and most famous of the dolphin 'draftees' was Notty, a Pacific white-sided dolphin that was enlisted from an aquarium in Los Angeles and taken to the Naval Ordnance Test Center at China Lake, California. The aim was to study the dolphin's sensory systems, sonar and diving physiology in order to develop more sophisticated naval equipment. However, the small enclosure at the centre was too restrictive for in-depth experiments to take place, and Notty was moved to the Office of Naval Research at Point Mugu, California. Meanwhile, the Navy had collected other dolphins, which it subjected to a battery of rigorous tests in order to learn more about their sonar, sensory systems and aquatic ergonomics. Much of this early research was fairly innocuous and dedicated to the study of swimming techniques and speed, but the main goal of the Point Mugu project was to train dolphins to retrieve, ultimately for more sinister purposes. Blair Irvine, a trainer who worked for the Navy from 1965 to 1969, used acoustic signals to give commands and fish as rewards in training these dolphins. The animals could apparently retrieve mines quickly and efficiently: 'Navy divers took half an hour to find one mine and put a line on it. We showed that a dolphin could potentially mark several mines much more quickly than that.'

Of course, it is true to say that this kind of research could save many lives, but the fact remains that dolphins are not free to choose whether they want to be involved in such activities.

One dolphin which captured the interest of the media at the time was Tuf Guy, also known as Tuffy, who was involved in a project at Sealab II in La Jolla, California. At the underwater base, Tuffy was trained to carry tools and messages between the laboratory and the surface. He was able to undertake tasks that were physically impossible for human divers, and of course suffered none of the ill-effects to which we are susceptible when diving back and forth from great depths to the surface for long periods of time.

In the late 1960s, with the advent of the Vietnam war, the Navy's attentions turned to more invidious research. According to Blair Irvine, the American government initially suggested deploying dolphins in Vietnam in the murky waters of Cam Ranh Bay. Trials to create an 'anti-swimmer system' to protect ships from enemy divers and a 'mine-hunting system' to locate hazardous hidden mines were carried out by dolphin-trainers. At the forefront of this research was James Fitzgerald, a manufacturer of sonic equipment. He claims that the experiments showed dolphins to be almost infallible. According to Fitzgerald, they were trained to pull the mouthpiece of a regulator from a hostile diver's mouth, or to push the diver to the surface and then to trigger an alert signal. In this regard, he commented that 'Between a man and a dolphin, there was no contest.' In an interview in 1985, Ken Woodal, who used to be part of SEAL, the Navy's Sea, Air and Land unit, revealed that he had worked with three dolphins in Vietnam who were trained to attach mines to enemy piers.

But the interest in 'dolphin warfare' did not end with the Vietnam war. In 1987, the Navy airlifted six Pacific bottlenose dolphins to the Persian Gulf, where they were used for underwater surveillance and to detect mines and missiles. Although these operations were 'top secret' at the time, Navy officials have now admitted that dolphins were present in both Vietnam and the Persian Gulf.

Top Secret

Undercover researchers now claim that the US Navy has at least 130 dolphins and a number of other sea mammals at its main bases in Hawaii, San Diego and Key West. The dolphins are caught by Marine Mammal Productions Inc. of Gulfport, Mississippi, one of the largest dolphin-catchers, and are then brought to Seaco Inc. in San Diego, where they receive basic training. From here they are dispatched to the naval bases for intensive training. Their main tasks include retrieving things that have fallen overboard and finding and recovering wayward torpedoes, but there is also a most disturbing suggestion that they have been trained to perform as 'kamikaze' missiles, swimming into enemy vessels whilst armed with explosive mines. However, there is little evidence to prove this theory and Navy spokesmen have claimed that it would be a waste of both time and money, as dolphins are expensive to buy and train. Other people have suggested that weapons have been designed to be fired solely by dolphins. According to Rick Trout, a former trainer who worked under contract for the Navy from 1985 to 1989, a 'Nose Cone' gun, a device designed to fit over the snout of the dolphin, has been designed. Attached to the fibreglass nose cone is a canister made of styrofoam, which could contain a spring-loaded firing mechanism that shoots a .45-calibre bullet on contact with its target. However, Trout doubts whether dolphins will actually carry out what is intended. In a trial in the Persian Gulf in 1987, a dolphin that he was training repeatedly failed to hit the target diver and, Trout says, 'The dolphin just laid its chin on the guy's shoulder.'

Nevertheless, the thought of employing dolphins to carry out this kind of mission is disquieting to say the least. It raises the question of where all such research will end. Dolphin experts say that the Navy's research is now focused on using the dolphin's incredible echo-locative facilities to detect long-range nuclear missiles, and there is additionally a growing fear that the Russians, who have also been exploiting the dolphin's abilities for warfare purposes, may use the animals to counter-attack the Americans. (Of course, for every new weapon that man creates, his enemies must then develop a counter-measure.) All this has led the US Navy to investigate devices which can jam the sonar of these 'enemy dolphins', so protecting its own interests. Far-fetched as it may seem, there are fears that the military deployment of dolphins will escalate, and there is already evidence that huge amounts of money are being invested in expanding the Navy's marine research.

Sam LaBudde, a conservationist renowned for his undercover exposé of the tuna-fishing industry, points out that this tactical use of dolphins has the potential to put wild dolphin populations at risk, although critics say that his theories are overly paranoid. 'This kind of operation could lead to the indiscriminate killing of dolphins. If both the United States and Russia are deploying dolphins for defence purposes, then any that happen to be unfortunate enough to be in an area where there is naval activity, run the risk of being annihilated – who's to know whose side they are on?' And even naval staff have commented on the dilemma presented by deploying dolphin weapon systems. In 1981, Navy Lt Commander Douglas Burnett wrote: 'In a hostile confrontation, both sides will have to consider dolphins as potential enemy biosensors or weapons. In some situations, there may be no choice except to destroy dolphins or any marine mammals presenting a similar threat . . . it may be a sound decision to protect shipping . . . by poisoning the surrounding waters to remove the threat of dolphin attacks, which would, coincidentally, remove a sizeable proportion of the area's ecology.'

Using dolphins for such warlike purposes has also created another problem. The Navy has admitted that some of its dolphins have permanently escaped from captivity. This raises the question, what potentially dangerous and offensive behaviour might such an escaped dolphin exhibit when encountering an innocent recreational diver? We shudder to think of the possible consequences.

Dolphin Sentries

More recently, the Navy proposed a project in which dolphins are to be used as sentinels at its Bangor base in Washington State. It plans to use 16 Atlantic bottlenose dolphins to guard a fleet of Trident nuclear submarines and to keep the dolphins in pens measuring approximately 25 ft sq. – a claustrophobic space for any creature used to the never-ending freedom of the ocean. One of the most galling aspects of this proposal was that these dolphins were to be removed from their natural habitat in the warm waters of the Gulf of Mexico, and transported to the freezing waters of the north-west Pacific. The temperature boundaries of the bottlenose dolphin range from between 10°C–28°C, which is considerably warmer than that of the Hood Canal at the Bangor base. One dolphin named Nalo had already died in naval captivity, only 11 days after being removed from Hawaii to the Puget Sound on a similar exercise. Unsurprisingly therefore, this recent proposal has caused a huge public outcry in America, whilst alerting dolphin-lovers throughout the world to these sinister events. In 1989, more than 15 environmental and animal rights groups filed a lawsuit against the Navy, the main charge being that in deploying dolphins at the Bangor base, they would be in violation of several federal statutes. Thankfully, their action has resulted in a 'major victory', according to Ric O'Barry. A federal court settlement in May 1990, ruled that the Navy must now get approval before it captures dolphins, and that it must do an Environmental Impact Study before using dolphins for any purpose whatsoever. 'At least this will help to monitor what the Navy is doing with dolphins,' commented O'Barry, 'For the first time, it must live within the guidelines of the 1972 Marine Mammal Protection Act like everyone else.' O'Barry has also pointed out that the idea of using dolphins as sentries is ridiculous. He challenged the Navy with a proposal that he could swim through any of its dolphin sentries and gain access to a submarine. 'It's so simple,' he explains, 'All I would need to do is to take a fire-extinguisher underwater with me and turn it on when I got close to the dolphins. A fire-extinguisher will make a really weird sound underwater, and anyone who knows anything about dolphins would know that strange noises scare them away. If I can do it, so could any potential saboteur!' Unfortunately, the Navy declined to accept his challenge.

But it is not just the ethics of using dolphins as instruments of war that are in question. Many people believe that the animals are actually badly abused in captivity. Rick Trout, appalled by the maltreatment of dolphins held captive by the Navy, made his allegations public, despite the fact that he put himself at great risk by breaching naval confidence. He has claimed that not only do some trainers use food deprivation, solitary confinement and muzzles, but also that corporal punishment and acts of physical aggression are used in the training process. Although the Marine Mammal Commission investigated the claims made by Trout and other naval employees, it apparently failed to acknowledge most of the alleged problems. However, the Commission did recommend that future captures were halted until adequate veterinary care was provided and new nutritional guidelines were drawn up.

This report unfortunately also ignored the high mortality rate of naval dolphins. According to the Navy's own Marine Mammal Inventory Report, 63 out of 138 dolphins have perished in captivity – a mortality rate of 45 per cent. Necropsy reports have highlighted a wide variety of causes of death, such as gastroenteritis, failure to adapt, pneumonia, stomach ulcers, and kidney failure. Experts believe that many of these illnesses are stress-related and indicate that the dolphins are living in conditions which are detrimental to their health.

Like many other trainers who have worked in conjunction with the Navy, Trout believes that the $30 million that it spent on its dolphin programmes during the Reagan administration was money down the drain. 'The animals are supposed to be protecting things,' he explains, 'But they're not prepared. The servicemen they are protecting would not survive . . . I don't think the projects are ethical and I don't think they work.' Dolphins are known to be independent and unpredictable, and are not the ideal sentinels, as they also lose interest in tedious tasks. Apt to 'wander off-duty', they can also be disobedient and contrary. Ric O'Barry confirms this. 'A dolphin is not like a dog,' he says, 'Once they've eaten 20 lbs of fish, they don't care what you try to get them to do. They'll take off. They'll disobey. I wouldn't want them guarding half of our nuclear arsenal.'

Against the Grain

Even those people employed by the Navy have strong reservations about the ethics of a dolphin defence/offence programme. Rear-Admiral Eugene Carroll, deputy director of the Center for Defense Information, has commented that 'Training an instinctively gentle, non-aggressive animal to conduct violent attacks against human beings would be an inherently difficult process.' Although much of the supposed 'information' about the Navy's involvement is merely conjecture, Carroll believes there is cause for concern: 'The fact that the US Navy takes dolphins under a special exemption from the Marine Mammal Protection Act and trains them and employs them without the supervision prescribed by the Act is a further indication of the potentially damaging consequences of sending dolphins to war. If we are wise enough to protect dolphins from this madness, then someday we should have the wisdom to protect humans as well.'

As Ric O'Barry points out in his book *Behind the Dolphin Smile*, 'It's wrong to train dolphins to kill frogmen with compressed air. It's wrong to imprison them in small pens. It's wrong to transport them from warm waters that are their natural habitat into the icy depths of northern water where they are doomed to perish. It's wrong to take these beautiful, intelligent, complex wild creatures from the oceans and make them serve our human schemes.' When are we going to put an end to these inhuman and sadistic practices, which exploit the intelligence and abuse the freedom and dignity of these benign marine mammals?

Chapter Eleven

....

CONSERVATION

INTRODUCTION

Traditionally, dolphins have always been regarded as a good omen, and fishermen have treated them with respect. In centuries past, fisherman and dolphin even sometimes worked together, helping each other to make a good catch, and although rare, such cooperation is still a part of certain native cultures.

However, through greed and competition for precious natural resources, many fishermen have turned against these kindly creatures in recent years. They deliberately set nets on schools of wild dolphins when fishing for tuna, and in the race to make ever-greater catches, employ vast 'drift nets' that sweep up all marine life, including dolphins. Every year 1,000,000 or more dolphins die throughout the world as a result of such practices. Meanwhile, noxious industrial chemicals and wastes poured into our oceans are polluting and poisoning the home of these marine mammals. As a result of such blinkered destruction of their natural environment, some rare species of dolphins now teeter on the brink of extinction.

AN ANCIENT ASSOCIATION

Behold now what manner of happy hunting the Dolphins kindly to men array against the fishes in the island of Euboea, amid the Aegean waves.

Oppian, *Halieutica, V.*

In a display of mutual trust and respect, dolphins and men often fished together in ancient times. Tales of such occurrences in the Mediterranean Sea are recorded in the classical texts. The Greek poet Oppian and the Roman writer Aelian tell how dolphins used to join in torchlit fishing expeditions off the Euboean shores. Their accounts relate how local fishermen would set out at night when the weather was calm. At a chosen spot, they lowered their sails and lit special lanterns which supposedly dazzled any nearby shoal of fish. Seeing the glow, dolphins hurried to the scene. Attempting to escape the approaching boats, the fleeing fish found themselves hemmed in by the dolphins. As the fish huddled together in fright, the fishermen made their catch.

According to Aelian, the fishermen's aquatic accomplices received a just reward for their assistance. 'The dolphins approach as though demanding the profits of their common labour due them from this store of food. And the fishermen loyally and gratefully resign to their comrades in the chase their just portion.'

In Greece, this fishing practice appears to have continued until the beginning of this century. In a book published in 1907, entitled *La Pêche en Grèce*, the author, Nicholas Apostolides, describes how fishermen of the Sporades would catch quantities of garfish on dark October nights, using a method similar to that described by the ancient scholars. However, he proposed that in fact the fishermen took down their sails and began to row so that they could listen for dolphins chasing their prey. On hearing the splashing sound, the men lit fires of resinous wood in iron grills fixed to their bows. The light attracted plankton, and consequently the fish that feed on them, to the boats. If any of the garfish made for the open seas, the dolphins prevented their escape.

Furthermore, if Pliny, the well-known Roman historian, is to be believed, in ancient times, dolphins could actually also be called upon to help catch fish. He records such an incident occurring in a marshy area near Nismes in the Province of Narbonne. At a certain season, countless shoals of mullet rushed from the narrow mouth of the marsh out to sea. In anticipation, the entire population would gather on the shore and begin loudly shouting 'Snubnose!' – the Romans' less-than-endearing nickname for the dolphin.

Pliny suggests that the dolphins heard the people's plea and hastened to the spot to give assistance. On arrival, the animals aligned themselves along the opening, barring the fishes' passage to the sea and driving them into the shallows. The fishermen then put down their nets. Those mullet that leapt over the obstacles were caught by the dolphins. Apparently, the trusting dolphins were 'delighted' to be caught in the nets too as they glided between the swimming fishermen and boats to stop the fish getting away. When the task was accomplished, the dolphins would ask for their fair share of the catch, which the fishermen gladly gave them, 'for if a man sin against them in his arrogance, no more are the dolphins his helpers in fishing,' Pliny (rightly) concluded.

The notion of summoning dolphins in this way may sound improbable, yet on the other side of the world, some Australian Aborigines have been calling the creatures to assist with fishing since time immemorial. Up until about 100 years ago, a quite unique rapport existed between the natives of Amity Point in Moreton Bay, on the Pacific Coast of Queensland, and their aquatic friends. The people would sit on small hillocks of sand looking out to sea, nets at the ready. On seeing a shoal of mullet, they ran down the beach and splashed the water with their spears. Suddenly dolphins appeared and formed a barrier to prevent the fish breaking away. In a scene of apparent confusion, men and dolphins were seen splashing about together, both parties receiving their share of the catch. It is said that the Aborigines had a special way of calling to the dolphins, and even had names for some of them. One elderly dolphin was well-known and fondly referred to as 'Big Fellow of the tribe of porpoises'. He was often seen taking fish offered to him on the end of a spear. The Aborigines forbade any man to kill a dolphin, believing that dreadful consequences would follow if this happened.

Even today, some Aborigines still depend on the dolphins' cooperation when fishing. An aboriginal elder called Gaboo Ted Thomas tells how, as a young boy, he received his first fishing lesson. 'I was told to grab a stick and wade into the water. The grandfathers then slapped the water with their sticks and soon a small school of dolphins appeared in the bay. The dolphins herded the smaller fish into the shallows, where we could flip them ashore with our sticks.' According to Gaboo Ted Thomas, his people have fished this way for as long as they can remember.

Similar stories come from other regions of the world, too. Native peoples living along the banks of the Amazon in South America say the pink-bellied river dolphin, locally known as the *boto*, goes to fishermen with its mouth open for help if it has a catfish or something else stuck in its throat. In return, it rewards them with a full catch of fish. And in 1954, an American forestry expert working in Brazil called F.B. Lamb observed an Amazonian fisherman whistling for 'his' *boto*, which then herded fish into nearby shallow waters where the man could spear them. The man then shared the fish with the dolphin.

In central Asia, home of the Irrawaddy dolphin, fishing villages reputedly had their own special 'guardian' dolphin which was given a particular name. The fishermen believed that the dolphin purposely drew fish into their nets, and sometimes suits were brought in native courts to recover catches that 'their' dolphin had unintentionally made for rival villagers.

Of course, not all fishermen in times past regarded dolphins as special. In some parts of the world, these creatures have traditionally been hunted for centuries. It is a sad fact that thousands of dolphins are presently being sacrificed purely for the sake of human greed and commercial gain.

A CRUEL CONSPIRACY

The hunting of Dolphins is immoral and that man can no more draw nigh the gods as welcome sacrificer nor touch their altars with clean hands but pollutes those who share the same roof with him, who willingly devises destruction for Dolphins. For equally with human slaughter the gods abhor the deathly doom of the monarchs of the deep.

Oppian, *Halieutica.*

Viewed in the light of stories about the helpful and trusting nature of these marine mammals, some modern fishing practices seem all the more disgraceful. Of these, deliberately setting nets on schools of dolphins to catch tuna fish is probably the most repugnant. Every year this results in the unnecessary death of an estimated 100,000 dolphins. Such killings have been going on since the 1960s, but only in recent years has the true horror of this practice come to our attention.

The man single-handedly responsible for exposing this scandalous affair is the biologist Sam LaBudde. As an observer for the US government's National Marine Fisheries Service, LaBudde suspected that dolphins might be dying in order to fuel catches of tuna fish in the Eastern Tropical Pacific, but he had no proof. When he left to join the Earth Island Institute, a San Francisco-based conservation group, LaBudde conceived a plan.

Masquerading as a cook, he got a job on board a Panamanian tuna-fishing boat called the *Maria Luisa*. Amongst his few possessions was a video camera, which he said was a gift from his father. The crew had no idea LaBudde was working undercover, and were happy to let him film events that took place on the four-month Pacific expedition during the winter of 1987. The footage LaBudde shot was to provoke a public outcry, for it showed hundreds of terrified dolphins drowning to death in a seething mass of panic and chaos. This is why.

In a quirky symbiosis, tuna fish swim beneath schools of dolphins in the waters of the Eastern Tropical Pacific, an area of ocean stretching from Southern California to Chile. This association is not common in other seas around the world. In the past, tuna were caught individually by small coastal fishing-boats using rod and reel. The dolphins were safe because they were too intelligent to be lured by the bait. However, the early 1960s saw the advent of purse-seine nets which were capable of catching many more fish than the old method. Once these mile-long nylon nets encircle a shoal of tuna, the bottom is closed by drawing in cables using the ship's powerful winches, as if pulling on the drawstrings of a purse.

Before long, unscrupulous fishermen took to setting their nets for schools of dolphins, hoping to haul in any yellow-fin tuna swimming under them. Inspired by greed, the fishing companies' catching methods became increasingly sophisticated. They started using helicopters in an aerial search for dolphins. Fishermen then dropped underwater explosives known as 'seal bombs' around the dolphin school. The 190-decibel blast, considerably louder than a jumbo jet at take-off, shocks and deafens dolphins. Thrown into a state of confusion and panic, they stop swimming and huddle together. Any tuna fish below them follow suit. Speedboats then move in on the dolphins, encircling them with the net and preventing any individuals from breaking away. The whole operation is like a naval assault.

'Dolphins trapped in a tuna seine net have little chance of survival. In panic, they propel themselves straight up in the air, lifting the net with their beaks through the mesh, gasping for air, squealing with terror. Those in the open section of the net are also distressed, leaping and rolling around in the water in total confusion. As the net is heaved in, things get worse. Soon there are dolphins draped on the net like on a Christmas tree, thrashing and flailing, if not already dead and hopelessly enmeshed. I scrambled to cut lifeless bodies free from the net, but it was usually too late. They would be thrown over the stern back into the water. Those lucky enough to escape being hauled up were thrown back into the ocean, but few survived,' says LaBudde, who is still shocked by the scenes he has witnessed. If fishermen obey the Marine Mammal Protection Act, they will lower one side of the net so that the dolphins can leap to freedom. But, as LaBudde points out, being exhausted by a chase that can last anything up to 90 minutes, and stunned by the deafening blast, very few of the animals escape to safety. On some occasions, the fishermen have set nets around a whole school of dolphins, only to find that there are no tuna fish with them as the nets were drawn up. Hundreds of dolphins are then simply discarded as waste.

LaBudde's footage forms the focus of a disturbing film, *Where Have All the Dolphins Gone?*, designed to bring these horrifying events to the attention of people throughout the world. With this evidence to hand, in 1988 The Earth Island Institute of San Francisco launched an all-out campaign against the US tuna industry, urging the public to boycott all companies selling tuna caught in this way. The message was effective. In the spring of 1990 the major American supplier, Heinz, was the first to announce that it would no longer buy tuna from fishermen who set their nets on dolphins. The Earth Island Institute has also set various criteria for 'dolphin-friendly' tuna fish. These guidelines have been adopted by various conservation societies around the world.

(a) Tuna should not be caught by setting purse-seine nets set on dolphins, or in drift or gill nets of any kind that may result in the accidental death of dolphins. Only fish caught by the old-fashioned pole-and-line method is acceptable.

(b) Any company claiming to sell 'Dolphin-Friendly' tuna must be able to prove that it buys from fisheries complying with these standards. This involves regular inspections at the canneries. Tuna fish caught in drift nets are detected by signs of bruising. The yellow-fin variety tends to be caught in the Eastern Tropical Pacific.

(c) As the US companies have banned all dolphin-deadly tuna, most currently floods into the European Community countries, particularly Italy. If you live in Europe, insist that the main tuna suppliers adopt a dolphin-friendly policy.

(d) If in doubt, do not buy tuna. When there is no longer any demand for their catch, fishermen will cease to set their nets on dolphins.

The US Congress is now taking measures to enforce legislation that prevents American fishing vessels from setting purse-seine nets on dolphins. At present this does not apply to other countries, and in the Eastern Tropical Pacific, dolphins are still at risk, mostly from Mexican and Venezuelan fishermen, who appear to be going about their business just as they did before the scandal came to light.

Sweeping the Oceans

> The Dolphins both rejoice in the echoing shores and dwell in the deep seas and there is
> no sea without dolphins.
>
> Oppian, *Halieutica*, I.

Throughout the world's oceans, dolphins are now also at risk of perishing in vast 'drift'
nets that hang in the sea, catching everything in their path. According to a cetacean expert,
Dr Roger Payne, these 'walls of death' are claiming even more victims than the purse-seine
nets deliberately set on dolphins.

Drift nets were first developed by the Japanese and have been in use since 1905.
Initially, they were made of natural fibres like cotton and hemp, but, with the invention of
cheaper plastics, a new breed of net arrived on the scene after the Second World War.
Modern versions are constructed of fine, mono-filament mesh, usually about 150mm (six
inches) square. Originally, these new, inexpensive 'plastic' nets were sponsored by the
FAO to assist developing countries in supplying their protein needs. Ironically, since the
1960s they have become the favourite method of fishing of many highly industrialized
nations who employ nets of anything up to 50km in length and 15km in depth to boost
their catches.

Japan, Taiwan and South Korea are the countries most responsible for using drift nets.
During the fishing season, more than 1,500 vessels from these countries have been setting
over 30,000 miles of net in the Pacific – enough to cross from Seattle to Tokyo and back
six times. Drift nets of smaller dimensions are also operated by other nations, including the
United States, the United Kingdom, Italy, France, Spain and Denmark.

Apart from their vast size, the main problem with drift nets is their inability to
discriminate between their intended catch and other forms of marine life. They may be
put out to catch albacore tuna or squid, but these nets destroy countless other sea-
dwelling creatures such as birds, dolphins, porpoises, seals, turtles and even whales. The
creatures become entangled in the mesh and drown to death. Usually, the nets are
released at dusk, left to drift with the currents overnight, then hauled in the following
morning. However, occasionally the nets break free or are abandoned by careless
fishermen. They are then carried along by the tides, endangering wildlife over vast tracts
of ocean as they drift aimlessly along.

Dolphins, possessed of a sophisticated echo-location system, should be able to detect
these nets. But despite its sensitivity, the dolphins' sonar cannot perceive the thin nylon
strands that make up the mesh, and in the darkness of night, these nets are effectively
invisible to any approaching dolphin. Once wrapped in the netting, any attempts to struggle
free simply make matters worse. Unable to surface for air, the animals suffocate and die.

Cetacean experts find it difficult to estimate just how many dolphins perish in drift nets, because the experts have to rely on figures given by fishermen. But, according to a report from the US National Marine Fisheries Service, in a six-week period during the summer of 1986, 53 dolphins and porpoises, as well as 14 fur seals, became entangled and died in the netting of just one Japanese squid-vessel. An example of how difficult it is to obtain accurate estimates of such destructive practices is the fact that, in an attempt to destroy any evidence of netting dolphins, Southern Italian fishermen hacked the dorsal fins and tail flukes off the animals while they were still alive, leaving them to spiral helplessly to the ocean floor. At least 4,000 dolphins caught off the French Riviera in the summer of 1989 perished in this way. In the North Pacific, too, the Dall's porpoise has been particularly hard-hit. In the last 20 years, hundreds of thousands have perished in nets set for salmon, squid and tuna. Because the porpoise population is dwindling so rapidly, they are now classified as an endangered species.

Australia was the first country to take a serious stand against drift-net use after Taiwanese fleets killed 10,000 dolphins, mainly the bottlenose, spinner and spotted varieties, while operating in Australian coastal waters between 1981 and 1985. When New Zealand authorities accidentally came across 180 fishing-vessels from Taiwan setting some 8,000km of net each night along the Subtropical Convergence Zone, the South Pacific countries decided to take further defensive action. They met at a convention in November 1989 and agreed to ban the use of drift nets in the entire region. Later that year, the global nature of this problem became the focus of discussions held by the United Nations General Assembly. In the face of mounting concern over how long the world's oceans can sustain such plundering of their resources before the finely-balanced marine ecosystem collapses, many countries now feel drift-net use should be restricted. As yet an international law banning these 'walls of death' from our oceans is still a long way off. The good news is, however, that Japan has now agreed to ban drift netting, a decision that will hopefully make a huge impression on marine life in the Pacific.

Local Concerns

Whereas drift nets wreak their havoc on the high seas, closer to shore, much smaller 'gill-nets' are a threat to dolphins and porpoises living in shallow coastal regions. Made from the same nylon mono-filament mesh as their giant counterparts, they are also undetectable to dolphins. Dr Stephen Leatherwood of the UN Environment Programme estimates that between 500,000 and 1,000,000 small cetaceans are caught in such nets each year. This means that many local dolphin populations may be under threat. As fishermen are not obliged to report such 'accidents', scientists can only guess at the kind of impact these nets may be having on the dolphins that live around our coasts.

The story of the tiny Hector's dolphin provides some vital clues. Found only off the coast of New Zealand, this exuberant creature, with its distinctive black-and-white markings, now has its own marine mammal sanctuary around the Banks Peninsula on the South Island. New Zealand's Department of Conservation took such action after 230 dolphins out of a breeding group of some 740 were killed in gill-nets between 1984 and 1988. As the females mature late and have a calf only once every one or two years, concerns were raised over whether the total population, which numbers only 3,000–4,000 dolphins, could survive such losses. Gill-nets are now banned from an area of prime dolphin habitat during the height of the fishing season.

The Gulf of California harbour porpoise or *vaquita*, which lives off the coast of Mexico, was severely affected by coastal gill-net fishing during the 1970s. No one knows for certain how many still survive, although 100 may be a generous estimate. Unless Mexico takes urgent steps to save the *vaquita*, it may soon be extinct.

Dolphin Alert

To prevent dolphins dying needlessly, some cetacean scientists are now looking at various ways to alert the animals to the presence of fishing nets. Dr Margaret Klinowska of the Marine Mammal Unit of Cambridge University in the United Kingdom, and David Goodson of Loughborough University (also in the UK), are currently investigating this field. One possible approach is to modify the nets in some way so that the dolphins can detect them with sonar. The idea is to attach to nets 'reflectors' that work on the same principle as cat's eyes. When the dolphin's echo-locating 'clicks' bounce back off these objects, it should give the impression that the animal is swimming towards a solid wall. An initial trial carried out in the Moray Firth in Scotland on a resident pod of bottlenose dolphins gave promising results. 'During the five-day study period, there was no sign that the dolphins were colliding or trying to go through the modified net,' Dr Klinowska claims.

This work is still in its early stages, and has obvious drawbacks. Sonar reflectors are only effective when the dolphins are using this sense for hunting. When merely swimming, the animals remain silent. There is also a danger that they may mistake the reflectors for fish. Other ways of tackling this problem may stem from studying the dolphins' swimming patterns. 'If nets were aligned parallel as opposed to across, their path of travel, they would not be at such risk of becoming entangled,' Dr Klinowska points out. 'Fishermen know an enormous amount about the habits of fish. We now need to understand more about dolphin behaviour and why they become entangled in the nets. Such knowledge is vital if fishermen throughout the world are to go about their work without harming dolphins.'

COLD-BLOODED KILLING

While some native cultures have always treated the intelligent, friendly, playful dolphin with kindness and warmth, others have shown it little respect. The ancient Greeks regarded the Mossynoccians living around the Black Sea, and the Thracians inhabiting the eastern border of Greece, as barbarians because these people hunted dolphins for their oil and meat. The Greeks believed that killing the 'divine' dolphin was a crime and sacrilege, reputedly punishable by death.

It may be that in their naïvety, people living in times past may have thought that dolphins were simply 'big fish'. But today we know better, and yet, throughout the world, some countries still permit the cold-blooded killing of these air-breathing mammals. According to Dave Currey and Allan Thornton, who run the British-based Environmental Investigation Agency, at least 500,000 dolphins die every year in uncontrolled slaughters. After travelling the world on fact-finding missions, Currey and Thornton have returned with countless tales of dolphins being stabbed, shot, speared, gassed, hooked, electrocuted, harpooned, blown-up and mutilated. They report that over five times as many dolphins and small whales are being killed each year as the number of great whales at the height of the whaling industry. At present, small cetaceans are not afforded any protection by the International Whaling Commission, and as a consequence, throughout the world many are hunted for food, fertilizer, and shark-bait.

Japan is responsible for the blatant killing of more dolphins than any other country. Between 1976 and 1987, Japanese fishermen killed over 200,000 small cetaceans off the shores of Japan. On one occasion, in November 1990, some 600 dolphins were clubbed and hacked to death on Shiragahama beach by the locals of Fukejima Island. Some doubt exists as to whether the dolphins were purposely driven ashore, or whether they beached themselves, but, regardless, they still met with a horrifying death. Dolphin meat is a popular delicacy in certain regions of Japan.

Some fishermen attempt to justify their actions by claiming that the dolphins deplete fish stocks and so threaten the men's livelihood. However, a more plausible explanation for such a threat lies with the vast fishing-vessels belonging to the major industrialized nations, which often set their nets off the coastline of poor 'Third-World' countries.

The collapse of the Peruvian anchovy industry in the 1970s left local fishermen in desperate need of alternative employment. They found it in killing dolphins for their meat. Every year, some 10,000 dusky dolphins, common dolphins and Burmeister's porpoises are slaughtered by being harpooned or caught in deliberately-set gill-nets. When Koen Van Waerebeek, founder of 'Grupo Cetaceos', a Lima-based conservation organization, visited the small fishing-port of Pucusana in November 1988, he found the market-floor covered with bloodied dolphin bodies. Most of this meat is sold fresh for human consumption in Lima, while the rest is dried and salted to produce *muchame*, originally an Italian delicacy, and now a popular snack amongst those who can afford it. As it is unspecifiably referred to as 'sea pig', many people are unaware that they are eating dolphin meat.

In other parts of the world, dolphins are not even killed in order for people to make a living. In the Danish-owned Faroe Islands, dolphins often die alongside long-fin pilot whales in a traditional slaughter that dates back centuries. After being driven into the bay, the creatures are hauled up onto the beach, where the islanders slit their necks and leave them to die. At one time the Faroese were a poor people who needed the whale meat and other by-products to survive. But with the development of a large-scale fishing-fleet, they now have high incomes. Yet this practice still continues, taking the form of an 'enjoyable' sport that often results in the death of over 500 dolphins in a single day.

THE STRUGGLE FOR SURVIVAL

As a result also of the destruction of their natural habitat, the survival of some dolphin species currently hangs precariously in the balance. With their comical pointed snouts and paddle-shaped flippers, the prehistoric-looking river dolphins of the family *Platanistoidae* now teeter on the verge of extinction.

Only a few years ago, for example, the distinctively pink-coloured Amazon river dolphin (*Inia geoffrensis*) seemed quite safe. Now it has become one of the most endangered species, due to the accelerated, commercialized 'rape' of the Amazon basin and the destruction of the South American rainforest.

Ever since the *Inia* entered the Amazon river basin from the Pacific coast, at least five million years ago, it has lived peacefully in the sheltered estuaries and lakes of this 4,000-mile-long river. Over the years the animal adapted to live in these somewhat murky waters, and these dolphins can swivel their heads a full 90 degrees and have superb sonar vision to improve their navigational powers.

More legends surround these creatures than any other animal in the forest. Fishermen and river people tell stories of how the *boto*, a local name for the *Inia*, saved them from drowning by taking them ashore when their boats turned over in this piranha-infested river. The dolphins are generally regarded as 'sacred people of the water', and to kill a *boto* is thought to incite bad luck. Legend has it that during the full moon, these dolphins can transform themselves into either a dashing, handsome man or a beautiful woman, either of whom lures victims to his or her underwater home. And if a husband had to leave his family for a while and returned to find his 'faithful' wife pregnant, this mishap was often blamed on the 'infamous pink dolphin'. Names like 'Carlos Bufeo' and 'Maria Boto' often appear on the birth certificates of such children.

The harmonious relationship between the native people and the river dolphin is now disintegrating. Due to exploitation of the forests, rainfall is declining and the river-level is dropping. Water pumped from its tributaries to irrigate massive agricultural projects exacerbates the problem, often leaving dolphins stranded in shallow pools to die of sunstroke and starvation. Low waters also attract commercial fishermen with gill-nets up to two miles long, which force the dolphins and the local people to compete for fish. The 'outsiders' also encourage locals to shoot, dynamite and poison their longstanding animal friends. Although outlawed in Brazil, unscrupulous poachers also hunt the dolphins and sell the creatures' bodily parts, particularly the eyes and genitals, in an expanding black market in *maccumba* or black magic, to North and South American, European and Japanese buyers.

Attempts to hold these particular dolphins captive invariably result in attempted suicide, so it is even more important to protect the *Inia* in its natural home. A naturalist called Roxanne Kremer has founded a conservation society called PARD (Preservation of the Amazonian River Dolphin) which is specifically focusing on saving the pink river dolphin from extinction. The main thrust of her work is to rekindle an environmental awareness and appreciation for the *Inia* among the people of Peru and Brazil.

Save the Seas

It is said that when the seas die, we die too. Yet for at least half a century, we have been treating the world's oceans as a dumping-ground for our unwanted wastes. It was as if we thought those vast expanses of water could swallow up any amount of rubbish we tipped into them without any dire consequences. Time is proving us wrong. Waves breaking along the coasts of many countries are now so unclean that they are a health hazard to humans. How long will it be before the dolphins that dwell in these seas also suffer the ill-effects of our pollution?

Indeed, dolphins are already dying through our negligence. Rubbish such as floating plastic bags, which may cover the animals' blow-holes, causing suffocation, is an ever-escalating cause for concern. The power-boats and jet skis that skim across the waves in holiday resorts generate high-pitched sounds that may affect the dolphins' sensitive hearing, causing distress and possibly disorientation. Seismic testing is guaranteed to do them much more harm.

Many noxious man-made chemicals flushed into the ocean may be insidiously taking their toll on the health and general wellbeing of cetaceans. A century ago, as many as 5,000 belugas or white whales lived in the Lawrence River in eastern Canada. Now, this local population numbers just 400 and is almost certainly doomed to extinction. The reason for this decline is pollution: for decades both Canadian and US industries have been pouring noxious chemicals into the Great Lakes which drain into this river. Belugas that die are so heavily contaminated that their bodies are classified as toxic waste and must be specially disposed of to keep the poisonous chemicals from returning to the environment. While some 24 different chemicals have been found in the affected animals' tissue, the most abundant are the PCBs (polychlorinated biphenyls).

For 50 years, PCBs were used in industry as cooling and insulating fluids in the manufacture of plastics, adhesives and lubricants. During that time, more than one billion kilograms of these highly toxic substances were produced. Although official manufacture of PCBs ceased in 1967, a certain amount leaked into the environment and these still linger in oceans and lakes throughout the world. PCBs entering the sea were taken up by plankton, which are in turn eaten by fish, the staple diet of dolphins and other marine mammals. Because PCBs are extremely stable and fat-soluble, they tend to accumulate in the dolphins' blubber. Dr Paul Johnston, Greenpeace Research Fellow at the School of Biological Sciences of Queen Mary College in London, feels that there is good evidence to suggest that PCBs have a detrimental effect on the health of all marine mammals. Research indicates that such chemicals may interfere with the healthy functioning of the liver, damage the endocrine organs, reduce fertility and weaken the immune system.

In the summer of 1987, hundreds of dead and dying bottlenose dolphins were washed up on the east coast of the United States from New Jersey to Florida. They were suffering from internal haemorrhaging, fluid in the lungs, enlarged spleens, bronchial pneumonia and peeling skin. Their immune systems had apparently broken down. Although official reports blamed poisonous algae in the fish that they had eaten, Greenpeace biologists found high levels of PCBs in the dolphins' tissues. Other industrial pollutants, including heavy metals such as copper, cadmium and mercury, were also present. A similar incident took place three years later, when a mysterious plague claimed the lives of 10,000 striped dolphins in the Mediterranean, arguably the most polluted sea in the world. Their deaths were attributed to an outbreak of the *morbilli* virus, which is similar to a killer 'flu.

The cetacean expert Bob Morris has little doubt that PCBs suppress the dolphin's immune system, making it more susceptible to such viruses. 'Because dolphins feed on oily fish like mackerel, herring, and bass, they are at risk of accumulating large amounts of PCBs. In the last 20 years tissue levels have been increasing by orders of magnitude of up to 100 times – much higher than we predicted. DDT residues may be present too, even though this chemical was banned in the early 1970s. Health problems are more likely during the winter, when the dolphins are forced to fall back on their fat reserves, or when the young are born. A female dolphin may off-load up to one-third of her PCBs onto a developing baby. Being rich in fat, mothers' milk also contains high concentrations of these chemicals. One baby dolphin born into the resident pod in Cardigan Bay in Wales, died of hepatitis when it was only six months old. An autopsy revealed the highest PCB levels ever found in any dolphin,' Morris reports. It is a disturbing and sobering fact that, due to our present-day pollution problem, the lives of future generations of dolphins may be at stake.

DOLPHIN INFORMATION AND WELFARE ORGANIZATIONS

DOLPHIN INFORMATION AND WELFARE ORGANIZATIONS

American Cetacean Society, PO Box 2639, San Pedro, California 90731, USA.

Animal Protection Institute, 2631 Fruit Ridge Road, PO Box 22505, Sacramento, California 96822, USA.

Appel pour les Baleines, 114 rue de Grenelle, 75007 Paris, France.

Bellerive Foundation, PO 6, 1211 Geneva 3, Switzerland.

Cardigan Bay Marine Wildlife, 44 Riverdale Road, Monkmoor, Shrewsbury SY2 STB, England.

Center for Coastal Studies, 59 Commercial Street, Provincetown, Massachusetts 02659, USA.

Cetacean Group, Department of Zoology, South Parks Road, Oxford OX1 3PS, England.

The Cousteau Society, 930 West 21st Street, Norfolk, Virginia 23517, USA.

Dolphin Circle, 8 Dolby Road, London Sw6, England.

Dolphin Database, PO Box 5657, Playa Del Rey, California 90296, USA.

Dolphin Network, 3220 Sacramento, San Francisco, California 94115, USA.

Dolphin Project, PO Box 224, Coconut Grove, Florida 33233, USA.

Earth Island Institute, 300 Broadway, Suite 28, San Francisco, California 94123, USA.

Environmental Investigation Agency, 208–209 Upper Street, London N1 1RL, England.

Greenpeace, 30–31 Islington Green, London N1 8XE, England.

Japan Environment Monitor, 400 Yamanashi-Ken, Kofu-Shi, 18–11 Kofu, Japan.

International Cetacean Education Research Centre, PO Box 110, Nambucca, New South Wales, Australia 2448.

International Dolphin Watch, Parklands, North Ferriby, Humberside HU14 3ET, England.

International Fund for Animal Welfare, Tubwell House, New Road, Crowborough, East Sussex TN6 2QH, England.

International Whaling Commission, The Red House, Station Road, Histon, Cambridge CB4 4NP, England.

Long Term Research Institute, 191 Weston Road, Lincoln, Massachusetts 01773, USA.

Marine Education and Research Ltd, 17 Harrington Park, Bristol BS6 7ES, England.

Oceanic Society, Fort Mason Center, Building E, San Francisco, California 94123, USA.

Orrca, PO Box E293, St James, NSWW 2000, Australia.

PARD (Preservation of the Amazonian River Dolphin), 3302 N. Burton Avenue, Rosemead, California 91770, USA.

Project Interlock, Box 20, Whangarei, New Zealand.

Project Jonah, 672B Glenferrie Road, Hawthorn, Victoria 3122, Australia.

Robyn des Bois, 15 rue Ferdinand Duval, 75004 Paris, France.

Sea Shepherd, (UK) PO Box 5, Ashford, Middlesex W15 2PY, England.
(USA) PO Box 70005, Redondo Beach, California 90277. (Canada) PO Box 48446, Vancouver, B.C. V7X 1AZ.

Society for the Protection of Marine Mammals, PO Box 348, D-200, NW Hamburg 55, Germany.

Whale and Dolphin Conservation Society, 20 West Lea Road, Bath BA1 3RL, England.

World Society for the Protection of Animals, Park Place, 10 Lawn Lane, London SW8, England.

Zoocheck, Cherry Tree Cottage, Coldharbour Lane, Dorking, Surrey, England.

BIBLIOGRAPHY

....

BIBLIOGRAPHY

Aelian. W. *Vol. 1. The Characteristics of Animals*. Books II, IV, V, X, XVI. Translation A.F. Scolfield. London: William Heinemann Ltd.

Aesop. *The Monkey and the Dolphin*. In *An Anthology of Fables*. London: Dent, Everyman's Library, 1913.

Alpers, Anthony. *Dolphins*. London: John Murray, 1960.

Anderson, H.T. (Ed.). *The Biology of Marine Mammals*. New York: Academic Press, 1969.

Aristotle. *The History of Animals*. Vol. 1. Books I–III. Translation A.L. Peck. London: William Heinemann Ltd.

Athenaeus. *The Deipnosophists*. Vol. VI. Book XIII: p. 606. Translation C.B. Gulick. London: William Heinemann Ltd.

Balaskas, Janet and Yehudi Gordon. *Water Birth*. London: Unwin Hyman Ltd, 1990.

Barton, Charles. 'The Navy's Natural Divers'. *Oceans*, July 1977.

Bastian, J. 'The Transmission of Arbitrary Environmental Information Between Bottlenose Dolphins'. R.G. Busnel (Ed.). *Animal Sonar Systems*. Vol. II: pp. 803–873. Jouy-en-Josas, France: Laboratoire de Physiologie Acoustique.

Booth, William. 'Unravelling the Dolphin Soap Opera'. *Oceanus*. Vol. 32, Nov. 1989.

Brower, Kenneth. 'The Destruction of Dolphins'. *The Atlantic Monthly*, July 1989, 35–58.

Bryden, M.M. and R. Harrison (Eds). *Research on Dolphins*. Oxford: Clarendon Press, 1986.

Bunnel, S. 'The Evolution of Cetacean Intelligence'. In *Mind in the Waters*. New York: Charles Scribner and Sons, 1974.

Burnett, Lieutenant Commander Douglas R. 'Dolphins, Naval Warfare and International Law'. *US Naval Institute Proceedings*, 1981.

Caldwell, M.C. and D.K. Caldwell. 'Individualised Whistle Contours in Bottlenosed Dolphins, *Tursiops Truncatus*'. *Nature*, 207: pp. 434–435, 1965.

———————— 'Vocal Mimicry in the Whistle Mode in the Atlantic Bottlenosed Dolphin'. *Cetology*, 9: pp. 1–8, 1972.

Cobet, E. and Harris. *The Handbook of British Mammals*. London: Blacknell.

Cousteau, Jacques. *The Ocean World of Jacques Cousteau: Mammals in the Sea*. London: Angus & Robertson, 1990.

Cox, Vic. *Whales and Dolphins*. London: W.H. Smith Books, 1989.

Davidson, John. *Subtle Energy*. London: C.W. Daniel.

Doak, Wade. *Dolphin, Dolphin*. Auckland: Hodder & Stoughton, 1981.
———— *Encounters with Whales and Dolphins*. Auckland: Hodder & Stoughton, 1988.
Dobbs, Horace. *Dance to a Dolphin's Song*. London: Jonathan Cape, 1990.
———— *Follow a Wild Dolphin*. London: Souvenir Press, 1977.
———— *Tale of Two Dolphins*. London: Jonathan Cape, 1987.
———— *The Magic of Dolphins*. Guildford: Lutterworth Press, 1984.
Donohue, Michael and Annie Wheeler. *Dolphins: Their Life and Survival*. Blandford.
Downer, John. *Supersense*. London: BBC Publications.
Ellis, Richard. *Dolphins and Porpoises*. New York: Alfred Knopf, 1982.
Evans, Dr Peter G.H. *The Natural History of Whales and Dolphins*. London: Helm, 1988.
Evans, W.E. 'Vocalisation Among Marine Mammals'. In W.N. Tavolga (Ed.). *Marine Bioacoustics*. Vol. II: pp. 159–186. Oxford: Pergamon Press.
———— 'Echolocation by Marine Delphinids and One Species of Fresh Water Dolphin'. *Journal of the Acoustics Society of America*, 54: pp. 191–9, 1973.
Fitzgibbon, Ronnie. *The Dingle Dolphin*. Athlone: Temple Printing, 1988.
Forcier-Beringer, Ann G. 'Talking With Dolphins'. *Sea Frontiers/Sea Secrets*, 32, March, April, 1986.
Funk and Wagnalls, Edited by Maria Leach. *Standard Dictionary of Folklore, Mythology and Legend*. New York: Harper and Row.
Gaskin, David. *The Ecology of Whales and Dolphins*. London: William Heinemann Ltd, 1982.
Gerber, Dr Richard. *Vibrational Medicine*. Santa Fe: Bear and Co., 1988.
Harrison, Sir Richard and Dr M.M. Bryden. *Whales, Dolphins and Porpoises*. London: Merehurst Press, 1988.
Hawkes, Jacquetta. *Dawn of the Gods*. London: Random House.
Herman, Louis. *Cetacean Behaviour: Mechanism and Function*. New York: Willey Interscience, 1980.
Herman, Louis and R.K.R. Thompson. 'Symbolic, Identity and Probe Delayed Matching of Sounds by the Bottlenosed Dolphin'. *Animal Learning and Behaviour*, 10, pp. 22–34, 1982.
Herodotus. Vol. 1. Books 1, 23 and 24. Translation A.D. Godley. London: William Heinemann Ltd.
Hesiod. *The Homeric Hymns and Homerica*. Hymn III. *To Pythian Apollo*. Translation H.G. Evelyn White. London: William Heinemann Ltd.
Holing, Dwight. 'Dolphin Defense'. *Discover*, October 1988.
Holmes, Brian. *Dorad an Daingin. The Dingle Dolphin*. Sonar 3, 1990.
Hutchison, Michael. *The Book of Floating*. New York: Quill, 1984.
Jeffrey, Francis and Dr John C. Lilly. *John Lilly, So Far. . .* Los Angeles: Tarcher, 1990.
Jerison, H. 'The Evolution of the Mammalian Brain as an Information-Processing System'. In J.F. Eisenberg & D.G. Klieman (Eds). *Advances in the Study of Mammalian Behaviour*. Special publication of the American Society of Mammalogists No. 7, 1983.
Johnson, William. *The Rose-Tinted Menagerie*. London: Heretic Books, 1990.
Klinowska, Margaret. *Dolphins, Porpoises and Whales of the World*. In *The IUCN Cetacean Red Data Book*. Gland, Switzerland.
Klinowska, Dr Margaret & Dr Susan Brown. London: *A Review of Dolphinaria*. For the Department of the Environment, 1985/86.
La Budde, Sam. 'Net Death: Net Loss'. In *Earth Island Journal*, 3 (2) spring 27–30, 1988.

Leakey, Richard E. and Roger Lewin. *Origins*. Futura/Macdonald, 1982.
———————— *Man: His Origins, Nature and Future*. London: Collins, 1979.
Leatherwood, Stephen and Randall Reeves. *The Bottlenose Dolphin*. London: Academic Press, 1990.
Lewin, Roger. *Bones of Contention*. New York: Simon and Schuster, 1987.
Lende, R.A. and S. Akdikman. 'Motor Field Cortex of the Bottlenose Dolphin'. *Journal of Neurosurgery*, 29: pp. 495–499, 1968.
Lilly, Dr John C. *Communication Between Man and Dolphin*. New York: Julian Press, 1978.
———————— 'Man and Dolphin'. *Worlds of Science*. New York: Pyramid Publications, 1961.
———————— *The Mind of a Dolphin*. New York: Doubleday, 1967.
McIntyre, J. (Ed.). *Mind in the Waters*. New York: Charles Scribner and Sons, 1974.
McLuhan, T.C. *Touch the Earth*. New York: Simon and Schuster.
Mannion, Sean. *Ireland's Friendly Dolphin*. Co. Kerry: Brandon, 1991.
Martin, Dr Antony R. *Whales and Dolphins*. London: Salamander Books, 1990.
May, John. *The Greenpeace Book of Dolphins*. London: Century, 1990.
Morgan, Elaine. *The Aquatic Ape, A Theory of Evolution*. London: Souvenir Press, 1982.
———————— *The Descent of Woman*. London: Souvenir Press, 1972.
———————— *The Scars of Evolution*. London: Souvenir Press, 1990.
Mugford, Roger. 'The Social Significance of Pet Ownership'. In *Ethology and Nonverbal Communication in Mental Health*. Pergamon Press, 1980.
Nayman, Jacqueline. *Whales, Dolphin and Man*. London: Hamlyn Books.
Nolman, Jim. *Dolphin Dreamtime. Talking to the Animals*. London: Anthony Blond, 1985.
Norris, Kenneth S. *The Porpoise Watcher*. London: John Murray, 1974.
Northridge, S. and Giorgio Pilleri. 'A Review of Human Impact on Small Cetaceans'. In *Investigations on Cetacea*. Vol. XVIII: pp. 222–261, 1986.
O'Barry, Richard. *Behind the Dolphin Smile*. Chapel Hill: Algonquin Books, 1988.
Ocean, Joan. *Dolphin Connection*. Hawaii: Dolphin Connection/Spiral Books, 1989.
Odent, Dr Michel. *Water and Sexuality*. Arkana, Penguin.
Oppian. *Halieutica*. Book I: pp. 383, 644, 673–684. Book V: pp. 416–588.
Overland, M. 'Cetacean Behaviour, Learning and Communication'. *Mammals in the Seas*. Vol. III.
Pausinias. *Description of Greece*. Laconia, in Vol. III, Book XXV: pp. 5–9; *Attica*, in Vol. I. Book XLIV: p. 8; *Corinth*, in Vol. II. Book I: pp. 2–4; *Arcadia*, in Vol. VIII. Book XLII. Translation W.H.S. Jones and H.A. Omerod. London: William Heinemann Ltd.
Pelletier, Kenneth R. *Mind As Healer, Mind As Slayer*. New York: Delacourt, 1977.
Plato. *The Dialogues*. 'Timaeus'; 'Critias'; 'Cleitophon'; 'Menexenus'; 'Epistles'. Vol. VII. Translation R.G. Bury. London: William Heinemann Ltd.
Pliny. *Natural History*. Vol. III. Books IX and VIII. Translation H. Rackham, M. A. London: William Heinemann Ltd.
Plutarch. *Moralia*. 'The Cleverness of Animals'. Translation Harold Cherniss and William C. Helmbold. London: William Heinemann Ltd.
Pryor, Karen, R. Haag and J. O'Reilly. 'The Creative Porpoise – Training for Novel Behaviour'. *Journal of the Experimental Analysis of Behaviour*. 12: pp. 653–661, 1969.
Robson, Frank D. *Pictures in the Dolphin Mind*. Dobbs Ferry. Sheridan House, 1988.

——————— *Thinking Dolphins, Talking Whales*. Wellington: A.H. and A.W. Reed, 1976.

Rose, J.E. and C.N. Woolsey. 'Organisation of the Mammalian Thalamus and Its Relationship to the Cerebral Cortex'. *Electroencephalog. Clin. Neurophysiology*, I: pp. 391–404, 1949.

Schusterman, Ronald J. 'Behavioural Methodology in Echolocation by Marine Mammals'. In R.G. Busnel & J.F. Fish (Eds). *Animal Sonar Systems*. New York. Plenum, 1980.

Schusterman, Ronald J., Jeanette A. Thomas and Forrest G. Woods. *Dolphin Cognition and Behaviour, A Comparative Approach*. Lawrence Eribaum Associates.

Shane, Dr Susan. *The Bottlenose Dolphin in the Wild*. United States: Hatcher Trade Press, 1988.

Sidenbladh, Erik. *Water Babies*. London: Adam and Charles Black, 1983.

Siegel, Bernie. *Love, Medicine and Miracles*. London: Arrow, 1986.

Smith, Dr Betsy. 'Project Inreach: A Programme to Explore the Ability of Atlantic Bottle-nose Dolphins to Elicit Communication Responses from Autistic Children'. In *New Perspectives on Our Lives with Companion Animals*. Philadelphia: University of Pennsylvania Press, 1983.

——————— 'Using Dolphin to Elicit Communication from an Autistic Child'. In *The Pet Connection*. Minneapolis Center for the Study of Human-Animal Relationships and Environments, 1984.

——————— 'Dolphins Plus and Autistic Children'. In *Psychological Perspectives*. Vol. 18, no. 2. Los Angeles: 1987.

Stenuit, Robert. *The Dolphin: Cousin to Man*. London: J.M. Dent, 1969.

Steurer, Karen L. *A Comparative Institutional Survey of Factors Influencing Mortality of Cetaceans in US Zoos and Aquaria*. Center of Coastal Studies, USA.

Temple, Robert. *The Sirius Mystery*. London: Sidgwick & Jackson, 1976.

Thompson, R.K.R. and Louis Herman. 'Memory for Lists of Sounds by the Bottlenosed Dolphin: Convergence of Memory Processes with Humans?' *Science*. Vol. 195: pp. 501–503, 1977.

Trout, Rick. '*Tursi Ops*, Exploiting A Gentle Intelligence'. *Testimony*. December 1988.

Tyack, Peter. 'Population Biology, Social Behaviour and Communication in Whales and Dolphins', *Tree*. Vol. I, no. 6. December 1986.

Vogel, Virgil, J. *American Indian Medicine*. University of Oklahoma Press, 1970.

Watson, Andrew and Nevill Drury. *Healing Music*. Bridport: Prism Press, 1987.

Wells, Randall and Michael Scott. 'Estimating Bottlenose Dolphin Population Parameters from Individual Indentification and Capture-Release Techniques'.

Williams, Heathcote. *Falling for a Dolphin*. London: Jonathan Cape, 1988.

——————— *Whale Nation*. London: Jonathan Cape, 1981.

Woods, Forrest G. *Marine Mammals and Man: The Navy's Porpoises and Sea Lions*. Robert B. Luce Inc, 1973.

Wursig, Bernd. 'Dolphins'. *Scientific American*. March 1979.

Wyllie, Timothy. *Dolphins, Extraterrestrials, Angels – Adventures Among Spiritual Intelligence*. Farmingdale: Coleman Publishing, 1984.